Existential
Therapies

Existential Therapies

Second Edition

Mick Cooper

Los Angeles | London | New Delhi
Singapore | Washington DC | Melbourne

Los Angeles | London | New Delhi
Singapore | Washington DC | Melbourne

SAGE Publications Ltd
1 Oliver's Yard
55 City Road
London EC1Y 1SP

SAGE Publications Inc.
2455 Teller Road
Thousand Oaks, California 91320

SAGE Publications India Pvt Ltd
B 1/I 1 Mohan Cooperative Industrial Area
Mathura Road
New Delhi 110 044

SAGE Publications Asia-Pacific Pte Ltd
3 Church Street
#10-04 Samsung Hub
Singapore 049483

© Mick Cooper 2003, 2017

First edition published 2003. Reprinted 2007, 2008, 2009,
2010 (twice), 2011, 2012 (twice), 2015
This second edition first published 2017

Editor: Susannah Trefgarne
Editorial assistant: Edward Coats
Production editor: Rachel Burrows
Marketing manager: Camille Richmond
Cover design: Lisa Harper-Wells
Typeset by: C&M Digitals (P) Ltd, Chennai, India
Printed and bound in Great Britain by Ashford Colour
Press Ltd.

Library of Congress Control Number: 2016934710

British Library Cataloguing in Publication data

A catalogue record for this book is available from
the British Library

ISBN 978-1-4462-0128-2
ISBN 978-1-4462-0129-9 (pbk)

At SAGE we take sustainability seriously. Most of our products are printed in the UK using FSC papers and boards.
When we print overseas we ensure sustainable papers are used as measured by the PREPS grading system.
We undertake an annual audit to monitor our sustainability.

In loving memory of my father, Charles Cooper (1910–2001), a communist and humanist, who taught me to value freedom, to question conventional wisdoms, and to honour the tragic side of life – an existentialist in spirit, if not in name.

CONTENTS

PRAISE FOR THE BOOK

'As always with Mick's work this is a wonderfully clear, accessible and engaging book, and an excellent starting point for anyone who is interested in existential therapy. As well as providing historical context and an overview of the existential approach and how it can be applied to therapy, this second edition expertly weaves in newer developments in the field including the existential-phenomenological approach, and time-limited existential therapy. Existential therapies are also brought to life with a case study that runs the whole way through the book. Overall a superb introduction and an important contribution to the field.'
Meg-John Barker, The Open University

'The second edition of *Existential Therapies* represents an important update of this important text. Mick Cooper respectfully examines the differences and similarities of the various major approaches to existential therapy. This should be required reading for all student and scholars in existential psychology.'
Louis Hoffman, Saybrook University

'Mick Cooper has done the counselling and psychotherapy community a great service by tracing the many influences that have shaped contemporary approaches to existential therapy. Cooper has woven together the various strands of thought into a coherent and lively presentation of how existential therapy is practised today. The book combines scholarship with a writing style that makes difficult concepts accessible. It should be required reading on any course where the existential tradition plays a part, and that includes person-centred courses and all sympathetic to the idea that psychotherapy is, in essence, a human encounter where warmth, understanding and a deep respect for the individual are key values.'
Tony Merry

'This is a book of superb thoroughness and scholarship – an unprecedented guide to existential therapy's chief positions and controversies.'
Kirk J. Schneider, President of the Existential-Humanistic Institute

'Though philosophers through the ages have practised existential counselling, it is only in the past hundred years that this approach has been formally developed and recognized as a form of psychotherapy. This publication marks a

milestone in the long history of the existential therapies in providing an excellent, clear and critical overview of the contrasting forms of the approach as it is currently practised. Cooper's special merit is to present the different flavours of existential therapy in an evocative and sometimes provocative fashion. He invites his readers to sample the whole range; he highlights potential bias, and then in true existential tradition leaves his readers to arrive at their own conclusions and work out their own versions of existential therapy.'
Emmy van Deurzen

'A very sympathic, personal and modern writing with a firm guiding hand leading through the complex diversity of existential therapies. The second edition brings a good adjustment to the actual situation with a remaining dominance of the British (and English language) perspective. Lively and practical book with reflected literature access - a perfect introduction, a perfect refresher!'
Alfried Längle, president of Gesellschaft für Logotherapie und Existenzanalyse, Vienna

ABOUT THE AUTHOR

Mick Cooper is a Professor of Counselling Psychology at the University of Roehampton and a practising counselling psychologist. Mick is an author and editor of a range of texts on person-centred, existential and relational approaches to therapy, including *Working at Relational Depth in Counselling and Psychotherapy* (SAGE, 2005, with Dave Mearns), *Pluralistic Counselling and Psychotherapy* (SAGE, 2011, with John McLeod), and *Existential Psychotherapy and Counselling: Contributions to a Pluralistic Practice* (SAGE, 2015). Mick has led a range of research studies exploring the process and outcomes of humanistic counselling with young people.

PREFACE TO THE
SECOND EDITION

I can't quite remember the moment, which isn't surprising as I have a terrible memory. I think I was sitting in a class at Regent's College, London, listening to Hans Cohn talk about Heidegger, when it dawned on me that different people actually used the term 'existential therapy' in very different ways. In fact, I think it might have been Hans who made that point himself, and something really clicked in me. Maybe I was a bit annoyed by the way that all these writers and teachers would tell you what existential therapy *was*, without really referring to what anyone else thought. Anyhow, once I finished my training as an existential psychotherapist in 1999, I approached Sage to see if they would be interested in a book about these different perspectives. To my amazement they said 'yes'.

The first edition of *Existential Therapies* was my first single-authored text. I was so anxious about what people might make of it. I remember going for a run along Brighton beach in the last few days before submission (this I do remember with crystal clarity), and being entirely consumed with anxiety over some finer detail of existential philosophy. I could just see, in my mind's eye, Emmy van Deurzen and the other greats of existential therapy crucifying me for getting my ontological mixed up with my ontico-ontological and my *gelassenheit* with my *gesundheit*. As it was, Emmy and many others were very supportive of the book when it came out, and the first edition even made it to number 15 in a recent worldwide survey of the most influential texts on existential therapists' practice (Correia, Cooper, & Berdondini, 2014a). I was also delighted to find the book translated into a range of languages: Greek, Danish, Persian, Arabic and Korean.

Although I've gone on to write several other books, I have always, perhaps, been most proud of *Existential Therapies*. It was the first time I really found my own voice in my writing. It is a voice that is slightly obsessional and likes to put things in boxes, but is also quite personal and tries to speak directly to the reader. And, I think, the book did help people to make some more sense of the existential therapy field. It created a map that showed what the different kinds of existential therapies were and how they fitted together, and perhaps helped others to feel that it did not all have to be crammed into one, homogeneous approach.

It is tempting to say that a lot has happened in the existential field since the first publication of this book in 2003. But that is kind of true and kind of not. In some ways, the existential field – like most psychotherapy approaches – is quite conservative, and there have not been that many major changes to the ways in which existential therapy is practised around the world. On the other hand, though, there have been a number of very interesting developments over the past 13 years; and there are also some aspects of the existential therapies field that have come more to the fore. These include:

- The proliferation of existential therapy groups, societies and institutes around the world.
- A growing body of research into the process (e.g., Wilkes & Milton, 2006) and outcomes (e.g., Vos, Craig, & Cooper, 2014) of existential therapies.
- An increasing recognition of the size, scope and contribution of Alfried Längle's post-Frankl school of existential analysis (see Chapter 4, this volume).
- The emergence, and evidencing, of meaning-centred therapies for people with chronic or life-threatening disease (e.g., Breitbart et al., 2010) (see Chapter 4, this volume).
- Cross-fertilisations between the existential-humanistic school in America and Chinese colleagues, as well as a growing emphasis on multiculturalism in the existential-humanistic field (see Hoffman, Yang, & Kaklauskas, 2009; see Chapter 5, this volume).
- The publication of several new books on existential therapy, particularly from within the UK-based existential-phenomenological school (e.g., Langdridge, 2012) (see Chapter 7, this volume).
- The hosting of the first World Congress for Existential Therapy, held in London during 14–17 May 2015 (with a second congress planned for Argentina, 2019); and the development of a collective statement on the nature of existential therapy (World Confederation for Existential Therapy, 2016).

In this second edition of *Existential Therapies*, my aim is to integrate these new developments into an updated review of the existential approaches. My hope is to give a 'state-of-the-art' presentation of where the existential field is at, and where it might be going to.

As part of this, I have made several terminological and structural changes from the first edition of the book. First, I have replaced the term 'British school' with that of the 'existential-phenomenological' approach (Chapter 7). Edgar Correia, a colleague and PhD student of mine, put the case for this to me on two grounds. First, the 'British school' has been spreading across Europe and other regions of the world, to the point where it would be somewhat inaccurate (if not imperialistic) to continue identifying it exclusively with the UK. Second, argues Edgar (personal communication, 29 January 2016), 'there are several societies with very similar visions to the British school but whose origins are not connected to the British school'. These include existential traditions in Brazil, Argentina and Chile. After many discussions, I have come round to agreeing with Edgar on this. As a replacement term, Edgar has been referring to the *existential-phenomenological* branch of existential therapy (e.g., Correia, Cooper, & Berdondini, 2014b). For me, this label is not ideal, and seems a bit too all-inclusive. But it feels the best one that we have for now, and it will be used throughout this text.

Second, in Chapter 4, I now speak of the *meaning-centred* approaches rather than 'logotherapy' *per se*. With the growth and diversification of therapeutic approaches inspired by Frankl – way beyond the limits of logotherapeutic theory and method – the use of a broader term seems essential.

Third, to make space to discuss some of these – and other – new developments, I have dropped the chapter on brief existential therapies (previously Chapter 9), and have integrated a discussion of Strasser and Strasser's time-limited approach into Chapter 7 on the existential-phenomenological approach.

Another change for this new edition is that I have used a fictional case study throughout, Siân, to try to illustrate how the different existential approaches might work with a specific client. I have to confess, I am slightly nervous about this, and worry that – as a fictional story – it may come across as somewhat contrived. However, my hope is that readers will bear with this, and find Siân a helpful addition to the book: concretising and bringing to life the different approaches to existential practice.

I hope that you will enjoy this book, and find it an informative, engaging and refreshing review of the existential therapy field.

Mick Cooper
Brighton, 2016

ACKNOWLEDGEMENTS

From an existential perspective, a human being is inseparable from their social context, and the writing of this book – both the first and second editions – would not have been possible without the emotional and intellectual support of numerous friends, colleagues, family members, and teachers.

Thanks, first of all, go to Helen Cruthers. Helen gave me enormous encouragement, love and help during the writing of the original book, and her comments and guidance on numerous drafts were invaluable. On the home front, I would also like to thank our four children: Maya, Ruby, Shula and Zac. Lost in tomes of Heideggerian and Kierkegaardian thought, nothing could have lifted my spirits more than to have a young toddler bound into my study, smile mischievously, and then proceed to pile all my philosophical books, one-by-one, onto the floor (now that Maya is almost 16, it is more a case of her bounding into my study and asking for money!). Special thanks also go to Jennifer Cruthers, Robert Cruthers, and Kitty Cooper, who grandparented our children so lovingly and diligently, and helped me find the time to complete the first edition of this book.

I am greatly indebted to Emmy van Deurzen. Not only has she been a central driving force behind one of the most vibrant and widespread branches of the existential world today; she was also incredibly generous with her time and support during the drafting of both editions of this book.

Many thanks also go to the following colleagues and friends for their informative, encouraging and challenging feedback on the first edition of this book: Ivan Ellingham, Alec Grant, Mike Harding, Angie Hart, Helen Hopkins, Tim LeBon, Paul McGahey, Tony Merry, Jacquy Paizas, Geraldine Pass, Kirk Schneider, Ernesto Spinelli, Freddie Strasser, Dominic Velarde, and Sarah Young. For the first edition, a number of therapists and academics generously gave me their time to talk through various aspects of the existential therapies, and to them I am grateful too: Hans Cohn, Erik Craig, Miles Groth, John Heaton, Wilhelm Maas, and Paul Wong.

For this second edition, I would like to say special thanks to Edgar Correia, a Portuguese existential psychotherapist and former PhD student (with Lucia Berdondini at the University of Strathclyde). Edgar's research into the practices and distribution of existential therapy has provided an invaluable source of understanding into the existential field today. I am also very grateful for the many colleagues who kindly gave their time to comment on chapters and drafts of the second edition: Martin Adams, Meg John Barker, Edgar Correia, Tamas Fazekas, Louis Hoffman, Alice Holzhey-Kunz, Alfried Längle, Kate Martin, Martin Milton, Mark Rayner, Kirk Schneider, Ernesto Spinelli, Alison Strasser, Michael Thompson, Emmy van Deurzen, Diego Vitali, and Joël Vos.

The majority of the first edition of this book was researched and written during a sabbatical semester, and for that I would like to thank colleagues in the School of Applied Social Science at the University of Brighton, who not only awarded me the sabbatical, but also covered my teaching load. I am very grateful to the learning resources team at the University of Brighton's Falmer Library too, who patiently processed for me numerous inter-library loan requests. For this second edition, I am very thankful to the ongoing support from my Department of Psychology at the University of Roehampton, and particularly the Head of the Department, Diane Bray.

Thanks, as always, to the team at SAGE, including Susannah Trefgarne, Edward Coats, Rachel Burrows, and Alison Poyner, and to Sarah Bury for her copyediting of the text. Also, I am enormously grateful to the translators of the first edition for taking the time to rewrite my words in their own languages: Kim Eunmi, Dimopoulou Mesenia, Charlotte Pietsch, Shin Seongman, and Ga Yohan.

Finally, I would like to say a special thank-you to Lucia Moja-Strasser, one of the great unsung heroes of existential therapy. Like many other UK-trained existential therapists, Lucia was a pivotal figure in my development as an existential therapist, and without her dedication, honesty and encouragement, I would not have been in a position to write this book.

Needless to say – and particularly from an existential standpoint – the contents of this book are my responsibility alone.

1

INTRODUCTION: THE RICH TAPESTRY OF EXISTENTIAL THERAPIES

This chapter discusses:

- The diversity of existential approaches to therapy.
- The rationale for writing this book.
- The book's aims.
- The structure and content of the book.
- The case study that will be used throughout the book to illustrate existential theory and practice.
- My personal biases and assumptions.

'What is existential therapy?' As a therapist and trainer, this is one of the questions that I have been most frequently asked. It has also been one of the questions that I have found the most difficult to answer. 'It's ... um ... about facing the reality of existence,' I have sometimes muttered, or come out with a stock response like, 'It's similar to person-centred therapy ... only more miserable!' Over the years, however, it has gradually dawned on me why this question has been so difficult to answer: because the term *existential therapy* has been used to refer to so many different therapeutic practices. Indeed, as Norcross (1987: 42) puts it, 'Existential therapy means something to everyone yet what it means precisely varies with the exponent.' Hence, while Yalom's (1980) existential psychotherapy encourages clients to face up to four 'ultimate concerns' of existence (death, freedom, isolation and meaninglessness), van Deurzen's (2012a) existential psychotherapy encourages clients to explore four dimensions of worldly being (the physical, personal, social and spiritual dimensions). And while Bugental's (1978) existential-humanistic approach encourages clients to focus *in* on their subjective experiences, Frankl's (1984) logotherapy often encourages clients to focus *out* on their responsibilities towards others. Today, then, it is widely accepted that it is not possible to define the field of existential therapy in any single way. Rather, it is best understood as a rich tapestry of intersecting therapeutic practices, all of which orientate themselves around a shared concern: human lived-existence. In other words, as Walsh and McElwain (2002: 254) conclude, it is more 'appropriate to speak of existential psychotherapies rather than of a single existential psychotherapy'; and this is the fundamental premise for the present book.

Of course, to a great extent, there is diversity within every form of therapy. Indeed, one could quite rightly argue that there are as many forms of therapeutic practice as there are therapists. Nevertheless, there are reasons why the field of existential therapy is more diverse than most. First, as Halling and Nill (1995: 1) write, existential therapy 'cannot be traced to a single authoritative source'. It has no founder, no Freud or Rogers, to give the approach a common theoretical and practical basis. Rather, since the first decades of the twentieth century, existential approaches to therapy have emerged spontaneously – and, at times, independently – in various regions of the world. Second, the philosophical field on which existential therapeutic practice is based (existential philosophy) is, itself, enormously diverse (Chapter 2, this volume). Hence, practitioners drawing from these ideas have tended to draw from very different beliefs and assumptions. Third, existential philosophical writings can be extraordinarily complex and difficult to understand. Hence, interpretations – and, at times, misinterpretations – of what existential philosophers have said have brought about a great diversity of therapeutic applications. Fourth, as Schneider and May (1995a) point out, existential therapists have spent much of their energies reacting against traditional approaches to therapy – particularly psychoanalysis – rather than proactively generating coherent, integrated models of practice. Finally, though, at the heart of an existential standpoint is the rejection of grand, all-encompassing systems, and a preference for individual and autonomous practices. Hence, few existential therapists have been concerned with establishing one particular way of practising existential therapy. Indeed, for most existential therapists, the idea that this approach can be systematised, or even manualised, is anathema to the very principles of the approach.

Despite this heterogeneity, the existential approach seems to be thriving today, with 136 existential therapy institutes in 43 countries across all inhabited continents (Correia, Cooper, & Berdondini, 2016a). Craig (2015: 81) writes, 'existential thinkers and practitioners today constitute a vibrant global community of individuals and groups who gather the meanings of lived experience wherever they find the human breath and heartbeat.' Indeed, there are claims that the existential approach is growing (e.g., Barnett & Madison, 2012; Craig, 2015); and the proliferation of existential texts, societies and training programmes would seem to testify to this (Correia, Cooper, & Berdondini, 2014b). Perhaps this is because of the intrinsically anti-conformist nature of the existential approach: its refusal to be categorised or defined. In an era of manualised, evidence-based 'treatments', existential therapy continues to provide counsellors and psychotherapists with an opportunity to express their independence, individuality and creativity; that is, to meet their clients as the unique human beings that they (as therapists) are, and not merely as the implementers of standardised treatment protocols. More than that, it provides a framework in which therapists can encounter each of their clients as the unique human beings that their *clients* are, and not merely as manifestations of particular psychological disorders.

Aims

The primary aim of this book is to introduce readers to the rich tapestry of existential therapeutic approaches. It aims to map out the different existential therapies, such that readers can learn to distinguish their Binswanger from their Bugental, and are able to identify the key dimensions along which these existential approaches differ. More than that, though, the book aims to stimulate and excite readers: to present the rich array of existential ideas and therapeutic practices in the hope that students and practitioners – of both existential and non-existential therapies – will find much here to incorporate into their own therapeutic work. A third aim of the book is to act as a signpost: to help readers identify areas of existential thought and practice that are of particular interest to them, and enable them to follow up these particular interests through further reading, or through contacting relevant organisations and/or websites. Finally, the book aims to contribute to a range of debates within the field of existential therapy, among them:

- What can clients hope to take from an existential approach?
- What are the strengths and limitations of the different existential approaches to therapy?
- What are the kinds of choices and dilemmas that existential therapists face?

Structure

Following this introduction, the book goes on to an overview of existential philosophy (Chapter 2). This is the kind of chapter that, as they say, you may want to come back to later. It's very 'theory-rich', and while you may want to learn about the philosophical ideas informing the existential therapies before looking at their actual practices, you may want to start with the practice, and then later come back to explore their philosophical roots.

After this chapter, the book goes on to look at a range of existential approaches to one-to-one therapy. Here, I have tried to focus on the most prominent, pervasive and influential approaches: those around which the greatest numbers of practitioners have constellated, and which have produced the greatest number of books, journals, conferences and training courses (Correia, Cooper, Berdondini, & Correia, 2016c, see Box 1.1). Wherever possible, I have also tried to include in these chapters brief descriptions of less prominent existential therapies which can be associated with these approaches. For instance, in the chapter on the existential-humanistic approach, I have also described Betty Cannon's (1991, 2012) 'Applied Existential Psychotherapy'.

Box 1.1   The 20 most influential authors on contemporary existential practice

In 2012, Edgar Correia, a Portuguese existential psychotherapist, surveyed over 1,000 existential therapists from around the globe to discover the authors that they considered most influential on their practice (Correia et al., 2014a). The top 20 are presented below, with the number of times that they were cited by respondents.

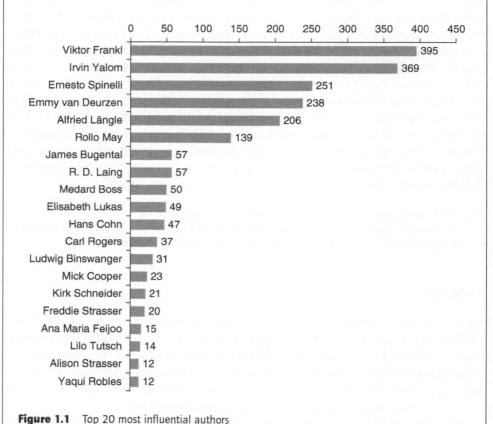

Figure 1.1   Top 20 most influential authors

Given that this book aims to act as a signpost, it also concentrates primarily on those existential therapies that readers are able to follow up, where there are books that are still in print (and in English) and professional bodies that can be contacted (see 'Recommended resources' at the end of each chapter). In some instances, I have included books that are no longer in print in the recommended resources because they are such key texts. Often, such books can be obtained through second-hand book-finding services (for instance, www.bookfinder.com), or through a university's inter-library loans service. These chapters also tend to focus on those existential approaches that outline specific forms of therapeutic practice, as opposed to purely psychological or psychiatric understandings.

Five existential approaches to therapy are examined in these chapters, roughly in chronological order of their origins. Chapter 3 looks at the *daseins-analytic* approach, which critiques many of the dominant assumptions within the field of psychoanalysis and psychotherapy, and encourages clients to open themselves up as 'Being-in-the-world'. Chapter 4 examines the *meaning-centred* approaches, based on Victor Frankl's logotherapy, which place particular emphasis on helping clients to discover meaning in their lives. In Chapter 5, the dominant brand of existential therapy in the United States, the *existential-humanistic* approach, is examined. This is an approach which places particular emphasis on helping clients to uncover their subjective experiences and to courageously face the givens of their lives. Here, the work of Irvin Yalom as well as Rollo May and other well-known American existential therapists will be explored. Chapter 6 looks at the work of R. D. Laing, who developed an existential model of schizophrenia, and outlined some of the knots and entanglements that interpersonal relationships can become tied up in. This chapter is somewhat different from the others, in that Laing did not develop a particular school of practice. Nevertheless, his work is of such importance to the field that it deserves a chapter in its own right. Finally, Chapter 7 looks at the development of the *existential-phenomenological* branch of existential therapy, with a particular focus on the work of two key figures in the UK: Emmy van Deurzen and Ernesto Spinelli. These approaches build on the work of Laing to develop a particularly descriptive, de-pathologising model of therapy.

To avoid repetition, I have tended to focus on the distinctive ideas and practices of each of these approaches, rather than those ways of working that they share with other existential (and non-existential) therapies. In fact, research indicates that there is a lot of overlap in the practices of therapists from different existential schools (Correia et al., 2016c) – aside from the meaning-centred approaches, which do tend to be quite distinctive (Correia et al., 2016c) – so this should be borne in mind when reading these chapters.

Of course, practitioners associated with each of the different approaches will also practise in very different ways, and they may also practise very differently with different clients. So while these chapters aim to identify the core beliefs and practices of each of the approaches, it is probably more useful to think of these different ways of thinking and working as existing on a range of dimensions, which will often cut across schools. This is explored in the penultimate chapter of the book (Chapter 8). Finally, Chapter 9 concludes by looking at some of the challenges and opportunities facing existential therapies in the years to come.

Each of the chapters begins with a series of bullet points describing the content of the chapters, and ends with recommended resources (primarily books and websites). There are also questions for reflections that some readers may find useful to stimulate further thought or discussion. In addition, within the chapters are some suggested self-reflective exercises. As the questions and exercises invite you to think about yourself personally, please ensure that you have appropriate support in place should you need it (for instance, a colleague who can be contacted). Of course, they are also optional and you may choose to skip them if you think they seem unhelpful.

With respect to terminology, throughout the book, I have used the term 'client' rather than 'patient', 'service user', 'analysand', etc. However, it should be noted that some of the different existential schools do use these alternative terms. The term 'therapy' is also used to refer to both 'counselling' and 'psychotherapy'.

Client study: Introducing Siân

For this new edition, a few people suggested that it might be helpful to have a client study running through it: something that could illustrate the different therapies and the way in which their practices might vary. So throughout the chapters of this book I will be using the case of Siân (pronounced 'Sharn') to illustrate the different existential methods and understandings. To preserve anonymity, and so that I can illustrate a range of practices (including those that I have not actually used in my own work), the case of Siân is fictional rather than actual. However, her characteristics, and her journey through therapy, are drawn from genuine clients who I have worked with over the years. In addition, wherever possible, the dialogues that I present with her are based on actual therapeutic work.

To introduce Siân, let's imagine a brief vignette of a first session together. We meet in a small room in a community-based counselling centre, and we are both sitting in comfortable armchairs. The room is softly lit with up-lights, with a large photograph of a cloudscape on creamy yellow walls. Siân has a shock of pink in her shoulder-length dark hair, and a brooch on her jacket that looks like it has been made out of plasticine. She fiddles with the ring through her nose. 'It was a long way down,' she says, about 20 minutes into the session, 'and … it was funny, I – I couldn't help laughing. It was the most weirdest thing.' I lean forward, hands clasped together under my chin. Siân continues: 'I just kept saying over and over in my head, "Siân, you're such an idiot, you're such an idiot, you're such a fuckin' idiot …. "' Siân glances up at me, smiling playfully, and then looks back down at the floor. Siân is describing a summer evening, a few months earlier, when she had sat on a window ledge outside her bedroom, wondering whether or not to jump. 'In the end,' continues Siân, 'I climbed back in and I thought, "Either I jump or I get into therapy … I don't know which is worse!"' She smiles at me again and I smile gently back.

Having established with Siân that she is not currently at risk of suicide or self-harm, we go on to talk about the issues that had brought her into therapy. Siân describes feeling depressed, stuck and lost in her life, as if she keeps hitting walls whatever direction she runs in. She says:

> If it was just one thing I could probably have dealt with it; but it's just … everything piled on top of me: like a big fat grey elephant sitting on my head. If I deal with one thing I've immediately got the next one to face. And then, when I've sorted out all these problems, I've got to work out what the hell I want to do with – with my life.

Siân looks at me, smiles wryly, then back down at the floor. She tugs at her shoelaces. After a short while she continues.

> Thirty … I'm 30 and I don't know what I want to do with my life yet. How stupid is that! I feel so empty and aimless. 'Life is passing me by' and everything like that. That's when I thought about just ending it all. That big bloody grey elephant sitting on my head. So heavy. And shitting on me too!' People must just be – they're so sick of me. Droning on. So boring. I used to be – just now a middle-aged, boring *schlump*.

Siân talks about being frustrated in her job: working from home as a web designer. She says that, when she was in art college in her early 20s, she had been in an indie folk band which she loved, but her father 'guilt tripped' her towards a career, so she had taken a college course in web design. Siân had hoped that this work would be an outlet for her creativity. Instead, however, she has found it all 'fonts and formatting', with hours spent writing in computer codes for companies and products that she has no interest in or care for. Siân goes on to say that, because she was also encouraged by her dad to take out a mortgage on a flat, and because she is working on a freelance basis, she has a lot of money worries. She describes having to constantly 'schmooze' people to get work, which she hates.

Siân says that her relationship with her girlfriend, Hanako, also feels like a dead end: 'I don't feel I get anything from her,' says Siân. According to Siân, they are constantly arguing, and she experiences Hanako as cold, distant and absent. 'I try *so* hard to get it right for her,' Siân says, 'but she just doesn't seem to like me. Whatever I do.' However, Siân says that she feels 'torn' about leaving Hanako, and it is something that keeps her up at night with worry. 'I just think,' says Siân, 'that maybe I'm the problem. I'm too passive, too girly, too commitment phobic – and totally fucked up by my past.' Siân describes how her mother died from breast cancer when she was two, and her father – struggling to cope with bringing up Siân and her younger brother – tended towards self-absorption, hopelessness and depression. Siân says that she can recall only a few times when her father had been loving, affectionate and focused on her – all after he had spent the evening drinking at a neighbour's house.

The one ray of light in her life, says Siân, is her six-year-old son, Kai. Siân says that she adores him, loves holding his little hand on the way to school in the morning, and kissing and cuddling him when she puts him to bed at night. But she worries that she is letting Kai down and is a 'bad mother'. 'I just can't bear him being around me when I'm so low all the time,' she says. 'He needs love, he needs fun. He needs something so different from me.'

So how might the different existential approaches understand some of the problems that Siân is experiencing, and help her to address them? This is something that we will explore throughout the chapters of this book.

Personal biases

Finally, a word about personal bias. From an existential perspective, bias is unavoidable: it simply isn't possible for me, or for anyone else, to stand above the world of existential therapies and give an objective 'God's eye account' (Merleau-Ponty, 1962) of the field. This means that the way I present the different approaches, the criticisms I raise, and even the approaches that I choose to present will undoubtedly be influenced by my own particular leanings. This I cannot change, but what I can do is two things. First, I can try to minimise any biases that I know are present. Second, I can alert you, the reader, to my own particular perspective, such that you are more able to put my biases and assumptions to one side.

My own approach to therapeutic practice tends to be at the gentler, more descriptive, less structured end of the existential spectra (see Chapter 8, this volume). I come from a family background that emphasised left-wing, progressive values (see Cooper, 2006), and have always be drawn to those therapies that emphasise relatively egalitarian, non-hierarchical client–therapist relationships. Hence, during my training in the existential-phenomenological approach at Regent's College, London, I found myself particularly drawn to Spinelli's relational-phenomenological approach (Chapter 7, this volume), and still see myself practising broadly in this way. This was further reinforced by many years in the world of person-centred training and writing (see, for instance, Cooper, Schmid, O'Hara, & Bohart, 2013; Mearns & Cooper, 2005). However, in the last decade or so, my interest in collaborative therapeutic relationships has taken me in the direction of *pluralistic therapy* (Cooper & Dryden, 2016; Cooper & McLeod, 2011; see Chapter 7, this volume). This holds that different clients are likely to need different things at different points in time – both existential and otherwise – and that the best way of working out what a client needs is to talk to them about it. Because this approach emphasises the potential helpfulness of multiple therapeutic practices, in recent years, I have become more open to the value that many different therapeutic understandings and methods can have, whether relational, existential or otherwise.

Another important bias that will become evident in this book – particularly in this second edition – will be my views on research, and especially the value of more quantitative, outcome-focused methods such as randomised controlled trials. Like many in the existential field (e.g., Schneider & Krug, 2010; Shapiro, 2016), I am deeply sceptical of the view that such methods have a privileged place on the 'hierarchy of evidence'. Quantitative outcome research, by its very nature, works in generalities, is reductionistic, and tells us very little about the value of particular therapies for particular individuals. At the same time, however, and unlike many others in the existential field, I *do* believe that such evidence can play a valuable role in helping us reflect on, and evaluate, our approaches (Cooper, 2004). Outcome research speaks in generalities but, as I have argued, so do most other things, like philosophy or psychotherapeutic theories (Cooper, 2004). That is, we will always come to our clients with generalised assumptions about what they might find helpful: 'it is never possible for us to encounter our clients from a neutral, un-tainted perspective' (Cooper, 2004: 7). Hence, for me, even the most quantitative, mechanistic research can help us to reflect on our *a priori* assumptions and biases, and challenge us to think in different ways. I may assume, for instance, that logotherapy is not that helpful, or that a relational approach is the most effective means of helping clients, but if the outcome research shows otherwise, I am afforded an opportunity to reassess my views, and to practise in ways that may be more genuinely responsive and helpful to my clients. Throughout this edition of the book, then, outcome evidence will be used as one means of critically reflecting on the different approaches, although I have also drawn on process research – both qualitative as well as quantitative – wherever possible, to inform the discussion.

Conclusion

The existential therapies are a rich and complex field, and the aim of this book is to map out the different approaches and compare and contrast them. Most importantly, though, the aim of the book is to bring the existential field to life in all its rich and colourful vibrancy. My hope is that readers will take, from this book, an increased interest in the existential field, and a greater understanding of how all the different approaches relate and interact.

Questions for reflection

- What are your aims for reading this book? What do you hope to get from it?
- What personal biases do you bring to reading this book? What do you think, for instance, makes therapy effective? And, are there any existential approaches that you are more or less drawn to?
- If you were going to write your own book about existential therapy (and haven't done so yet), what would you want to say?
- What would be your initial response to meeting Siân?

Recommended resources

Barnett, L., & Madison, G. (Eds.). (2012). *Existential psychotherapy: Vibrancy, legacy and dialogue*. London: Routledge.
Wide-ranging collection of papers that reflects the current state-of-the-art of existential therapy.

Correia, E., Cooper, M., & Berdondini, L. (2014). The worldwide distribution and characteristics of existential psychotherapists and counsellors. *Existential Analysis, 25*(2), 321–337.
Data on the global distribution of existential therapists and approaches.

Correia, E., Cooper, M., Berdondini, L., & Correia, K. (2016). Existential psychotherapies: Similarities and differences among the main branches. [doi: 10.1177/0022167816653223] *Journal of Humanistic Psychology*.
Survey-based study of the similarities and differences across the existential schools.

Craig, M., Vos, J., Cooper, M., & Correia, E. (2016). Existential psychotherapies. In D. Cain, K. Keenan & S. Rubin (Eds.), *Humanistic psychotherapies* (2nd ed., pp. 283–317). Washington, DC: American Psychological Association.
An evidence-based review of contemporary existential thought and practice.

Iacovou, S., & Weixel-Dixon, K. (2015). *Existential therapy: 100 key points and techniques*. London: Routledge.
Pithy summary of the key elements of existential thought and practice.

van Deurzen, E. (Ed.) (in press). *World handbook of existential therapy*. London: Wiley.
Definitive and comprehensive guide to existential thought and practice across the major schools.

A full list of existential societies and training institutes around the globe, compiled by Edgar Correia of the *Sociedade Portuguesa de Psicoterapia Existencial*, is available at: sppe.pt/publicacoes. Also published as Correia, Cooper, & Berdondini (2016a, 2016b).

2

EXISTENTIAL PHILOSOPHY: THE MEANING OF BEING

This chapter discusses:

- The nature of an existential philosophical perspective.
- The existential focus on questions of existence.
- The phenomenological foundations of an existential approach.
- The characteristics of existence, as described by existential philosophers: unique, verb-like, freely-choosing, towards-the-future, limited, in-the-world, with-others, embodied, and inherently anxious and guilty.
- The potential for authentic and inauthentic modes of existing and relating.
- Critiques of existential philosophy.

At the most general level, existential therapy can be defined as 'a form of therapeutic practice that is based, primarily or wholly, on the assumptions associated with the existential school of thought' (Cooper, Vos, & Craig, 2011). To understand the nature of existential therapies, therefore, it is essential to understand something of the philosophical tradition from which these ideas arise.

Unfortunately, the field of existential philosophy is surrounded by much confusion and misunderstanding. For many people, it is associated with images of gloomy cafés in post-Second World War France, and Gauloises-smoking intellectuals furtively discussing the meaningless of existence. Many people also associate it with such concepts as nihilism, angst, atheism and death. These images and associations have tended to arise because existential philosophy is sometimes equated with the existential*ist* movement of Jean-Paul Sartre and his circle, who did, indeed, develop their writings in France around the end of the Second World War, and took a relatively melancholic – though by no means pessimistic (Heidegger, 1996a) – view of existence. Today, however, the term 'existential philosophy' tends to be used in a broader sense, to refer to the writings of a loosely connected group of thinkers who are neither predominantly French nor atheistic, nor concerned with the meaninglessness of existence (Guignon, 2002) (see Box 2.1). Indeed, while many of these thinkers were active around the first half of the twentieth century, existential ideas have a lineage that 'can be traced far back in the history of philosophy and even into man's pre-philosophical attempts to attain some self-understanding' (Macquarrie, 1972: 18). Existential ideas, questions and ways of philosophising have been identified in the teachings of such notable figures as Socrates, Jesus and the Buddha (Macquarrie, 1972), as well as in such ancient philosophical systems as Stoicism (van Deurzen, 2002).

Box 2.1   Key existential philosophers

- **Søren Kierkegaard** (1813–1855): Danish philosopher and father of modern existentialism. Criticised the lack of passion and the conformity of nineteenth-century Christendom, as well as the all-embracing, abstract philosophising of Friedrich Hegel. Argued that human beings needed to turn towards their own subjective truths, and make a personal leap of faith towards God.
- **Friedrich Nietzsche** (1844–1900): German philosopher. Attacked the slavish, herd mentality of conventional Christianity, and preached an atheistic gospel of aspiration towards the Übermensch: the autonomous 'overmen' who create their own values and morality, and live earthly lives of passion and commitment.
- **Martin Buber** (1878–1965): Jewish philosopher and theologian. Emphasised the relational nature of human existence, and the distinction between 'I–Thou' and 'I–It' modes of relating (see below).
- **Karl Jaspers** (1883–1969): German psychiatrist-turned-philosopher, whose ideas underpinned many twentieth-century developments in existential philosophy, among them the unavoidable 'boundary situations' that human beings face.
- **Paul Tillich** (1886–1965): German protestant theologian who fled to the United States in the 1930s, bringing with him the existential style of philosophising. Advocated courage in the face of the anxiety of non-being, and distinguished between *existential* and *neurotic anxiety* and *guilt*.
- **Gabriel Marcel** (1889–1973): French philosopher, playwright and Christian. Emphasised the mysteriousness and immeasurability of existence, and the importance of fidelity and openness to others, as well as the primacy of hope.
- **Martin Heidegger** (1889–1976): German philosopher, and the most influential thinker on contemporary existential practice. Earlier work emphasised resolution in the face of anxiety, guilt and death, while later work placed a greater emphasis on language and an openness towards Being.
- **Jean-Paul Sartre** (1905–1980): French philosopher, novelist, playwright and social critic. Probably the best-known existential philosopher, who emphasised the freedom at the heart of human existence, and the angst, meaninglessness and nausea that it evokes.
- **Maurice Merleau-Ponty** (1907–1961): French philosopher, particularly recognised for his emphasis on the embodied nature of human existence.
- **Simone de Beauvoir** (1908–1986): French philosopher, writer and activist, who developed an existential ethic of freedom and wrote about the social and historical factors that could limit choice.
- **Albert Camus** (1913–1960): French novelist and philosopher. Emphasised the absurdity of human existence, but the possibility of creating meaning in a meaningless world.
- **Frantz Fanon** (1925–1961): Afro-Caribbean philosopher and psychiatrist, whose work extended existential ideas to anti-colonialist thought and revolutionary practice.

The confusion surrounding existential philosophy, however, has not been helped by existential philosophers themselves. Many of these philosophers' writings are exceedingly opaque; and some, such as Kierkegaard (1992), have deliberately aimed to express their ideas indirectly. Take the following passage, for instance: 'The self is a relation that relates itself to itself or is the relation's relating itself to itself in the relation; the self is not the relation but is the relation's relating itself to itself' (Kierkegaard, 1980b: 13). The fact that 'Existentialists disagree with one another, at least in part, on virtually every philosophical issue imaginable' (Wartenberg, 2008: 3) also makes it difficult to develop a coherent understanding of the approach. For instance, while some existential philosophers are deeply religious (such as Kierkegaard, Buber and Marcel), others are committed atheists (such as Sartre, Nietzsche and Camus). Similarly, while some emphasise the need for individuality (such as Kierkegaard and Nietzsche), others emphasise the need for relationship (such as Buber, Marcel and Jaspers). And while some consider existence to be ultimately meaningless (such as Sartre and Camus), others place great emphasis on the primacy of hope (such as Marcel). One can only speak of existential philosophers in the loosest sense, then, as a group of thinkers – across history – who show some 'family resemblances' in their outlook and style of philosophising.

The fact that existential philosophy is a difficult, contradictory and ill-defined field of inquiry, however, is in no way grounds for dismissing it out of hand. Indeed, as a philosophy that emphasises diversity over uniformity, concreteness over abstractness, dilemmas over answers, and subjective truths over grand-encompassing theories, such complexity is the very lifeblood of existential philosophy itself. Existential philosophy is difficult to understand, in part, because it is a difficult set of ideas – ideas that challenge our very assumptions about how things are. Indeed, it is difficult to understand because existence, itself, is difficult to understand! To engage with these ideas, then, requires a willingness to step into an uncertain and dimly-lit world, and to put to one side a need for certainty and quick, easily-digestible answers.

Existence

What, then, is the family resemblance that all existential philosophers share? A useful starting point is to consider existential philosophy as an approach that, as the name suggests, takes as its primary concern the *existence* of human beings (Ellenberger, 1958).

This notion of *existence* can be compared against its traditional counterpart, *essence*. The essence of an entity is *what* it is – the universal, abstract and unchanging characteristics that make it one kind of entity rather than another (Macquarrie, 1972). For instance, we might say that the essence of this book is that it is about existential therapy. By contrast, the existence of an entity is the fact *that* it is, that it has a particular, concrete being. The existence of this book, then, is that it is this particular book that you have in front of you, with all its particular sentences, scribbles in the margins, and coffee stains. This existence is more than a collection of abstract, essential qualities; it is the reality of the actual entity in front of you.

Figure 2.1 is an attempt to diagrammatically represent existence and essence. As this diagram suggests, an entity's essence is what it is made up of, and one must imagine each of these 'internal' essences being common to a whole range of entities. By contrast, the existence of this entity is how this particular entity manifests itself in its totality: it is the unique way in which this particular entity encounters its world.

Try looking over this book for a minute or two, focusing on its particular concrete existence. If such a way of looking at it seems unfamiliar to you, it is probably because, in our culture, we tend to focus on essences rather than existence. Since the time of Plato (around 400 BCE), philosophy has searched for the universal, abstract and unchanging truths that lie behind manifest existence (Macquarrie, 1972). Science, borne from within this tradition, has emerged as the essentialist project *par excellence*, breaking 'reality' down into ever-more fundamental laws and components. Within this essentialist world-view, an entity's existence is little more than a superficial mask that conceals its 'true' reality.

Over the course of the nineteenth and twentieth centuries, this essentialist outlook has become increasingly applied to an understanding of human beings. Positivism, developed by Auguste Comte (1978–1857), proposed that human society and human beings could be understood in terms of their underlying laws and rules (Mautner, 1996). This led to the development of such essentialist psychologies as behaviourism and classical psychoanalysis,

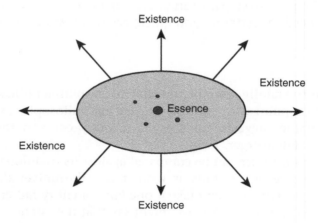

Figure 2.1 Existence and essence

where the concrete individual was broken down into such constitutive parts as stimulus and response, or id and superego (respectively, Watson, 1925; Freud, 1923). Similarly, Friedrich Hegel (1770–1831), one of the most influential philosophers of the nineteenth century – and to whom much contemporary existential thought is a reaction – developed a philosophical system in which concrete, individual human existences were subsumed within a model of highly abstract and universal processes.

Few existential philosophers have questioned the value of studying inanimate objects in an essentialist, scientific way. What they vigorously reject, however, is the extension of this outlook to an understanding of human beings. Indeed, some existential philosophers, such as Heidegger (1962), use the term 'existence' to refer solely to human existence. Existential philosophy, then – particularly in its nineteenth- and twentieth-century form – can be understood as a reaction to philosophical and scientific systems that focus on the universal, abstract and unchanging essences behind concrete human existence: that treat particular human beings primarily as members of a genus or instance of universal laws (Guignon, 2002). Such essentialist approaches are rejected because, from an existential perspective, the concrete reality of human existence is irreducible to a set of essential components. That is, even if I could list every one of your essential qualities – for instance, your level of extraversion, your 'intelligence quotient', and the neurochemicals passing through your brain – I would still not be describing *you*, because the actual, concrete *you* that you are is more than all these essential components put together. In this respect, an existential approach may best be described as a particular *ethic*: that human beings should be treated, first and foremost, *as* human beings, and not as something other than human (Cooper, 2015).

This existential stance can be illustrated by looking at what it would mean in working with our client, Siân. Here, first and foremost, it would mean trying to encounter Siân *as* Siân – the concrete human existent that she is: that is, the person who feels a great adoration for her son, Kai; who lies awake at night with worry next to her partner, Hanako; who struggles over computer code in her web design work. And even if, for instance, it turns out that Siân meets criteria for depression, or has an 'avoidant' attachment pattern, an existential approach would mean that we do not approach Siân chiefly, *as* a depressive or *as* an avoidant attachment type. These might be aspects of Siân, but Siân, from an existential standpoint, would be understood as so much more than that: as a unique, integrated, irreducible whole.

The phenomenological method

A key contribution to an understanding of this human existing comes from the field of phenomenology, as developed by the German philosopher Edmund Husserl (1859–1938). Following in the footsteps of the French philosopher

René Descartes (1596–1690), Husserl adopted a standpoint of radical doubt, arguing that all we can know is what we experience: the 'inner evidence' that is given to us intuitively in our conscious experiencing of things. In other words, to truly know ourselves and our world, we need to turn our attention to our conscious, lived-experiences.

To do so, Husserl outlined a range of methods or *reductions*, starting with the *phenomenological method*, which Spinelli (2005), drawing on Ihde (1986), describes in terms of three interrelated steps. The first of these steps is the *rule of epoché*, whereby we are urged to 'set aside our initial biases and prejudices of things, to suspend our expectations and assumptions, in short, to *bracket* all such temporarily and as far as it is possible so that we can focus on the primary and immediate data of our experience' (Spinelli, 2005: 20). In particular, Husserl urges us to set aside our *natural attitude* – the assumption that objects in the external world are objectively present in space and time – and instead focus solely on our immediate and present experiencing of them. It is important to note here that Husserl is not suggesting that we should try to deny, negate or eradicate our assumptions. Rather, he is suggesting that we 'bracket', 'suspend', 'withhold' or 'parenthesise' them, such that we can consider alternative possibilities, and develop a deeper understanding of how we actually experience our world. The second step in the phenomenological method, according to Spinelli, is the *rule of description*, the essence of which is '*Describe, don't explain*' (Ihde, 1986: 34). Here, we are urged to refrain from producing explanations, hypotheses or theories as to what we are experiencing, and instead to stay with the lived-experiences as they actually are. Third, there is the *rule of horizontalisation*, which 'further urges us to avoid placing any initial hierarchies of significance or importance upon the items of our descriptions, and instead to treat each initially as having equal value or significance' (Spinelli, 2005: 21). To this can be added a fourth step, *verification*, whereby we 'keep checking back ... whether our observations and descriptions are true to the actual phenomena perceived and experienced' (van Deurzen, 2012b: 9). This phenomenological reduction may then be followed by attempts at an *eidetic reduction*, which aims to identify the universal essences underlying things (van Deurzen & Kenward, 2005), and by the *transcendental reduction*, which aims to identify the essence of 'pure' consciousness (Linsenmayer, 2011).

Drawing on phenomenology, twentieth-century existential philosophers – such as Sartre, Merleau-Ponty and Heidegger (who was an assistant to Husserl) – have all argued that, to understand human existence, we need to put to one side abstract hypotheses, analytical procedures, and philosophical theories, and instead focus on human existence as it is actually lived. Indeed, these philosophers are often referred to as existential-phenomenologists.

If we go back to Siân, then, a phenomenological perspective would argue that, if we really want to understand her, we need to understand how she *experiences* her world. We need to know, for instance, what it is like for her lying there next to Hanako: what is she thinking, what is she feeling, what is she wanting to do? And, it would suggest that the way that we can do this is, first, by bracketing any assumptions we might have about that experiencing. For instance, as her therapist, I might assume that Siân is feeling alone and sad as she lies there, but perhaps she is actually feeling scared that Hanako is going to make a sexual 'move' towards her. Second, from this phenomenological standpoint, if I want to know about this experiencing, I should ask Siân to *describe* what that is like, rather than analysing or offering an interpretation of what she is saying. In addition, from a phenomenological standpoint, I should try to treat everything Siân says as being of equal validity, and reflect back to Siân my understanding of her experiencing for verification. From here, I might then want to go on and explore potentially universal essences behind Siân's experiencing: for instance, that human beings feel anxiety when they experience themselves as the objects of others' desires.

This phenomenological process can help us understand more about people's existences as actually lived, but there are a number of important differences between an existential philosophical outlook and a Husserlian phenomeno-logical one. First, existential philosophers have tended to reject the idea that, through the various reductions, we can arrive at a pure consciousness (i.e., a transcendent ego). Rather, they have argued that human existence is funda-mentally and inextricably immersed in its world. Second, existential philoso-phers have moved away from the Husserlian emphasis on cognitive, conscious processes to focus on embodied, practical, concrete involvement in the world.

Existential philosophers, as with some phenomenologists, have also gone on to try to say something about the universal, invariant qualities of this human existence. (Heidegger uses the term *ontological* to refer to such charac-teristics, reserving the term *ontic* for the activities of each particular human existence within these givens; Cohn, 2002.) Different existential philosophers have emphasised different – and, at times, contrasting – *givens*, but there are a number of commonalities across the existential spectrum, and these will be explored in the following sections.

Existence as unique

One of the characteristics of each human existence that existential philosophers have most consistently pointed to is its uniqueness. Each of us, it is argued, is distinctive, irreplaceable and inexchangeable (Macquarrie, 1972): with a unique potential that we bring into the world. This is an inevitable corollary of a philo-sophical outlook that emphasises concrete, particular actualities over shared, universal essences. If, for instance, you and I were understood in terms of such universal characteristics as levels of extraversion or neuroticism (for instance, Goldberg, 1990), then it might emerge that we are relatively similar people. If, however, I am understood as me-writing-this-now, and you are understood as you-reading-this-then, then we are all of a qualitatively distinctive order.

For some existential philosophers, this emphasis on the uniqueness of each human existence is coupled with a highly individualistic outlook. Kierkegaard, often considered one of the most individualistic existential philosophers, held that each person is a solitary being, with no connections to anyone or anything else apart from God (Guignon, 2002). Within every human being there is a 'solitary wellspring' within which God resides, he writes, and he derides those who treat immortality or faith as socially-shared affairs (Kierkegaard, 1992).

On the bases of such writings, it is often assumed that all existential philosophers hold that 'the individual is inexorably alone' (Yalom, 1980: 353). Many existential philosophers, however, hold that the basic state of human existence is to be with-others (see 'existence as with-others', below). As Macquarrie writes, then, there is a 'deep tension to be found among existential philosophers, even sometimes in one and the same philosopher, as they are torn between the individual and communal poles of existence' (1972: 84). As we shall see, this tension is also evident in the contrasting practices of some existential approaches (Chapter 8, this volume).

Existence as a verb-like flow

Virtually all existential philosophers have also argued that human existence is not a noun-like thing, but a verb-like happening. This is a challenge to the commonly held assumption, derived from a natural science worldview, that human beings are entities alongside other entities in the world: fixed, static, substance-like objects that can be studied in the same way that atoms or tables can (Heidegger, 1962). In contrast, existential philosophers have argued that human existence is fundamentally dynamic in nature, that it is a flux (Merleau-Ponty, 1962), an unfolding event (P. Hoffman, 1993), a path (Jaspers, 1986) or a process (van Deurzen, 1998). Indeed, the very word 'exist' comes from the Latin verb *existere*, which means to stand out or emerge (Macquarrie, 1972). Existence, then, can be conceived as an upsurge (Sartre, 1958), a becoming, a bursting forth into the world. In this respect, it is not just that we can understand people in terms of their moment-to-moment living existing, but that, ontologically, people *are* their lived existing. So, from this existential perspective, we would understand Siân *as* that lying-in-bed-feeling-the-coldness-of-the-sheets-worrying-Hanako-will-pounce-on-her. From this standpoint, it is not that Siân *has* this experiencing, or that this experiencing is the product of some deeper, realer, entity-like Siân. Rather, from this existential perspective, this experiencing *is* Siân.

A phenomenological exercise may help to illustrate this point. Reflect, for a moment, on what you are experiencing as you read these words. Initially, you may perceive yourself as a thing-like self encountering another thing: this book. If you try to bracket this natural attitude, however, and simply focus on what you are experiencing, you may come to see that your experiencing is a reading-of-these-words-now, or a wondering-what-this-is-on-about, rather than a fixed thing encountering another fixed thing.

From an existential perspective, then, we are first and foremost a verb-like being, and it is only subsequently that we may define ourselves as a noun-like thing, such as 'an extrovert' or 'a therapist'. This is the meaning of the well-known Sartrean (1958: 568) phrase: 'Existence precedes essence' (see Figure 2.2). In other words, human beings are not fixed selves, but a relationship towards their own being; or, as Kierkegaard puts it, 'a relation that relates itself to itself' (1980b: 13). For Heidegger, too, the essence of human existence is 'self-interpretation' (Dreyfus, 1997). As human beings, we are constantly making sense of ourselves and understanding who we are – even if this is not at a level of reflective self-awareness.

Existence as freely choosing

At the heart of existential philosophy is also the assertion that human exist-ence is fundamentally free (Macquarrie, 1972). This directly challenges the assumption – particularly prevalent among scientific psychologies – that human thoughts, feelings and behaviours are always determined by a prior set of circumstances or conditions, such as unconscious drives or external stimuli. For existential philosophers such as Kierkegaard (1980a) and Sartre (1958), human existence erupts into the world out of no-thingness, and thereby cannot be reduced to a set of determinative causes. From this per-spective, freedom is not an 'add-on' to being, but the essence of being itself (Sartre, 1958). Sartre writes: 'Man does not exist *first* in order to be free *sub-sequently*; there is no difference between the being of a man and his *being-free*' (1958: 25).

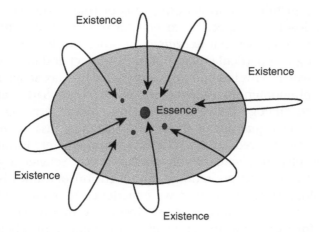

Figure 2.2   Existence precedes essence

While empirical debates rage about the reality of human freedom (e.g., Bargh, 2004; Ryan & Deci, 2004), phenomenological reflection reveals that such freedom is an integral part of human lived-experience (Guignon, 2002). As you are reading this, for instance, you are unlikely to experience yourself as being impelled by a set of causes to act in a particular way. You are unlikely to feel, for instance, that you are *determined* to turn the page, or *caused* to adopt the particular beliefs outlined in this book. Rather, you are likely to experience yourself as having the possibility of making choices. You may feel, for instance, that you could choose to stop reading this book and make yourself a cup of tea, or tear up the pages of this book and burn them. Of course, you may not want to behave in this way, but *wanting* is a very different notion from being deterministically *impelled* to do one thing or another.

Of all the existential philosophers, it is Sartre (1958) who places the greatest emphasis on human freedom. In asserting that existence precedes essence, he is suggesting not only that we are an upsurge of nothingness prior to any fixed identity, but also that 'Man is nothing else but what he makes of himself' (1996: 259). In other words, we *are* our choices: our identity and characteristics are a consequence – and not causes – of the choices that we make. From this perspective, then, there is nothing that caused you to become the person you are, whether therapist, parent or extrovert. Rather, you became you by virtue of the choices that you have made in your life. That is, these identities are only an outcome of the (ultimately groundless) decisions that you have made. Applied to Siân, then, an existential perspective would reject the idea that there is something intrinsic to her that has *made* her 'passive', 'girly' or 'commitment phobic'. Rather, it would hold that she has chosen to behave in particular ways throughout her life, from a plethora of possibilities, and has also come to define herself in particular ways that could always be otherwise.

Sartre (1958: 38) also argues that human beings are the creators of their own values: 'my freedom is the unique foundation of values and ... *nothing*, absolutely nothing, justifies me in adopting this or that particular value.' Not all existential philosophers agree, however. Marcel (1949), in particular, argued that values are not chosen but *recognised*. In other words, we do not decide to value something in a particular way, but have a direct and immediate intuition of its intrinsic worth. This is a point of view shared by Max Scheler (1874–1928), a prominent phenomenologist, who influenced both Sartre and Heidegger. Scheler drew an analogy between values and colours, arguing that both are directly experienced qualities of things. For instance, just as we immediately intuit that an object is red, so, for Scheler, we immediately intuit whether it is pleasant or unpleasant, valuable or worthless, etc. Scheler argued that this immediate, intuitive and pre-rational apprehension of values is given in our feelings (Dunlop, 1991), such that we experience happiness when we intuit pleasantness in a thing, or bliss when we intuit spirituality. The significance of this position for existential therapy will become apparent when we go on to look at logotherapy in Chapter 4 of this book.

Existence as being-towards-the-future

In challenging a causal, deterministic understanding of human beings, existential philosophers – most notably Heidegger (1962) – have also challenged traditional assumptions about the nature and movement of time. In general, we tend to think of past, present and future as three consecutive regions on a time-line, with the present moving imperceptibly from what was to what will be. If we start with how human beings actually experience their world, however, this conceptualisation would no longer seem satisfactory. As you read these words, for instance, your initial experiencing is not something that is past, but something that is in the present. You are reading *these words here*, not the words in the sentence before. In this sense, then, one might say that the present tends to precede the past: existence begins with an eruption in the immediate now, and only subsequently goes back to its prior state of being.

Contrary to popular myth, however, existential philosophers do not 'begin by isolating man on the instantaneous island of his present' (Sartre, 1958: 109). Rather, they see existence as inextricably past, present *and* future. While the past, then, is not seen as causing the present, it is still seen as being fundamentally woven into its woof. As you read this sentence, for instance, you do so in the present, yet the way you presently experience it is inextricably related to what you have experienced in the past. Had you been brought up only learning Swahili, for instance, then your experiencing of these words might be very different, for instance as meaningless blurs. Hence, existence may emerge in the present, but it always 'takes up' its own past (Heidegger, 1962).

For Heidegger, however, '*Everything begins with the future!*' (2001: 159). In taking up our past, we do not simply apply it to the present, but use it to act towards future goals, meanings and possibilities. 'Man first of all,' writes Sartre, 'is the being who hurls himself towards a future and who is conscious of imagining himself as being in the future' (1996: 259). From an existential perspective, the basic ground for human action is motives rather than causes (Heidegger, 2001): we pull ourselves from ahead, rather than being pushed from behind. In other words, your reading of this book is not, first and foremost, something that was caused to be, but something that is orientated towards an end goal such as achieving a greater knowledge of existential therapy.

Sartre (1958) uses the term *projects* to refer to the kinds of plans that we have for the future, and suggests that they may be of a higher or lower order. The project of reading this book, for instance, may be part of a higher-order project of becoming a better therapist, which might, itself, be part of a higher-order project, such as 'contributing to a better society'. As with our freedom, however, Sartre argues that our projects – right up to our highest-order, 'original' ones – are ultimately groundless. That is, they have no externally-given, extrinsic foundations: nothing outside ourselves on which they can be based. In other words, from a Sartrean perspective, our lives have no given, automatic meaning – there are only the meanings that we choose to endow them with. Viktor Frankl (1986), founder of logotherapy, likens this self-creation of meaning to the illusion of the Indian fakir, who throws a rope up into the air and then proceeds to climb up it himself; and, like the fakir's illusion, Camus (1955) and Sartre conclude that life is essentially absurd. For them, there is no profound reason for living, for going through the agitation of daily living and suffering. While we strive towards meanings and purposes, there are none to be found – only those that we have created ourselves out of nothing. This leads Camus (1955: 11) to state that: 'There is but one truly serious philosophical problem and that is suicide. Judging whether life is or is not worth living amounts to answering the fundamental question of philosophy.' Later on in this chapter, we will see how Camus attempts to answer this question.

It should be noted again, however, that not all existential philosophers share this belief. For Marcel, for instance, the hope that there is an order and integrity to the universe is 'oxygen for the soul' (Blackham, 1961), and not something to be disparaged. Buber (1958: 140), too, emphasises the fact that, in the presence of a Thou (see below), there is an inexpressible confirmation and assurance of meaning, such that 'The question about the meaning of life is no longer there'. We will come back to this viewpoint when we look at the meaning-centred approaches in Chapter 4.

Existence as limited

While existential philosophers argue that human beings are fundamentally free to choose their own future, it would be wrong to assume that they see human beings as free to do whatever they want. For Jaspers (1986), for instance, human existence runs up against numerous *limit-situations* – such as death, suffering, struggle and guilt – which cannot be transcended, avoided or resolved. In such respects, existential philosophers have consistently emphasised the fact that human freedom is 'hedged in' in innumerable ways (Macquarrie, 1972). Hence, an understanding of the limits of human existence is as important to existential philosophers as an understanding of its freedom. For Kierkegaard (1980b), both 'possibility' and 'necessity' are intrinsic aspects of our existence, and the 'mirror of possibility', alone, reflects only half the truth.

Heidegger (1962) and Sartre (1996) use the term *facticity* to designate the limiting factors of existence (Macquarrie, 1972). The factical is the given, and some of the factical aspects of human existence have already been examined in this chapter, such as the fact that we are free. From an existential perspective, for instance, we cannot choose not to be free: even if we choose not to choose, we are still making a choice. Facticity also refers to the fact that we always find ourselves in a particular concrete situation. For example, right now I am surrounded by a computer, a desk, a phone and walls, none of which is of my making, and all of which limit my freedom in some way. I cannot just walk through the space where the wall is to get directly to my kitchen. My freedom is bounded in a very real way.

Heidegger (1962) uses the term *thrownness* to refer to the fact that existence, right from its very start, finds itself thrown into a particular factical situation that is not of its making. We did not choose, for instance, to be born to our particular parents, nor did we choose the particular social, historical and cultural context in which we emerged. The term 'thrownness' also refers to the fact that, like the throwing of a dice, there is no reason for why we should find ourselves emerging in one particular situation rather than another (Macquarrie, 1972).

Hence, from an existential perspective we do not determine the beginning of our existence, and neither do we determine its end. Death, as Heidegger (1962) and other existential philosophers have emphasised, is the inescapable, immovable boundary at the end of our lives. Like a road block beyond which we cannot pass, it brings to an end all our projects and possibilities. It is the 'congealing point of existence' (Jaspers, 1932), which summarises and completes our being. For Heidegger, this death is of particular importance because of his emphasis on being as being-towards-the-future. Hence, for Heidegger, our being is a being-towards-death. In this respect, death is not only an unavoidable event at some point in our future, but also an intrinsic component of our every moment of being.

Thrownness and death, then, are like two bookends on either side of existence – boundaries that our freedom and choice cannot extend beyond – and circumscribing these two boundaries is the boundary condition of chance (Jaspers, 1932). There is no reason why we are thrown into our particular beginnings; often no reason why we meet our particular end; and, in between, we are constantly encircled by a 'huge tide of accident'. Opportunities come to us or evade us in ways that are beyond our control: a chance meeting sets the beginnings of a life-long relationship; we lose our job because of a fall in shares on the Tokyo stock market; cells mutate in our body and we are afflicted with cancer.

From an existential perspective, then, we cannot fully control our beginnings, our endings, or much of what happens in between, but what we can choose is how we *face* these ontological limitations. Even a person who is imprisoned, writes Sartre (1958), is free to decide whether to stay put or to try to escape. Hence, while we might say that human existence is constricted like a rat in a cage, this is very different from saying that a human being *is* a cage: that it is fixed and determined without any possibility of movement and choice.

Existence as in-the-world

While earlier existential philosophers tended to emphasise the individuality and aloneness of each human being, later existential thinkers, most notably

Heidegger (1962) and Merleau-Ponty (1962), have emphasised the in-the-worldness of human existence. '[T]here is no inner man,' writes Merleau-Ponty; 'man is in the world, and only in the world does he know himself' (1962: xi). In other words, existence is not located *within* the individual, but *between* the individual and their world. Indeed, Heidegger uses the term *dasein* – literally translated as 'being-there' – to refer to the specifically human form of being; at other times, he writes of the hyphenated *being-in-the-world* to emphasise the indissoluble unity of person and world. In other words, he is suggesting that your reading-these-words-here is not something that takes place in your head, but between you and the words on this page: it is located on the inter-worldly, rather than intrapersonal, plane. Such an assertion is a radical challenge to another pervasive assumption within Western culture: that we can talk about human beings in isolation from their context.

The roots of this philosophical standpoint can be found in the phenomeno-logical concept of intentionality, which proposes that consciousness is always consciousness *of* something (Spinelli, 2005). My awareness is always directed to something outside myself – whether real or imagined – and if my conscious existence is my very being, then those external entities are a fundamental part of who I am. Heidegger (1962) developed this standpoint by arguing that, in our everyday existence, we are constantly appropriating objects and tools without being aware of them as separate entities. As I write these words, for instance, I am not experiencing my computer as something that is separate from me: at the level of existence, it is a fundamental part of my very being. Only when it goes wrong do I then experience it as something distinct: as *that* useless pile of plastic and silicon. Hence, if my very being is my concrete doing, then these objects within the world are a primordial part of my existence.

In his later writings, Heidegger (1996b) moved away from an understand-ing of human beings as the manipulators of their world, and towards an understanding of human beings as the 'custodians', 'guardians' or 'shepherds' of Being as a whole. That is, *dasein* is like the guardian of a clearing in the forest, where the Being of the world can be seen for what it is; or like an 'aperture', in which the truth of Being can be revealed. From this perspective, man is not the 'Lord of Being', but its servant, who is entrusted with the most dignified of tasks: of bringing the truth of Being to light. This notion of human being as an openness to the world is of particular importance to the daseinsanalytic school of existential therapy, which will be examined in Chapter 3 of this book.

Existence as with-others

Along with arguing that human existence is fundamentally in-the-world, later existential philosophers have also argued that human existence is fun-damentally with-others. This philosophical position – generally referred to as an *intersubjective* one (Crossley, 1996) – further challenges the dominant Western belief that human beings are separate and distinct identities. It proposes that each of our existences is fundamentally and primordially intertwined with the existences of others. In other words, you are not simply you. Rather, you are a meeting point across a complex network of relationships, inextractable from your interpersonal context.

Heidegger's (1962) account of this intertwining is rooted in the fact that the way we appropriate entities in the world is based on public – rather than private – understandings. The way I type on my computer, for instance, is not something that I determined alone, but is based on how my culture has deemed it appropriate to type: for instance, with five fingers, putting spaces between words, etc. Indeed, the very language that I use to write this book is not something that I have evolved independently, but is acquired from my socio-cultural nexus. If, then, my very existence is a typing-these-words-here, it is fundamentally infused with the being of those others, and can never slip out of its cultural context.

On this basis, Heidegger (1962), like Sartre (1958), argues that our existence is fundamentally contingent and groundless. By this, Heidegger means that our being-in-the-world is not rooted in some personal truth or reality, but in interpretations that are public and non-specific to us (Dreyfus, 1997). We are, as Dreyfus (1997: 25) puts it, 'interpretation all the way down': our very being is permeated by social, generic, impersonal understandings. Heidegger refers to these understandings as the world of *the they* or *the One*. It should be noted here, however, that Heidegger is not simply talking about a tendency to conform. Rather, he is saying that we are fundamentally and unavoidably infused with the being of others. In other words, the way that we play sports, the way we talk to each other, and the way that we relate to our children are all grounded in a socially-constructed nexus of meanings and interpretations that are not solely of our making.

Heidegger (1962) also presents some preliminary ideas about concrete relationships with others, and identifies two particular modes of relating: *leaping in* and *leaping ahead*. Leaping in involves taking over the other person's concerns and projects for them, and handing the task back to them when it has been completed, or disburdening them of it altogether. So with Siân, for instance, leaping in might involve telling her how she should sort out her relationship. In such relating, writes Heidegger (1962: 158), 'the Other can become one who is dominated and dependent, even if this domination is a tacit one and remains hidden from him'. For him, this is the most prevalent form of relating to others. By contrast, in leaping ahead, we help the other to do things for themselves, to address their own concerns and projects (1962: 159). So, for instance, this might involve providing Siân with an opportunity to think things through for herself. For Heidegger, such a form of relating helps the other to open up to their possibilities for being, and to exist in a more authentic manner (see below). This distinction is of clear relevance to the practice of therapy, and is particularly emphasised by the daseinsanalytic approach (see Chapter 3, this volume).

Of all the existential philosophers, however, it is Buber (1958) who examines concrete relationships with others in most detail. Like Heidegger (1962), Buber holds that the I is always in relation to an Other, but he makes a fundamental distinction between *I–It* and *I–Thou* attitudes to this Other. In the I–It attitude, the other is experienced as a thing-like, determined object: an entity that can be systematised, analysed and broken down into universal parts. We might perceive the Other, for instance, as a neurotic whose adult ego is constantly threatened by their unconscious drives. By contrast, in the I–Thou attitude, we behold, accept and confirm the other as a unique, un-classifiable and un-analysable totality: as a freely-choosing flux of human experiencing. For Buber, such an I–Thou attitude requires a meeting with the Other as they are in the present, rather than in terms of our past assumptions or future needs. It is an opening-out to the Other in their actual otherness – and a loving 'confirmation' of that otherness – rather than a self-reflexive encounter with our own stereotypes and desires. Buber also argues that such an I–Thou attitude requires the I to take the risk of entering itself fully into the encounter: to leap into the unpredictability of a genuine dialogue with all of its being (including its vulnerabilities) and to be open to the possibility of being fundamentally transformed by the encounter. Buber is not talking here about a merging with the Other – we cannot encounter what we are – nor is he suggesting that we can, or should, always relate to others in an I–Thou way. What he is suggesting, though, is that we have the potentiality of experiencing moments of deep, I–Thou connection with Others. We shall explore the relevance of this assertion to therapy later on in the book.

For Sartre (1958), too, human existence is inextricably social; yet, in contrast to Buber (1958), he tends to see relationships as inevitably 'it-ifying'. For Sartre, the 'look' of the other constantly threatens to turn the I into an object, into a fixed thing that is devoid of freedom and possibilities. Suppose, for instance, that as you are reading this book, you become aware that someone is standing behind you, observing your every movement. Now, instead of experiencing yourself as a reading-this-book, you become aware of yourself as an object to this person's gaze: a 'thing' with such characteristics as sloppy posture or unkempt hair. In attempting to defend ourselves against such objectification, Sartre suggests that human beings may try to objectify the other instead, and get locked in a battle of objectify-or-be-objectified.

For Sartre, this struggle is particularly complex in intimate relationships where we want to possess the love of another, yet want this love to be 'freely' given. It is of little value, for instance, to know that someone loves us because they *have* to, yet it can be equally frustrating to feel that someone else's love is beyond our control. For Sartre, then, relationships are almost inevitably frustrating, unfulfilling and conflict-ridden. 'Hell', he famously suggests, 'is other people.' This perspective is of particular importance when we go on to look at Laing's description of interpersonal relationships in Chapter 6 (this volume). As Fanon (1991) suggests, it may also be helpful in understanding the experiences of clients from Black and other oppressed minorities, who are objectified through 'the look' of the dominant majority. Fanon (1991: 82), describing his experiences as a Black Caribbean in France, writes, 'I came into the world imbued with the will to find a meaning in things, my spirit filled with the desire to attain to the source of the world, and then I found that I was an object in the midst of other objects.'

Existence as embodied

Many existential philosophers, most notably Merleau-Ponty (1962), have emphasised the fundamentally embodied nature of human existence. That is, we are inextricably bodily beings; we *are* our bodies; and it is only through our bodies that we can engage with, encounter and 'rise towards' our world. This can be illustrated through phenomenological reflection. If you focus on what you are experiencing as you read this, you will become aware that it has an ineradicably bodily dimension. For instance, you may notice that you experience a slight straining at the side of your eyes, or a gnawing in the pit of your stomach. You will also become aware that these bodily experiences cannot be entirely separated off from your 'mental' experiences: at every moment, your experiencing has the quality of a psychosomatic whole. Such a standpoint, then, challenges the traditional Cartesian assumption that mind and body are qualitatively distinct entities, and that the former is in some way superior to the latter.

In fact existential philosophers, such as Heidegger (1962), have argued that the very way we *understand* our world is embodied. As you read this chapter, for instance, you will be intellectually processing these words; but you will also be experiencing them in a bodily-felt way. For instance, you may experience feelings of excitement in response to some of these ideas, or frustration in response to others. From a traditional, Cartesian standpoint – one that puts mind over body – such bodily-felt experiences are little more than secondary, irrational responses. However, from an existential perspective, our bodily-felt experiences are an immediate, direct and intuitive apprehension of our world that may precede our intellectual grasp (as per Scheler, see above). Rather than being derivative, then, they can be considered *equiprimordial* (i.e., of equal priority); and rather than being considered irrational, they can be considered of equal validity to our intellectual understandings. Indeed, as Nietzsche (1967: 71) writes: 'There is more wisdom in the body than in thy deepest learnings.'

The idea that we apprehend our world in a direct and bodily way leads Heidegger (1962) to state that we are always 'in a mood'. By this, he does not mean that we are always grumpy, but that human existence is intrinsically *attuned* to its world. Furthermore, these moods – as immediate, intuitive ways of recognising particular facts (Warnock, 1970) – give us vital access to the truth of our being (Guignon, 2002). This embodied understanding of being is particularly significant in the 'focusing'-orientated approaches to existential therapy (see Madison, 2015; Madison & Gendlin, 2012).

Existence as anxious

Of all the moods that can help us recognise the truth of our being, existential philosophers – most notably Heidegger (1962) and Kierkegaard (1980a) – have placed particular emphasis on anxiety. While it may seem that existing as a unique, no-thing-like, freely-choosing happening is relatively agreeable, existential philosophers have argued that such a being-ness brings with it profound feelings of dread and angst. This is particularly the fact that we are freely choosing beings. '[F]reedom's possibility announces itself in anxiety', writes Kierkegaard (1980a: 74); and he goes on to argue that the more we acknowledge and act on our freedom, the more we will experience angst.

Why should this be the case? First, as Yalom (2001: 148) puts it, 'alternatives exclude'. In choosing one thing, I am always choosing against something else, and there is always the possibility that I will choose against the better alternative. An illustration of this is Siân feeling torn about separating from Hanako. On the one hand, if she chooses to leave Hanako, she may free herself from the pain and anguish of being in that relationship; but, in doing so, she is also excluding the possibility of a deepened relationship with someone she loves. And for Siân, as is so often the case in life, the reality is that she does not know, and *genuinely cannot be certain*, which is the best option to choose. She must make decisions, and vitally important decisions, in the midst of uncertainty. For Sartre (1958), what makes these choices even more anxiety-evoking is the fact that we choose not only for ourselves, but also for others as well. So, from this perspective, Siân's feelings of anguish may be intensified because she knows that her choices will affect Kai's life as well as her own. Hence, from an existential standpoint, while we, alone, are responsible for our decisions, we also carry a responsibility to the rest of the world on our shoulders. No wonder, then, that Sartre describes human beings as 'condemned', rather than 'blessed', to be free.

From an existential perspective, what further exacerbates this anxiety is the fact that we have nothing solid on which to base these choices. As Sartre (1958) argues, we have no fixed identity, no given meanings to guide us – or on which we can blame our choices. Like a person lost in the jungle, we are forced to cut our own path through life, with no directing signs or maps to point us in the right direction. Indeed, from a Heideggerian (1962) perspective, the most fundamental anxiety comes from a realisation that all those signs and maps that we thought were givens are ultimately only socially agreed conventions. With a flash of dread, we realise that all those activities we assumed were intrinsically meaningful – the way we do our jobs, the way we treat our friends, the way we think and write – have no ultimate grounding, and could easily be other. It is as if we suddenly realise that our whole world is nothing but a theatre stage and we are merely playing a part: absorbed in a world of empty constructs and roles that only give the illusion of some ultimate meaning-motivating action (Dreyfus, 1997).

From an existential perspective, however, it is not only that freedom and nothingness bring with them anxiety, but also the fact that our existence runs up against unmovable boundaries, such as death and chance. Indeed, it is only because of these boundaries that our choices are infused with angst. If, for instance, we lived forever, we could make all the choices that we wanted to, and alternatives would not exclude. In other words, anxiety is the 'dizziness of freedom' (Kierkegaard, 1980a: 61) in the face of limitations.

Existence as guilty

For Heidegger (1962), freedom brings with it not only anxiety, but also guilt. Here, Heidegger is not using *guilt* in the traditional sense of having wronged others, but in the sense of having wronged oneself: of having failed to fulfil one's ownmost potential. Yalom (1980) suggests that we might think of such existential guilt as 'regret' or 'remorse'. For Heidegger, such guilt is unavoidable. As we have seen, in making choices, we are always excluding certain alternatives, such that we are always in debt to ourselves for not carrying out all our possibilities in life. In other words, we always lag behind who we might have been. In choosing to follow an academic path, for instance, I renounced the possibility of developing my potentiality as a journalist. Such a possibility continues to haunt me: perhaps I could have been the editor of a national newspaper by now – I will never know. From an existential perspective, however, one thing is certain: were I the editor of a national newspaper, I would still be experiencing guilt about something else, such as my failure to actualise my academic potential.

Existence as inauthentic

From an existential perspective, then, anxiety and guilt – as well as other 'negative' feelings, such as dread, despair, unsettledness and a sense of absurdity – are responses to the reality of our human condition. They are intrinsic, and *intelligible* (i.e., meaningful), parts of our *primary experiencing*: our immediate feelings, thoughts and desires towards-the-world (Cooper, 2015). It is also argued, however, that few of us welcome the emergence of such feelings. Rather, we try to quell them; and we do so by turning a blind eye to the reality of our existence: pretending to ourselves that things are other than they really are. Heidegger (1962) refers to such self-relating as *inauthentic*, while Sartre (1958) writes of *self-deception* or *bad faith*.

At the heart of such self-deception is a denial of our freedom and responsibility, and we may do this in a number of ways. Supposing, for instance, that in the midst of my annual diet, I am visited by a friend, who brings with him a large bar of chocolate. I am then faced with a choice: do I eat some of the chocolate and undermine my diet, or do I commit myself to spending the whole evening staring longingly at it? One strategy that I may adopt to attenuate the anxiety that this choice evokes is to turn myself into a 'thing' (Sartre, 1958). For instance, I may tell myself that I am 'someone with no will-power', such that the eating of the chocolate becomes a *fait accompli*. Alternatively, I may tell myself that I am 'a committed dieter', such that there is no chance of me eating the chocolate. Either way, by objectifying myself, I am denying the reality that, at that point in time, I am entirely free to choose how I behave, and am compelled to behave in neither one way nor the other.

If I subsequently eat the chocolate, I may then adopt a number of strategies to deny my responsibility for doing so. For instance, I may blame my friend for bringing the chocolate around, or I may blame it on some unconscious, inner urge: 'I just couldn't stop myself'. Adhering to an ideology or dogma may be another form of denying my true freedom and responsibility. I might say to myself, for instance, that 'inner desires should always be followed' – such that there is no question of choice whenever they emerge.

From an existential perspective, another means of denying the freedom and responsibility that I, as an individual, hold is by falling in with 'the crowd'. I might think to myself, for instance, that if my friend is eating the chocolate, then it is OK for me to do the same: 'We couldn't all possibly get obese'. That way, I do not need to think for myself, but can simply adhere to the behaviours and values of others. For Heidegger (1962), the essence of inauthenticity is such a falling-in with the world of *the One*, but it is important to remember here that he is not simply talking about conforming. Rather, he means the tendency to fall in with the socially agreed nexus of meanings, and to take them as givens, rather than recognising their fragility and contingency. It is not just a question, then, of me eating the chocolate as my friend is doing; rather, it is my falling in with the whole world of dieting, and the fact that I do not question whether being thin is really so meaningful. I have simply assumed I should try to lose weight, rather than questioning the whole validity of this cultural assumption.

Here, it is important to note that, for Heidegger, we do not start off as true to ourselves and only later become inauthentic (cf., Rogers, 1959). Rather, from his perspective, we are primordially fallen prey to the social world, and can only subsequently gain some distance from it.

Self-deception may also involve trying to deny the given restrictions and limitations of our lives. I know, for instance, that my friend's chocolate bar is enormously high in calories, but I may try to pretend to myself that things really aren't quite so fixed. I might say to myself, for instance, that it's probably a relatively low-calorie chocolate, or that the peanuts in it reduce the calorific intake. In terms of denying the givens, Heidegger (1962) puts particular emphasis on the way that we tend to deny our impending demise. We talk of death, for instance, as something that only happens to other people; or we paint the faces of the deceased for funeral viewings, such that we can pretend death is a peaceful state of slumber, rather than the complete absence of all existence (Farber, 2000). Indeed, for Sartre (1958) bad faith is ultimately a continual slippage between a wholly deterministic understanding of our being and a wholly volitional one. We veer from seeing ourselves as totally determined, to seeing ourselves as totally free, such that we can never get pinned down to the anxiety-evoking reality of our being: that we are free to choose within a given set of limitations.

Hence, from an existential perspective, human beings have a tendency to try to hide from the reality of their existence; but, they argue, we pay a heavy price for such self-deception. For philosophers like Heidegger (1962) and Sartre (1958), when we deny our freedom and responsibility, we also deny our possibility of freely choosing towards our own future, and actualising our ownmost potentiality for being. Instead of developing our unique possibilities, we become 'levelled down': 'dispersed' within a public world that reduces everything down to a bland, uniform averageness. Here, we lose the possibility of a life infused with passion, creativity and vitality, and instead become deadened, domesticated, tranquillised and alienated from ourselves (Guignon, 2002). In essence, we live only half a life rather than a full one. We can see this in the case of Siân. With her website design career and her mortgage, Siân has the 'comfort' of doing things like everyone else, but she is miserable doing it, and feels like her life is passing by.

From an existential standpoint, when we are not engaging with life as it really is, we are also less capable of meeting the challenges and givens that will inevitably confront us. What is more, the kinds of defence that we put up to protect ourselves from the existential reality inevitably falter, such that *existential* anxiety, guilt or shame become *neurotic* manifestations of these moods (Holzhey-Kunz, 2014; Tillich, 2000). For instance, from an existential standpoint, we might hypothesise that Siân's adoption of a girlish, 'likeable' persona is a way of trying to avoid her existential responsibilities. It is as if she is saying, 'I'm sweet, I'll do what you say, I'm not in charge.' Existentially, however, it could be argued that, at some level, Siân knows that this is not the entire truth: that is, she knows that she *is* an adult woman; she does have feelings like anger; she shares responsibility for a child; and she does have to make choices in her relationship. This awareness, we might hypothesise, creates anxiety for Siân; and one way that she might attempt to deal with it is by trying to shore up her girlish, likeable persona even further. So, for instance, she tries harder to be seen as playful and fun, and worries more and more that people do not really like her. Here, Siân's existential anxiety (of being responsible) gets sublimated into a neurotic anxiety (of people not liking her). And, from this perspective, because being liked by others is not really Siân's fundamental issue, however much she achieves it, her deeper existential concerns may continue to haunt her. In this respect, we can think of anxiety problems as 'failed efforts to confront and solve a finite number of unavoidable existential dilemmas that every human being will experience' (Wolfe, 2008: 204).

Existence as authentic

How, then, can we forge a life that is intense, passionate and whole? In moving towards a more authentic way of being, Heidegger (1962), like many other existential philosophers, has emphasised the importance of adopting an attitude of courage and resolve: a willingness to 'stand naked in the storm of life' (Becker, 1973: 86). In particular, it has been argued that we need to be willing to face our anxiety. For Kierkegaard (1980a: 156), the courageous person does not shrink back when anxiety announces itself, 'and still less does he attempt to hold it off with noise and confusion; but he bids it welcome, greets it festively, and like Socrates who raised the poisoned cup, he shuts himself up with it and says as a patient would say to the surgeon when the painful operation is about to begin: Now I am ready.'

Through facing up to such anxiety, it is argued that we are 'jerked' out of our pseudo-securities – out of our absorption in pseudo-familiar tranquillity (Macquarrie, 1972) – and summoned to face our ownmost freedom and possibilities (Heidegger, 1962). In this respect, then, existential anxiety is not irrational or a sign of pathology, but a teacher and guide. 'Whoever has learned to be anxious in the right way,' writes Kierkegaard (1980a: 155), 'has learned the ultimate'; and he goes on to state that, 'the more profoundly he is in anxiety, the greater is the man'. In the case of Siân, then, we might say that it *is* anxious for her to acknowledge that she has some choices, and that the decisions she makes *will* affect herself and those around her. And, to some extent, any choice she makes is a frightening leap into the dark. But, at the same time, by grasping her life 'by the scruff of the neck', Siân can start to decide who and how she wants to be.

In this respect, an attitude of resolve also involves courageously facing one's existential guilt. As we have seen, to some extent, we will always experience a sense of guilt over our unfulfilled possibilities, but the more that we hide from our freedom and potentiality, the more this sense of guilt will grow. For Heidegger (1962), this guilt is revealed to us in the call of our 'conscience': 'an abrupt arousal' that calls us back to ourselves, that reminds us of our debt to our own being. It is a summons – albeit a silent one – out of our lostness in the One. And although, for Heidegger, we can never entirely stand outside the nexus of social meanings, we can 'choose to choose' which social practices and possibilities we take up, rather than blindly falling in with the One.

Like existential anxiety, then, existential guilt is not considered a negative experience, but a mentor on the path towards greater freedom. 'The more profoundly guilt is discovered,' writes Kierkegaard, 'the greater the genius' (1980a: 109).

Existential philosophers have also argued that an authentic self-relational stance involves resolutely facing the fact that there are no ultimate grounds for our projects, meanings and interpretations. This is not to suggest, however, that we should adopt a nihilistic or hopeless attitude towards life. As Camus (1955) states, we can still live and create in the very midst of a desert. A resolute attitude, then, means committing ourselves to projects *despite* their absurdity. It involves 'a decisive dedication to what we want to accomplish for our lives. And our stance towards the future is that of "anticipation" or "forward-directedness": a clear-sighted and unwavering commitment to those overriding aims taken as definitive of one's existence as a whole' (P. Hoffman, 1993: 229). Camus likens this commitment-in-absurdity to the activities of the mythological Sisyphus, who is condemned by the Greek gods to ceaselessly roll a rock to the top of a mountain, whereupon the stone falls back under its own weight. Sisyphus' task is absurd and unceasingly meaningless, and yet he does not falter or give up. 'The struggle itself towards the heights is enough to fill a man's heart,' writes Camus (1955: 111), and he suggests that, through being conscious of his fate, Sisyphus gains a strength and dignity, such that he can descend the mountain in joy as well as sorrow.

In adopting a more authentic self-relational stance, Heidegger (1962) also puts particular emphasis on resolutely facing our mortality. Here, however, he is not suggesting that we should be broody or pessimistic, but that we should live every day in the knowledge that we are moving towards an inevitable – and indeterminable – ending. For him, it is through such an acknowledgement that we can make the most of our days: it is as if we darken the background behind our existences such that the foreground of our being comes to light more fully. To know that our existences may end at any moment also means that we cannot continually defer our choices and projects. It means that we must get on with life. From this perspective, then, Siân is quite right to acknowledge that her life is passing her by. It *is*, and she could carry on in this state of indifference for the rest of her life. But by acknowledging that her life is finite, and that she only has a limited time on earth to do the things that she wants to do, it is argued that Siân has the potential to make different choices: to forge for herself an existence that is more vibrant, meaningful and alive.

Furthermore, from an existential standpoint, in acknowledging our being-ness-towards-death, we are lifted above the world of the One, for, according to Heidegger (1962), our being-towards-death is a journey that we must take alone. No one can die for us; no public body or group of friends can protect us from our inevitable demise (Hoffman, 1993); and no one else can draw together the totality of our lives in the face of this final ending. Hence, through acknowledging that we are on an individual and unique journey towards death, we also come to realise the individuality of our lives, and with it the possibility of actualising our ownmost potential.

In striving towards a more authentic way of being, many other existential philosophers have also emphasised the importance of distancing ourselves from the One. For Kierkegaard (1992), our true and highest task is to be a single individual: to turn towards ourselves, to think for ourselves, and find truth in aloneness rather than in 'chumminess with others'. This authentic individual, for Kierkegaard, has a great love of and need for solitude, and he compares him to those '"Utterly superficial nonpersons and group people"' who experience, 'such a meagre need for solitude that, like lovebirds, they promptly die the moment they have to be alone' (1980b: 64). For Kierkegaard, then, 'Everyone should be chary about having dealings with "the others" and should essentially speak only with God and with himself' (quoted in Buber, 1947: 208). Similarly, for Nietzsche, 'the one essential for the morally adult man is to create his own values and reject the stock morality of his group' (Warnock, 1970). To be authentic is to be obedient to one's own ideals, values and beliefs rather than those of 'the herd'.

Authenticity as towards otherness

For some existential philosophers (such as Sartre, 1958), authenticity tends to end here: with a commitment to one's own projects and possibilities in the face of absurdity. As we have seen, however, for many philosophers of existence, such as Buber (1958), human existence is not a self-contained phenomenon, but something that reaches out beyond its own being. From this standpoint, then, to exist authentically is to acknowledge and actualise one's connectedness with something – or someone – beyond one's own self.

For Kierkegaard, for instance, resolutely facing one's anxiety and withdrawing from the crowd are not ends in themselves, but first – albeit essential – steps on a journey towards an authentic relationship with God (Macquarrie, 1972). Tillich (2000), too, highlights the possibility of moving beyond self-acceptance towards acceptance by a transcendent other, and, like Kierkegaard, challenges traditional conceptions of faith and God. For Tillich (2000: 186), absolute faith is not a belief in some kind of concrete, ego-like patriarch – or what Kierkegaard (1980b: 123) calls a 'super-father Christmas'. Rather, it is an openness to 'the God above the God of theism'. Tillich describes this God above Gods as a kind of acceptance or forgiveness, a transcendence that cannot be demonstrated or proved. For him, then, absolute faith is the 'acceptance of acceptance without somebody or something that accepts' (2000: 185): it is an openness to being accepted and forgiven, even though one cannot identify the source of that unconditional love.

Another philosopher of existence who has placed great emphasis on the transcendence of the self towards God is Buber. In direct contrast to

Kierkegaard, however, Buber (1947) argues that the way to God is not through renouncing relationships with others, but through developing closer and more intimate interpersonal relationships. For Buber (1958: 99), God is the 'eternal Thou', the 'Centre' where the 'extended lines of relation' meet. Hence, in developing and maintaining I–Thou relationships with other human beings, he suggests that we have an immanent and immediate experience of God. Buber (1988: 61) argues, then, that 'the inmost growth of the self is not accomplished, as people like to suppose today, in man's relation to himself, but in the relation between one and the other'.

For Marcel (1949), whose brand of existential philosophy shares many similarities to Buber's, such a reciprocal relationship of presence also requires a *fidelity* to the Other: a faith in the presence of an other-than-me to which I respond, and to which I continue to respond (Blackham, 1961). For Marcel (1949: 72), such fidelity is 'like the faithful following, through darkness, of a light by which we have been guided and which is no longer visible to us directly'. It is an unwavering loyalty to the other, whether human or supra-human. For Marcel, such fidelity also involves an *availability* to the other: a being-at-the-'disposal' of the Other when they are in pain or in need; and a 'receptivity' to the Other, in the sense that one might actively receive a guest. Marcel writes that such an understanding of human existence and relating is a way out of the 'extravagantly dogmatic negativism which is common to Sartre, to Heidegger and even to Jaspers' (1949: 65), in that it forms the basis for a genuine hope. Through loving and being loved by something outside myself, my existence no longer feels superfluous, but 'upheld', 'willed' and 'justified'. This leads on to the work of such post-existential philosophers as Levinas (1969), who develop this concept of Being as an availability to the Other.

In his later writings, Heidegger (1996b) also emphasises the importance of an openness to something beyond the self – an emphasis which balances his earlier focus on resolve (van Deurzen, 1998). For him, however, this something is not God, but Being itself. Human beings, as we have seen him suggest, are the 'shepherds' of Being; and in his later writings, he outlines a stance by which *daseins* can authentically fulfil this role. This is an attitude of *gelassenheit*, which might be translated as a stance of 'abandonment' or 'releasement' towards things (Macquarrie, 1972). It is a non-manipulative, non-imposing serenity that lets things be what they are – an openness to the Being of beings, a meditative letting-oneself-into-nearness of Being (Heidegger, 1966). Such a way of being accords with a mindful form of thinking: a waiting upon thoughts to come, rather than a wilful generation of ideas and representations. It is also a form of thinking characterised by composure, calmness and concern – a slowing-down of pace – and contrasts with 'calculative', scientific thinking, which manipulates its world and races from one idea to the next. We will see how these ideas can be therapeutically applied in Chapter 3 of this book on daseinsanalysis.

Existence as unresolvable

From the preceding sections, one might conclude that existential philosophers have proposed an essentially linear view of human development: that human beings, fallen into a world of inauthenticity and alienation, have the possibility of recovering themselves through an attitude of resolve and openness to others. In many respects, however, existential philosophy arose as a reaction to those modernist narratives – most notably Hegel's philosophical system – that place human beings, both collectively and individually, on an ever-forward-moving trajectory. From an existential perspective, life is not a unidirectional process, and it is also not perfectible (Cox, 2009). Rather, it is inherently and unavoidably caught in a web of multiple tensions. There is, for instance, the tension between freedom and limitations, between self and others, between the I–Thou and the I–It (Buber, 1958), and between hope and despair (Marcel, 1949). Furthermore, at the heart of an existential outlook is the assertion that there are no intrinsically 'right' answers. Rather, there is only a constant pull from one side to the other. Such tensions are paradoxes: contradictions that cannot be overcome. Jaspers (1932: 218) calls these *antinomies* and writes that, 'They are not resolved but only exacerbated by clear thinking, and solutions can only be finite, can resolve only particular conflicts in existence, while a look at the whole will always show the limiting insolubilities.'

Ultimately, even authenticity and inauthenticity can be seen as two poles of a dilemma, neither of which is intrinsically 'better'. Heidegger (1962) explicitly rejects the idea that a moral judgement is associated with either of these terms, as well as the idea that authenticity is some kind of goal that we can attain. Rather, as Moran (2000) suggests, authenticity is probably best understood as something that we may have moments of: for we can never stand naked in anxiety for more than a flash of time before falling back into a more comfortable and protected state of being (Tillich, 2000). From an existential perspective, then, authenticity should not be perceived as the end-point of some linear journey, like the summit of a mountain that we can reach and rest upon. Rather, as in Camus' (1955) myth of Sisyphus, it is probably better understood as those moments of insight and awareness in which we face up to the reality of our condition and possibilities, before falling back into the world of everyday understandings and practices. From this perspective, then, therapy – existential or otherwise – may be able to help our client Siân to become more assertive in her life, but there is an acknowledgement that she may always feel pulled back into more passive and deferential ways of being. And, in addition, while therapy may be able to help her find some meanings in her life, there is also an acknowledgement that she may always experience moments of futility and emptiness. In other words, from an existential standpoint, therapy can never help Siân entirely overcome or resolve her feelings of distress. But what it can do, from this perspective, is to help her understand them more and feel more accepting of where she is in this web of possibilities, and to make choices that may be more likely to help her find greater fulfilment and aliveness.

Critical perspectives

Criticising existential philosophy, as a whole, is not an easy task because of the great diversity of existential viewpoints. As Macquarrie (1972: 219) writes, 'Criticisms that may be very much to the point as regards some form of existentialism miss the mark when extended to others.' Nevertheless, a number of criticisms have been – and can be – made, and some of the key ones are outlined below.

First, there would seem to be something of a contradiction between the anti-essentialist starting point of existential philosophy and its attempts to describe the common characteristics of human existence. Specifically, 'if each individual existent is unique and cannot be regarded as a specimen of a class, how can one generalise about human existence, as a philosophy of existence seems compelled to do?' (Macquarrie, 1972: 55). To suggest, for instance, that human existence is a being-towards-death (Heidegger, 1962) would seem to be putting universal statements about human existence before the concrete individuality of each unique human existence. Macquarrie counters this critique by suggesting that what existential philosophers are describing here are not the *properties* of human existence, but their *possibilities*. In other words, existential philosophers have not attempted to reduce human existence *down* to a set of finite, essential characteristics, but rather to build it *up* through outlining some of the interwoven layers of human complexity. There is no suggestion, then, that existence is 'nothing but' being-towards-death, embodied, etc. Rather, existential philosophers have suggested that existence is an embodied-anxious-being-towards-death, *ad infinitum*. Nevertheless, there is an undeniable tension within existential philosophy between the emphasis on universal characteristics and the emphasis on unique, personal ones, and this is something that also arises in the existential approaches to therapy.

This leads on to a second contradiction that is apparent in some of the more proselytising, 'hard-line' existentialist writings (Cox, 2009). On the one hand, there is the invitation to turn away from the crowd and towards one's 'innermost truths' (for instance, Kierkegaard, 1992), yet such an invitation, in itself, would seem to be an admonishment to follow a particular path. Neither Kierkegaard nor Nietzsche was blind to this contradiction, and Nietzsche specifically implored people to find their own way rather than following his. Nevertheless, in the writings of some existential philosophers and therapists, there would seem to be limited respect for people who make particular choices, such as a life of conformity, passionlessness or obedience.

A third criticism of existential philosophy is that it is overly morbid: that it tends to focus on such experiences as despair, anxiety, and mortality to the neglect of more positive and pleasurable experiences. As Schrader (1967: 13) writes: 'some readers have concluded that to be an existentialist one needs simply to accentuate in a rather brooding way the darker side of life and cosmologize his anguish.' Indeed, even Abraham Maslow (1968: 16), founding father of humanistic psychology, wrote that we should not take too seriously 'the European existentialists harping on dread, on anguish, on despair and the like'. As we have seen, however, some existential philosophers have written about the more positive moods, such as joy and hope (for instance, Marcel, 1949). Furthermore, those existential philosophers who do tend to place greater emphasis on the bleaker aspects of existence do not see these as ends in themselves, but as routes towards a more fulfilling, intense and alive way of being. Indeed, the emphasis on 'negative' experiences is often an attempt to counterbalance the tendency within modern culture to deny the more painful and discomforting sides of our lives. Existential philosophy, then, is less a philosophy of doom and despair, and more a philosophy of balance (Kohn, 1984).

There is also the question of how well-evidenced the existential theories actually are. It is one thing to claim, for instance, that Siân will better off facing up to her freedom, or finding meanings in her life, but is that actually the case? As we shall see in later chapters of this book, in some areas the existential assumptions – and ways of working with them – are well-evidenced. For instance, it is true to say that human beings, in general, feel happier when they have a sense of meaning and purpose in their lives (see Chapter 4, this volume). But there are many existential hypotheses for which empirical evidence is lacking or where the prevailing evidence actually challenges an existential worldview. For instance, recent neuropsychological evidence suggests that the experience of choice may be an illusion, and that decisional activity is occurring in our brains long before we are aware of making a choice (e.g., Bargh, 2004; Soon, Brass, Heinze, & Haynes, 2008). There is also evidence to suggest that the more choices we have, the more overwhelmed and miserable we can end up feeling (Schwartz, 2005; Vohs & Baumeister, 2004). In most cases, then, we need to be very cautious in distinguishing between what existential philosophers have claimed and what might actually be true for a particular client. Probably, at best, what we can say is that some of these existential ideas may be helpful – and sometimes very helpful – to some clients some of the time.

This leads on to a fifth criticism of existential philosophy: that in prizing passionate inquiry over objectivity and systematic thinking and research, it is essentially irrationalist (Macquarrie, 1972). Again, there is some truth in this: existential philosophers have emphasised the importance of being open to the non-rational and mysterious (for instance, Marcel, 1949). This is not, however, a rejection of the rational, but an attempt to see the other side of it. As Macquarrie writes: 'existentialism at its best is neither irrational nor anti-rational but is concerned rather with affirming that the fullness of human experience breaks out of the confines of conceptual thought and that our lives can be diminished by too narrow a rationalism' (Macquarrie, 1972: 221).

At the other end of the scale, however, is an equally serious criticism. Existential philosophy is grounded in the assumption that existence is 'real', that it is a phenomenon that is 'there', and which transcends the particular words or discourse we use to describe it. Postmodern philosophers such as Derrida (1974) and Lyotard (1984), however, have argued that any knowledge is always contained within a particular language system or 'discourse', and that it is not possible to stand outside this system and prove the reality of a phenomenon. In other words, we cannot go beyond the bounds of our language to show that existence *really* exists: it is, ultimately, only a particular narrative that we adopt. This criticism has serious repercussions for a philosophy that invites people to authentically acknowledge their true existence, and is by no means easy to respond to. Indeed, to answer – in words – the postmodern critique would be to prove the very postmodern point: that our arguments are always constrained within the boundaries of language. Nevertheless, what is important to note is that, whether it is real or not, human beings' existences are of great significance to themselves. Hence, even if we cannot prove existence exists, we can certainly show that it is of great relevance to human beings – and thus to the process of therapy (Cooper, 1999).

Conclusion

Existential philosophy, by its very nature, is a vast and sprawling edifice, replete with debates, contradictions and half-completed arguments. As we have seen, however, what each philosopher of existence shares is a concern with the nature of human existence: that unique, concrete, indefinable totality. Existential philosophers have depicted this existence in many different ways, but what is common to each of their descriptions is a radical challenge to many of our contemporary assumptions about what it means to be human. At times these challenges can be more critical than constructive but, together, they create a radically new, and radically humanising, image of what it means to exist. What better foundations then, on which to construct the most human of professional practices: counselling and psychotherapy.

Questions for reflection

- To what extent do you agree that human beings are fundamentally free? What about the other characteristics of human existence, as described by existential philosophers (unique, a verb-like flow, towards-the-future, limited, in-the-world, with-others, embodied, anxious and guilty)?

(Continued)

(Continued)

- Do you agree that human beings tend to be better off if they experience greater levels of authenticity? If so, why do you think this is the case?
- If you were to be more authentic in your own life, how would you be different?

Recommended resources

Introductions and overviews

Cohn, H. W. (2002). *Heidegger and the roots of existential therapy*. London: Continuum.
Clearly and simply outlines some of Heidegger's key concepts and their implications for therapeutic practice. Polt's (1999) *Heidegger: An Introduction* is more in-depth, and a brilliantly lucid introduction to his works; as is Dreyfus's (1997) *Being-in-the-World*, which systematically outlines key aspects of Heidegger's thinking.

Cooper, D. E. (1999). *Existentialism*. Oxford: Blackwell.
Useful introduction to the principal concepts of existentialism.

Cox, G. (2009). *How to be an existentialist: Or how to get real, get a grip and stop making excuses*. London: Bloomsbury.
Hugely witty, irreverent and accessible: a brilliant introduction to Sartrean-based existentialism. See also Cox (2012), which extends these reflections.

Guignon, C. B. (2004). *Existentialism*. From: www.rep.routledge.com.
Very brief, but enormously lucid, accessible and incisive summary of existential thought.

Moran, D. (2000) *Introduction to phenomenology*. London: Routledge.
Comprehensive, accessible and in-depth introduction to the writings of Husserl and the key phenomenologists, including such existential-phenomenologists as Heidegger and Merleau-Ponty.

Panza, C., & Gale, G. (2008). *Existentialism for dummies*. New York: Wiley.
An accessible, informed and comprehensive introduction, though not as funny as it tries to be.

Spinelli, E. (2005). *The interpreted world: An introduction to phenomenological psychology* (2nd ed.). London: Sage.
Very clear introduction to phenomenology, specifically orientated towards therapists and psychologists.

van Deurzen-Smith, E. (1997). *Everyday mysteries: Existential dimensions of psychotherapy*. London: Routledge. (Section 1.)
Useful summary of the ideas of key existential philosophers and their relevance to therapeutic practice.

Warnock, M. (1970). *Existentialism* (rev. ed.). Oxford: Oxford University Press.
Classic introduction to key existential thinkers.

Wartenberg, T. E. (2008). *Existentialism: A beginner's guide*. London: Oneworld.
Succinct, informed and very readable: one of the best contemporary introductions to existential philosophy.

Existential Comics: existentialcomics.com
Existentialism in bite-sized graphics.

Research

Greenberg, J., Koole, S. L., & Pyszczynski, T. (2004). *Handbook of experimental existential psychology*. New York: Guilford Press.
Rich collection of research-based chapters on many different aspects of existential thinking, including death awareness, freedom and authenticity.

Original texts

None of the following texts are easy, and some can seem impenetrable at times, but there is nothing like reading a philosopher's original works to give you a sense of their outlook and style of philosophising. Don't worry too much if you can't understand all of what you read – or even most of it – some of the greatest minds of our century have struggled with these works.

Buber, M. (1923/1958). *I and Thou* (2nd ed.) (R. G. Smith, Trans.). Edinburgh: T. & T. Clark.
Poetic, passionate and relatively accessible – Buber's essential work contrasting the I–Thou and I–It ways of being.

Camus, A. (1942/1955). *The myth of Sisyphus* (J. O'Brien, Trans.). Harmondsworth: Penguin.
Camus' key philosophical work. Succinct and relatively accessible; asks whether life is worth living, and concludes that human beings can still create meaning and an intensity of living in a meaningless universe.

Friedman, M. (Ed.). (1964). *The worlds of existentialism: A critical reader*. Chicago, IL: The University of Chicago Press.
Anthology of existential writings, with a whole section on existentialism and psychotherapy. Kaufman's (1975) anthology has fewer readings, but they are more in-depth.

Heidegger, M. (1959/1966). *Discourse on thinking* (J. M. Anderson & E. H. Freund, Trans.). London: Harper Colophon Books.
Relatively accessible introduction to, and presentation of, Heidegger's later thought, contrasting 'meditative' and 'calculative' thinking.

Heidegger, M. (1962). *Being and time* (J. Macquarrie & E. Robinson, Trans.) Oxford: Blackwell.
Probably the single most important and influential existential text. Brings to the fore the question of existence, highlights its 'in-the-world'-ly nature, and outlines its authentic possibilities. Tough-going, but enormously stimulating and thought-provoking. Stambaugh's (Heidegger, 1996a) more recent translation has been very well-received.

Kierkegaard, S. (1846/1992). *Concluding unscientific postscript to philosophical fragments* (H. V. Hong & E. H. Hong, Trans.) Princeton, NJ: Princeton University Press.
Generally recognised as Kierkegaard's *magnum opus*, emphasising the subjective, individual nature of truth and the path towards God. Turgid and taxing, but surprisingly humorous at times, and with remarkably vivid insights into the human condition.

(Continued)

(Continued)

Merleau-Ponty, M. (1945/1962). *Phenomenology of perception* (C. Smith, Trans.). London: Routledge.
Merleau-Ponty's most important work, emphasising the fundamentally embodied nature of human existence. A brilliant and original analysis, but extremely tough-going – makes *Being and Time* look like *Heat* magazine.

Nietzsche, F. (1967). *Thus spake Zarathustra* (T. Common, Trans.). London: George Allen and Unwin.
Nietzsche's classic work, filled with aphorisms on the body, courage and the will to power.

Sartre, J. P. (1943/1958). *Being and nothingness* (H. Barnes, Trans.). London: Routledge.
Turgid, dense and highly inaccessible, but Sartre's *magnum opus* provides a brilliant analysis of the human condition – in all its freedom, absurdity and nothingness – and is one of the most important and influential existential texts.

Tillich, P. (1952/2000). *The courage to be* (2nd ed.). New Haven, CT: Yale University Press.
Popular and relatively accessible work that advocates a stance of courageousness and faith in the face of moral, spiritual and ontological non-being.

3

DASEINSANALYSIS: FOUNDATIONS
FOR AN EXISTENTIAL THERAPY

This chapter discusses:

- The history and development of the daseinsanalytic approach to existential therapy.
- Key influences on the approach.
- Daseinsanalytic revisions to core psychoanalytic concepts and practices – psyche, the unconscious, transference, causality and interpretation – and implications for practice.
- Daseinsanalytic dreamwork.
- Criticisms of the daseinsanalytic approach.

It is something of a paradox that one of the earliest attempts to develop an existential approach to therapy is primarily grounded in some of the latest existential thinking. Daseinsanalysis draws extensively from Heidegger's later teachings (Cohn, 2002). As such, it places a great deal of emphasis on helping clients to 'open up' to their world in order to lead an authentic life (see Chapter 2, this volume). This makes it very distinctive among the existential therapies. What also makes it very distinctive is the depth and thoroughness with which it has critiqued the theoretical foundations of classic Freudian psychoanalysis.

Ludwig Binswanger (1881–1966), a Swiss psychiatrist, founded the daseins-analytic movement in the early 1930s, and is still considered one of its most influential authors (Correia et al., 2016c). Binswanger was a close friend of Freud, but felt that Freud's attempts to understand human beings scientifi-cally had led him to reduce human being to a distinctly inhuman collection of causal mechanisms, instincts and formulae (see Binswanger, 1963). Binswanger also felt that Freud had split human beings off from the world that they inhabited – referring to this subject–object divide as 'the cancer of psychology' (Spiegelberg, 1972). In an attempt to construe a more dignified and holistic understanding of human existence, Binswanger turned to the work of such existential-phenomenological philosophers as Kierkegaard, Buber and Heidegger, and developed an approach that he termed 'daseins-analyse' or 'phenomenological anthropology'. Here, he attempted to describe the nature of human psychopathology in terms of the sufferer's way of being-in-the-world – a descriptive enterprise that did not attempt to reduce human suffering to deterministic, world-less mechanisms. Drawing on Buber, Binswanger also critiqued, and attempted to develop, Heidegger's work on interpersonal relationships. He argued that the highest and most original form of human existence is the reciprocal love relationship: the 'dual mode of love' (Frie, 1997).

It was one of Binswanger's followers, the Swiss psychiatrist Medard Boss (1903–1990), however, who was to become the pivotal figure in the development of daseinsanalysis as a form of psychotherapy, and he remains the most influential author in the field (Correia et al., 2016c). While Binswanger was primarily interested in understanding psychopathology from an existential and phenomenological perspective, Boss went on to consider the implications of Heideggerian thought for therapeutic practice. Binswanger's denunciation by Heidegger (2001) – for fundamentally misinterpreting *Being and Time* in individualistic and subjectivistic terms – also led to his increasing marginalisation within daseinsanalysis. In contrast, Boss maintained a close friendship and collaboration with Heidegger for many years, and between 1959 and 1969 hosted a series of seminars by his mentor (Heidegger, 2001). Even in his later years, Boss felt that there was nothing that he could criticise or modify in Heidegger's thought (Craig, 1988b). Indeed, such was Boss's devotion to Heidegger that one of Boss's (1979) key works, *Existential Foundations of Medicine and Psychology*, was written under Heidegger's watchful eye.

In 1971, Heidegger encouraged Boss to establish the first daseinsanalytic training institute – the Daseinsanalytic Institute for Psychotherapy and Psychosomatic Medicine in Zurich, Switzerland. Today, there are around eight daseinsanalytic institutes worldwide, primarily in Europe (Correia et al., 2014b). However, research suggests that the numbers of contemporary daseinsanalysts are fairly limited (Correia et al., 2014b) and possibly in decline, with around 40 participants at the biannual fora of the International Federation of Daseinsanalysis (E. Craig, personal communication, 8 February 2016).

Today, the field of daseinsanalysis is also somewhat divided. On the one hand, there are the followers of Boss, and subsequently the Swiss psychiatrist Gion Condrau (1919–2006) (see Condrau, 1998), who are primarily influenced by the later Heidegger and his emphasis on a serene openness to being. On the other hand, there is the Swiss psychotherapist Alice Holzhey-Kunz (1943–) and her followers (see Holzhey-Kunz, 2014; Holzhey-Kunz & Fazekas, 2012), who are more influenced by the early Heidegger, Binswanger, and Lacanian and intersubjective psychoanalysis. In contrast to Boss's *classical daseinsanalysis*, Holzhey-Kunz puts particular emphasis on the necessity of psychological suffering (Fazekas, in Holzhey-Kunz & Fazekas, 2012). She has also developed her own theory of the origins of psychological distress (see Box 3.1).

Box 3.1   Ontological traumatisation

Alice Holzhey-Kunz argues that people who experience neurotic problems have 'a special sensitivity [*Hellhörigkeit*] to the fundamental [ontological] truths that concern his human being' (2014: 270). That is, as suggested in Chapter 2 (this volume), most 'non-neurotic' people are able to shield their eyes from the reality of the human condition: such as their inevitable being-towards-death, the 'unavoidable uncertainty' within which they have to choose, and the 'yawning abyss' of being. But the neurotic person is too sensitive; they 'hear something that dares not be heard' (E. Craig, personal communication, 8 February 2016); they are unable to drown out the noise of their ontological concerns with everyday chatter and 'common sense'. They are, suggests Holzhey-Kunz (2016: 24), 'ontologically traumatised', and their symptoms are a desperate attempt to fight this truth 'in the illusory hope to defeat it'. In direct contrast to approaches like cognitive therapy, then, which hold that people experience psychological distress because they incorrectly perceive reality (Beck, John, Shaw, & Emery, 1979), Holzhey-Kunz argues that people experience psychological distress because they perceive reality *too* accurately, and are not sufficiently able to delude themselves. How and why they may have become such 'reluctant philosophers', however, she is yet to explain.

As the former, Bossian, approach appears to be the dominant strand in daseinsanalysis, and because translated texts from this standpoint are more widely available, this will be the principal focus of the present chapter. However, more information about Holzhey-Kunz's approach can be foundin her recently published English-language book, *Daseinsanalysis* (2014). In addition, it should be noted that there are leading figures in the contemporary daseinsanalytic field, such as the Austrian psychotherapist Tamas Fazekas, who are searching for a 'united daseinsanalytic school' (Holzhey-Kunz & Fazekas, 2012: 45).

Influences

As indicated above, classical daseinsanalysis is primarily grounded in the philosophical perspective of Martin Heidegger, and particularly the ideas that he developed in the later years of his life (when he was most closely in contact with Boss). Indeed, the name of the approach, *daseins*-analysis, makes it clear that it is primarily concerned with an analysis – in the sense of an exposition – of human *da-sein* ('being-there'). Daseinsanalysis, then, does not start with the notion of human beings as entities that are separate and distinct from their world. Rather, it starts from the notion of human existences that are fundamentally connected to their world: an 'openness' towards Being.

The other major influence on the development of daseinsanalysis was Freud's psychoanalytic approach, and to a much lesser extent Jung's analytical psychology. Boss claimed to have been in training analysis with Freud himself (Craig, 1988b), and for many years practised as a classical psychoanalyst, before developing an interest in Jungian analysis in the 1930s. Such a steepening in traditional psychoanalytic practice has left an indelible mark on daseins-analysis, which, in its practical aspects, bears a strong commitment to classic Freudian analysis (Holzhey-Kunz, 2014). As with psychoanalysis, for instance, daseinsanalytic patients are encouraged to follow the fundamental rule of *free association*: saying whatever passes through their heart or mind, without censorship or exception. Their analyst, meanwhile, listens attentively with 'evenly hovering attention' (cf. Heidegger's *serenity* for the deep ground of being together; T. Fazekas, personal communication, 10 February 2016). As with classic Freudian or Jungian analysis, daseinsanalysts may also be keen to direct their clients towards exploring and understanding their dreams (Holzhey-Kunz, 2015). In many respects, then, daseinsanalysis can be considered a branch of psychoanalysis (Holzhey-Kunz, 2015), but with a vigorous purging of the theoretical superstructure on which psychoanalytic techniques are based. In other words, daseinsanalysis aimed to 'dispense with the tedious intellectual acrobatics required by psychoanalytic theory' (Boss, 1963: 234), and instead to develop a grounding for analytical practice that was rooted in the phenomenological lived-actuality of human existence. Indeed, it was Boss's hope that, not only daseinsanalysts, but therapists of all persuasions would eventually turn to his Heideggerian foundations as the basis for their therapeutic practice.

From psyche to being-in-the-world

Freudian psychoanalysis (Freud, 1923) – like many other forms of 'psycho'-therapy, such as transactional analysis (Berne, 1961) – is based on the analysis of a 'psyche'. This is conceptualised as a self-contained, thing-like entity, within which various parts (such as an id and ego, or adult and child ego-states) exist and interact. In drawing on an existential-phenomenological standpoint, however, daseinsanalysts fundamentally reject this concept of a world-less, isolated psyche, and with it such notions as 'intrapsychic parts' and 'intrapsychic dynamics' (Boss, 1963, 1979). Not only, then, do daseins-analysts draw on the existential-phenomenological argument that we do not experience existence as a *thing inside* our head, but they go on to argue that we do not experience existence as a collection of *sub-things* interacting inside our head, like balls on a snooker table. Rather, existence is *dasein* and, as such, is fundamentally in-the-world.

While daseinsanalysts, therefore, continue to invite their clients to free-associate, the way they understand what they are hearing – both during the therapeutic session and later in supervision – tends to be very different from a psychoanalytic, or other psyche-centred, perspective (Boss, 1963, 1979). Gone are attempts to understand clients' experiences in terms of intrapsychic parts such as id, ego and superego (Freud, 1923), critical Parent and free Child (Berne, 1961), or internal objects (Greenberg & Mitchell, 1983). Gone, too, are attempts to understand the clients' experiences in terms of intrapsychic processes, such as repression, denial and sublimation. Instead, daseins-analysts aim to 'stay open' to their clients' in-the-world experiences as they are described.

An illustration of this comes from a second session of therapy with Siân, as she talks about a recent difficult experience with Hanako:

Siân: We were sitting in the waiting room at the doctors for Kai, and I ... was just so stupid for agreeing to Hana[ko] coming along. I was, you know, really anxious – and instead of her being supportive she's just sat reading something stupid – like *House and Gardens* or something. Wouldn't talk to me. Or Kai. And every so often she's asking me how we're doing but it's ... and, like, Kai's so bored and spilling his juice on the floor and trying to open the door to the doctors. ... I – I just – all the way back I just stared out of the bus thinking, 'Who are – why did you do that to me? Do you hate me or something?' But I was – the anger was really at myself. I just think, 'I – I'm such an idiot to let her treat me like that.'

Here, from an intrapsychic perspective, we might hypothesise that Siân's 'inner critic' is attacking her 'experiencing self', or that she is repressing her anger and then projecting it on to Hanako (or introjecting it towards herself). But from a daseinsanalytic perspective, the focus remains more on Siân's experiencing of her world: for instance, her experiencing of Hanako as cold and insensitive.

This replacement of the psyche with being-in-the-world has major implications for the classic daseinsanalytic understanding of psychological difficulties. From a psychodynamic, or other psyche-centred, perspective, psychological problems tend to be construed in terms of conflictual relationships within the psyche: a struggle, for instance, between Siân's 'inner critic' and her 'adapted child self'. In daseinsanalysis, however, psychological difficulties tend to be construed *in terms of an individual's 'closedness' to their world*. For Boss (1988), the human being is a bundle of possibilities for relating to the world, and 'mental illness' is the privation, blocking or constriction of these potentialities. With Siân, then, we might hypothesise that she is closed to the love and care that other adults hold for her (note: Hanako *did* ask her several times how she was doing), and can only experience their coldness and distance. Metaphorically, the psychologically distressed individual is like a clearing in a forest, surrounded by keep-out signs.

As the converse to this, psychological health, from a daseinsanalytic perspective, is construed as a state of openness and letting-be – both mentally and physically (Boss, 1963, 1979) – and particularly an openness to loving and trusting others (Condrau, 1998). It is a way of being in which all that 'stakes a claim' on the beingness of *dasein* can be perceived and responded to in all its richness and complexity: an attitude of serenity and *gelassenheit* (see Chapter 2, this volume). This does not mean experiencing everything at once – at any point in time, in any mood, we will always be closed to certain aspects of our world – but it does mean having the openness and flexibility to move around our whole spectrum of world-disclosing possibilities. For Siân, then, this might mean being more open to the warmth and care that others might hold for her, as well as being open to acknowledging coldness and distance when it is there. Metaphorically, the psychologically healthy individual is like a clearing in a forest which stays open to all the different beings that wish to pass through (see Box 3.2). More than that, it welcomes them: acknowledging and validating their existence.

Box 3.2   Welcoming the being of beings

Imagine that you are a clearing in a forest.

• To what extent do you think that you are open, or closed, to allowing different aspects of your world to pass through?
• Which aspects of your world do you tend to stay open to?
• Which aspects of your world do you tend to shut out?

You may find it useful to think about this question in relation to the four dimensions of worldly being outlined in Table 7.1 (page 144): the natural world (such as your environment), the social world (such as your relationships), the personal world (such as your dispositions), and the spiritual world (such as your values). You may also find it useful to think about this question in relation to your clients: which aspects of their world do they allow into their clearing of being, and which do they tend to shut out?

From unconscious to closedness-to-the-world

In rejecting the notion of intra-psychic parts and dynamics, most daseinsanalysts also reject the notion of *an* 'unconscious' – a part of the psyche which, by its very definition, is not phenomenologically experienced (Boss, 1963, 1979). Daseinsanalysts, as discussed above, accept the idea that human beings may close themselves off to certain aspects of their world, but they vehemently reject the idea that these aspects are hidden away in some box-like, intrapsychic container; or that forces within this container can cause individuals to feel and behave in certain ways. So, from a daseinsanalytic perspective, it would not make sense to think of Siân as holding an unconscious anger towards Hanako; and to interpret this anger as the expression of a 'deeper',

suppressed rage towards her father, for instance, would also be entirely incon-
sistent with daseinsanalytic thinking.

This replacement of 'the unconscious' with 'closedness to the world' has
subtle but important implications for therapeutic practice. Take the following
dialogue:

Therapist: Siân, I noticed you haven't said much this session.
Siân: It's OK. I'm just – I feel quiet at the moment. Just don't – feel like there's not
             much to say right now. Everything feels – it's all very flat. [One minute pause.
             Siân looks up.]

Here, a therapist who believed in the unconscious may be inclined to wonder,
and encourage Siân to wonder, what is 'underneath' this quietness. If, for
instance, the therapist was about to go on holiday, they might wonder if Siân's
silence is, perhaps, an expression of her resentment at being left alone (as we
have seen, she does seem to expresses her anger through silence). And the fact
that Siân denies this would not necessarily be seen as an indicator that it is
not true: if this anger is 'in' her unconscious, then Siân may simply not be
aware of it. By contrast, a therapist who rejects the notion of the unconscious
may be more likely to trust the client's awareness of their own experiencing,
and help them develop a deeper and broader understanding of what this experience actually is. Here, a therapist might simply sit quietly with Siân, or ask
her to say more about that flatness. So the aim, from this standpoint, is not to
help the client find some hidden motive or force that is causing them to
behave or feel in a particular way, but to help them develop a greater awareness of their experiences as they are actually experienced.

From transference to real relationships

Given that daseinsanalysts reject the notion of intrapsychic, unconscious
dynamics, it should come as no surprise that they also vigorously reject the
notion of transference – one of the most cherished of psychoanalytical concepts (Boss, 1963, 1979). For Boss, the idea that clients might transfer onto their
therapist feelings and ideas which derive from previous figures in their lives is
yet one more piece of psychoanalytic 'ballast', which fails to accord with the
phenomenological reality of the client's lived-experiences, and degrades the
actuality of the therapist–client encounter. Furthermore, it implies that human
beings can somehow have impartial, non-transferential relationships with
other people – an assumption that contradicts the Heideggerian, intersubjective assumption that human beings are always, inextricably tied up with others
in their world.

Daseinsanalysts, however, are still very interested in how clients perceive
and behave towards their therapists, and what these perceptions and
behaviours might say about their wider being-in-the-world (Boss, 1963, 1979).

Instead of being interpreted as projections of clients' feelings towards parental figures, however, they are understood in terms of clients' openness or closedness towards others. That is, clients, like all human beings, are open to some aspects of the people they encounter in their world, and closed to others – and this openness and closedness will be extended to their relationships with their therapists. Supposing, for instance, that Siân's quietness in the sessions continues, and she seems to be becoming increasingly withdrawn. One session, Siân turns up ten minutes late and slumps down in her chair.

> Siân: Sorry ... buses ... I don't – Hana's got the car so I was on the bus. I just – I was thinking about what to talk about on the bus and I just – feels like I shouldn't be here.
>
> Therapist: You're feeling like you shouldn't be here? Can you – can you say more about that?
>
> Siân: I just – I think I'm wasting your time. Like I try and talk about stuff, but I was – I was just thinking, 'I feel so flat. So down', and everything. I just think you're sitting there – you know, you say all the right therapy-type touchy-feely stuff, but I just think you must be thinking, 'Jesus ... what a bore!' Like, 'Shut up and let someone with some real problems talk.'

Here, from a transferential perspective, we might begin to wonder who Siân is seeing the therapist 'as'. Is she, for instance, seeing the therapist as a critical and punishing parent, and might this be derived from her experiences of her father in earlier life? By contrast, a daseinsanalytic perspective would be more inclined to bracket such hypothesising: it would note that Siân seems very open to potential criticism and anger from her therapist, but closed to the genuine care, patience and acceptance that the therapist might hold for her, particularly when feeling flat or low.

This daseinsanalytic reinterpretation of transference has subtle but important implications for how therapists might act towards their clients. For a start, it means that therapists would be much less likely to offer transferential interpretations: directly making links back to clients' parental figures (for instance, 'Siân, you seem to imagine that I'm very critical towards you, and I just wonder if that's how you experienced your father'). It also has implications for the therapist's general stance towards their clients. From a classic psychoanalytic perspective, the more 'neutral' a therapist can be, the more a client's projections can be discerned upon the 'blank screen' of their being. If, from a daseinsanalytic perspective, however, a therapist can never be other than an integral part of a unique, complex and fundamentally two-way relationship, then it is meaningless to suggest that they should – or would ever be able to – maintain an impartial, objective stance. Hence, from a daseinsanalytic position, there is little value in the therapist attempting to attain the mirror-like impassivity prescribed – but not always enacted – by Freud (Friedman, 1985). Indeed, Boss (1963) suggests that such an attitude is, itself, an inadequate and restricted mode of relating, with the potential to close clients even further to their worlds. Rather, from a daseinsanalytic perspective, therapists should be genuine and real, capable of modelling for their clients ways of being that are responsive and open to their world. For instance, the therapist might say something like, 'Siân, it sounds like it's really hard for you to be open to the care and interest I'm feeling for you now.'

Along these lines, Boss (1963) suggests that therapists should be supportive and warm, encouraging their clients to ever-greater levels of openness. From a daseinsanalytic perspective, it is an attitude of loving acceptance to all aspects of a client's existence – not unlike Rogers' (1957) 'unconditional posi-tive regard' – that plays a major role in helping clients to gradually open themselves up to the totality of their world. As the earlier extract suggests, for instance, Siân finds it difficult to be in the world in a quiet or flat way – she feels that she has to entertain. Here, by conveying an acknowledgement and acceptance of this way of being (for instance, 'Siân, it's OK for you to be quiet and contemplative here; you don't need to entertain me'), the hope is that Siân might become increasingly open to this mode of engaging with the world. The aim of the daseinsanalyst, therefore, is to create a 'trial world' in which clients can begin to experience a more open way of being: to create an atmosphere of permissiveness which 'enables the patient to unfold all his world-disclosing possibilities of relating toward the particular beings which he encounters' (Boss, 1963: 253). In other words, just as psychologically healthy individuals are shepherds to the Being of the world, so effective therapists are shepherds to the *dasein* of their clients: creating an open and free space in which they can experience all of their world-disclosing possibilities. Indeed, such is the importance of creating a permissive environment that Boss sums up the difference between psychoanalysis and daseinsanalysis by saying that, while the former asks the question 'Why?', the latter asks the question 'Why not?' A daseinsanalyst, for instance, might ask their client, 'Why not allow yourself to trust others?' or 'Why not allow yourself to be quiet here?'

Such a stance of 'Why not?'-asking also means that, when clients are 'acting out' their problems towards their therapists, they may be positively encour-aged to do so. Rather than seeing this 'acting-out' as the repetition of repressed emotions – as Freud did – Boss (1963: 240) writes that: 'Acting-out may indi-cate that something is unfolding for the *first time* in the analysand's life. He dares to behave in a manner which has never been permitted him (at least not sufficiently).' Hence, as with Siân being encouraged to inhabit her quieter mode of being, the daseinsanalyst 'will let the acting-out continue to the greatest extent possible without violating his own integrity, inner freedom, and selfless concern for the analysand'. Boss goes on to warn against the dangers of trying to defuse or interpret a client's acting-out (for instance, by suggesting to Siân that her quietness towards the therapist is a manifestation of anger or resistance). He writes that it may be experienced by clients as a further prohibition on their behaviour, pushing them back into a narrowly intellectual mode of relating, or keeping them locked in the false hope that if they can find an answer for why they do what they do, all their problems will be solved.

To illustrate his approach, Boss (1963) gives the example of a 'sadistic pervert' who experienced intense and, at times, overwhelming feelings of violence towards others. This client had, indeed, attempted to strangle a young woman, but for the vast majority of his existence he restricted himself to an attitude of aloofness, intellectual speculation and cool indifference, fiercely struggling against his world-hating possibilities. For Boss, an important part of the therapeutic work involved allowing the client to gradually begin acting out – in a non-physical way – his hatred towards the therapist. Boss (1963: 195) writes:

> For weeks on end, our work in the analytic sessions consisted in simply allowing the patient to revile the analyst, the entire staff of the asylum, and the world in general. Every time we suspected that he was hesitating before some especially crass insult to ourselves, we encouraged him to still greater bluntness by asking him why he would not speak out. Thus for a long period he was allowed for the first time in his life, and within the safe realm of the analyst–analysand relationship, to learn to know the possibilities of hating the world openly and to appropriate this way of relating to people as belonging to his existence, too.

Clearly, such openness to a hateful way of relating to the world was not the end-point of this therapeutic process. However, in allowing the client to openly hate the world, the client's (unsuccessful) attempts to close himself off to hate-disclosing possibilities were diminished. Now, he was no longer locked into a battle against his experiencing of hate, and this meant that he could open himself up to further ways of relating to his world, such as tenderly and vulnerable (Boss, 1963).

For the daseinsanalyst, however, such an attitude of permissiveness should not be confused with one of complete sympathy or collusion; nor should it be confused with one of 'doing the work for the client' (Boss, 1963). Drawing on Heideggerian thought – and, according to Boss, in complete accord with psychoanalysis – Boss suggests that a therapist's stance towards their client should be one of leaping ahead rather than leaping in (see Chapter 2, this volume). That is, therapists should anticipate their clients' potential for being, and provide a space in which they can come to fulfil it (Condrau, 1998). The therapist should not, however, leap in to rescue, reassure or give the client answers – a form of relating that is seen as having the potential to undermine the client's own freedom and responsibility.

Given this emphasis on the therapist's genuineness, warmth, permissiveness and non-directiveness, daseinsanalysis can be described as a primarily 'relational' approach to therapy (Fazekas, in Holzhey-Kunz & Fazekas, 2012). This is confirmed by research, which shows that many contemporary daseinsanalysts see their work as characterised by relational practices, including the attitudes and skills associated with the person-centred approach to therapy (Correia et al., 2016c). Concomitant with this, daseinsanalysts tend to eschew more structured techniques or interventions.

From causality to agency and freedom

Drawing on existential philosophising (see Chapter 2, this volume), another key aspect of classic psychoanalytic thinking that daseinsanalysts forcefully reject is the notion that people's thoughts, feelings and behaviours are caused, or determined, by their pasts. States Boss (1979: 152): 'Any psychological theory that translates a motive or motivational context into a psychic cause or a psychodynamic causal chain destroys the very foundations of human being.' In other words, the daseinsanalytic approach is not primarily concerned with the childhood origins of clients' distress, but rather their here-and-now means of relating to their worlds (Condrau, 1998).

This is not to say that daseinsanalysts reject the idea that individuals' presents are *influenced* by their pasts. As Fazekas puts it, 'In the here-and-now, the past is always present and the future is always being anticipated' (personal communication, 10 February 2016). Indeed, like psychoanalysts, they firmly root the sources of most individuals' psychological difficulties in early childhood experiences. From a daseinsanalytic perspective, however, individuals' life histories are 'formative' rather than 'determinative' (Hicklin, 1988). Boss (1979: 192) writes:

> A Daseinsanalytic study of pathogenesis does not aim to trace phenomena back to causes, but is concerned with discovering biographical incidents which then motivated a human being to conduct himself in a certain way and which still motivate him to perpetuate these modes. Pathogenic, biographical motivating incidents are motives which induce a person to restrict, or partially blind him to, the abundance of his inborn possibilities of relating so that he fulfils only a few neurotic modes of relation to his world.

Hence, for instance, daseinsanalysts would avoid supposing that the death of Siân's mother *caused* her to want affection from others, or *made her* see others as disinterested or critical. What they might suppose, however, is that Siân, as a young child, sought out affection and approval from others – perhaps to compensate for her lack of parental love – and continued to seek this out as an adult. In addition, it might be hypothesised that, given Siân's early experiences, she failed to experience the possibility of being deeply loved, nurtured and cared for as a child. Hence, from this daseinsanalytic standpoint, while Siân might be seen as someone who seeks out love and affection, she may also be understood as someone who is relatively closed to receiving it.

As with Siân, and in line with much psychodynamic and humanistic thinking (Rogers, 1959), daseinsanalysts tend to construe problematic childhood experiences in terms of inadequate parenting, in which the client feels unloved, criticised or punished for experiencing the world in a particular way (Boss, 1988). Individuals who trust no one, for instance, may have been hurt and betrayed by their parents so many times that, as adults, they come to believe that an openness to loving relationships will only lead to more pain. Indeed, according to daseinsanalysts, if the inadequacy of the individual's parenting is acute, then the adult may have effectively remained in a child-like state of stunted world-openness (Boss, 1963; Condrau, 1998) – closed to more adult and mature possibilities. Here, the role of the daseinsanalyst is essentially to re-parent the client: to create a permissive, warm environment in which the client can let the past be present and mature properly, with their full plethora of world-disclosing possibilities intact.

The connection that daseinsanalysts draw between clients' pasts and their present also means that daseinsanalysts will not shy away from helping clients to reflect on their pasts, and to see how their freedom to experience the full richness and complexity of their world has become malevolently impaired and constricted (Boss, 1963). As with transferential interpretations, therapists may also help clients to examine the early life experiences that have led them to be open or closed to their therapist in particular ways. Siân, for instance, might be encouraged to consider whether her closedness to the therapist's care arises from a fear that, as with her dad, the therapist will ultimately be more interested in themselves. Unlike more classic psychoanalytic interpretations, however, daseinsanalysts would be extremely careful to avoid implying that clients' presents are *caused* by their pasts, and would steer clear of such phrases as '*x made* you *y*', or '*because* of *x* you now do *y*'. Daseinsanalysts would be concerned that, as well as being seen as inaccurate, such deterministic invocation would undermine the client's sense of autonomy and responsibility.

In shifting from a causal to an agentic theoretical framework, daseinsanalysts are also interested in helping their clients examine what choices they have in their world, and perhaps to see that they have more choices than they imagine they do (Boss, 1963). Siân, for instance, says that she feels that she 'can't say anything' when Hanako upsets her: she does not want to shout at her or 'make her in the wrong'. But, from a daseinsanalytic perspective, perhaps there is a different way she can respond here, like speaking gently to Hanako or showing an understanding of Hanako's perspective as well. In this respect, Condrau (1998: 36) states that: 'The entire purpose of the psychotherapeutic relationship lies in mobilizing and directing the capabilities of two persons (the therapist and client) in order to free the one (the client).' This is entirely consistent with the daseinsanalytic aim to help clients open themselves up fully to their worlds; for, from a Heideggerian (1949) position, to be free is to allow what-is to manifest itself. With Siân, for instance, a daseinsanalyst might hypothesise that the more she can be open to the care and love that those around her feel towards her – as well as their criticism and disinterest – the freer she may be to respond to them in a multiplicity of ways.

Daseinsanalytic dreamwork

Like the classic Freudian and Jungian psychotherapies from which it has evolved, much of daseinsanalysis is concerned with helping clients to explore and make sense of their dreams (Boss, 1957, 1977). Given, however, daseins-analysis's rejection of the unconscious, it should come as no surprise that it also rejects the Freudian assumption that dreams are a symbolic representation of unconscious forces and intrapsychic dynamics. Rather, from a daseinsana-lytic perspective, the manifest content of a dream is simply what it is – a carrot is a carrot – there is nothing behind the manifest phenomena (Boss, 1977). Furthermore, from a daseinsanalytic perspective, dreams are not considered 'minor, truncated, spectral reproductions of waking life' (Stern, 1977: xv), but modes of experience that are autonomous and authentic in themselves (Boss, 1977). A dream no more points to meanings in waking life than waking life points to meanings in dreams: they are two forms of experiencing of equal validity and legitimacy. A dream, in other words, *is* real life (T. Fazekas, per-sonal communication, 10 February 2016).

Nevertheless, from a daseinsanalytic perspective, what a human being's dreaming and waking experiences share are relatively similar spectra of world openness (Boss, 1977). From a daseinsanalytic standpoint, for instance, we might expect that Siân's dreams are full of persecuting and threatening fig-ures, and that she is nearly always alone – there is no one caring, comforting or loving her. Hence, for daseinsanalysts, the enormous significance of dreams is that they can reveal much about a client's spectrum of world-openness, in two senses. First, it is in terms of what is allowed, or not allowed, to manifest itself in the individual's dream-world. A person who dreams of a kindly old man, for instance, would seem open to experiencing the caring tenderness of the world, while a person who only ever dreams of desolate, uninhabited landscapes would seem closed to the possibility of intimate human contact. Second, it is in terms of how the dreamed-self responds to whatever is revealed in the dream-world. A person who dreams of embracing a beautiful peacock, for instance, would seem open to the splendour and exquisiteness of the world, while a person who dreams of killing or running away from such a bird would seem closed to this worldly splendour. Daseinsanalysts also seem par-ticularly interested in dreamed-entities that are boxed, caged or locked in – pointing to potential ways of being-in-the-world that have not yet achieved their freedom.

The significance of dreams for the daseinsanalyst, however, is not just that they mirror the client's spectrum of openness and closedness in the waking world. Rather, 'it often happens that previously unknown significations and referential contexts address the human being and become existent *for the first time* during dreaming' (Boss & Kenny, 1987: 160, italics added). Among streams of excrement and blood, for instance, a depressed individual may dream of meeting a beautiful peacock, a manifestation of the fact that they are beginning to be able to experience the beauty and splendour of the world. From a daseinsanalytic perspective, the fact that this quality is encapsulated within a particular dream entity or person – rather than the dreamer herself – suggests that it is still a very latent possibility. But if the client, in their waking life, can be encouraged to explore this worldly possibility, then perhaps they will be able to experience it more directly in subsequent dreams: as an entity they run towards, feel a sense of joy towards, or, perhaps, as something that they embody themselves. In this respect, daseinsanalysts are particularly interested in clients' dream series, and what this may indicate about their increasing openness to their worlds.

**Box 3.3   Exploring your own dream from
a daseinsanalytic perspective**

This exercise is an opportunity to explore one of your own dreams from a daseins-analytic perspective. It can be done on your own or with a partner, whose role is to help you unpack and understand your dream through the steps below:

- Briefly describe your dream.
- Now describe your dream again, in the first person (e.g., 'I could see … ', 'I went to … '). Try to describe it in as much detail as possible.
- Reflect on the following questions:

    o   *Where* are you in the dream?
    o   *What* do you perceive and encounter?
    o   *How* do you experience this?

- Consider what your dream might say about the aspects of your world that you are open to. What is it that you dream about? Is there anything in your dream you are embracing?
- Consider what your dream might say about the aspects of your world that you are closed to. What do you not dream about? Is there anything in your dream that you try to push away, or that is locked/hidden from you?
- Consider if there are any elements of your dream that may indicate a 'growing edge' of openness to certain aspects of your world.

Daseinsanalytic dreamwork starts by asking clients to give increasingly detailed accounts of the dream that they have brought to the session, supple-menting the first sketchy remarks with more refined statements (Boss, 1977). The initial goal is to 'put together as clear as possible a waking vision of what actually has been perceived in dreaming' (Boss, 1977: 32). In this first stage, the daseinsanalyst will avoid commenting on the specific content or narrative in the dream, and they will avoid any interpretation. Rather, the focus is on attuning to the dreamer, and restricting themselves to questions that help clarify the dream experience. In particular, Condrau (1998) suggests that the therapist should ask the tripartite question: what? where? and how? In other words: *Where* is the dreamer in the dream? *What* do they perceive and encounter? And *how* is this experienced? To facilitate this process, the dasein-sanalyst may also ask the client to re-visualise the dream, or elements of it, as a means of building up an increasingly detailed picture of it.

Daseinsanalyst and client may then go on to explore the analogies between this dream and the client's waking life. A therapist may say, for instance, 'In your dream, you only seem to experience your world as desolate and uninhab-itable, and I wonder if there is an element of this in your waking life too?' Alternatively, the therapist might say, 'In your dream, you ran away from the seductress, and I wonder if, in your waking life, you find it difficult to be fully open to the erotic and sensual too?' Daseinsanalysts will also be very keen to help their clients identify latent potentialities in their dreams, and perhaps to suggest that these are ways of being that they can become more fully in touch with. With a 'highly timid' client who dreams about sharing his room with the Persian King Cyrus, for example, Boss suggests asking:

a. Don't you find it very satisfying that in your dreaming you are now already able to stand very near to Cyrus-like strength and sovereignty?
b. Of course, in your dreaming that strength and sovereignty both exist only outside of yourself still. Are you more fortunate in your waking life, in that you perceive some of that masculine strength in yourself? (1977: 94)

As this example demonstrates, Boss also suggests that clients should be praised for the new potentialities that emerge in their dream-world – just as they should be encouraged and praised for the new potentialities that emerge in their waking life. To a depressed client who dreams of eating a hot dog, for instance, Boss (1977: 79) suggests responding: 'I think it is wonderful that, at least while dreaming, you allow yourself the deep, though unshared, sensual pleasure of eating a juicy hot dog.' As discussed earlier, through such loving acceptance of the client's experiences – whether waking or dreamed – the client can begin to unfurl their full potential.

To illustrate this process of daseinsanalytic dreamwork, let's look at how it might be conducted with our client, Siân. Around three months into the therapy work, Siân asks if she can talk about a dream that she has had the night before. She describes being in a concrete, basement-like room: a bit like her first primary school. It is somewhere very familiar – somewhere that often features in her dreams. There is the smell of school dinners, but she also notices a well in the middle of the floor. Siân describes going over to the well and looking down it. She says that she expected it to be very deep, but instead it is quite shallow and it looks as if people have been throwing money in. She can see bronze and silver coins, lying in a shallow layer of water, under a cast iron grid.

Working with this dream in a daseinsanalytic way, Siân would be first invited to retell the dream in the first person: 'I was standing in a concrete room ... I walked over to the well ...' She would then be asked how she experienced this dream-world. Siân says:

> At first it just felt, I dunno, normal, like I'd always been there. I felt a bit nauseous – sick with the smell of school dinners, but – and I was really aware that no one else was about but – it was OK, I didn't mind. And I felt quite intrigued by the well and, you know, surprised it was so shallow and – at first, I thought, 'Who's been here?' like, 'There's people been here before,' and that actually felt quite cool – quite good.

As with many clients, as Siân explores the dream in this descriptive, phenomenological way, new elements of it begin to come out. 'It's funny,' Siân says, 'but at the end, when I was looking into – into the well. I did start wondering – "Could I get that money?" There were actually some pound coins down there' [laughs].

Having described the dream in detail, Siân goes on to draw parallels with her everyday existence. 'I have a lot of friends around me,' she says, 'but ... I think the loneliness in the dream says something of what I do feel very deeply. Like no one really knows or cares for me. I am alone.'

'I'm noticing, though,' says the therapist, 'that towards the end you – there were some other – traces of other people there. And that felt good. Golden coins beneath the iron grid ...'

'Yeah, I guess so,' says Siân, 'even trying to get the coins out!' From here, Siân goes on to talk about how, perhaps, she could allow herself to be more fully open to people in her life, and not to push their warmth and affection away. 'I –,' she says, 'It's only really Kai that I can let myself feel totally loved by. I – my mates have been really worried about me, but I – I just don't get back [to them].'

Towards the end of the session, however, Siân acknowledges that there is one other person who she can allow herself to be cared for, and this is an ex-girlfriend, Rachel. In fact, to the therapist's surprise, Siân admits that she has been having an 'on-off' affair with Rachel for the past six months. 'I get a softness there,' Siân says, 'It's just a love and a warmth and a comfort that – maybe I haven't acknowledged how much I need.' This opens up a whole new area of the therapeutic work that will be discussed in subsequent chapters.

From interpretation to description

Perhaps the best way of summing up the daseinsanalytic approach is that its concern is 'to *see*, not to explain' (Condrau, 1998: xi). That is, the aim of daseinsanalysis is not to help clients discover *why* they have the experiences they have: whether because of unconscious forces or past experiences. Rather, it is to help them build up an increasingly detailed and complex picture of the way in which they experience their world; for, by doing so, they can begin to break through their areas of world-closedness and un-freedom. And, indeed, research indicates that contemporary daseinsanalysts considered phenomeno-logical methods and attitudes by far the most characteristic practices in their work (Correia et al., 2016c).

As daseinsanalysts sit with their clients, then, they are not primarily think-ing, 'I wonder why my client behaves in that way.' Rather, they are likely to be thinking, 'I wonder how my client is experiencing their world.' Hence, the questions and observations emanating from the therapist are all likely to be aimed at broadening the client's awareness of their way of being, including those questions and observations concerning the client's past. In other words, the daseinsanalytic approach stands in direct opposition to the Freudian (1916: 67) maxim that 'the phenomena that are perceived must yield in importance to trends which are only hypothetical'. Rather, the therapist must start with the client's experiences as perceived, and attempt to bracket any hypothetical or abstract interpretations.

Critical perspectives

While daseinsanalysis' greatest contribution to psychotherapy may be its crit-ique of psychoanalysis, it has been argued that the psychoanalysis it criticises is 'only the most narrow, orthodox and stereotypical of psychoanalytic formu-lations, formulations which were more characteristic of psychoanalysis as it was practiced in the first half of the [twentieth] century' (Craig, 1993: 265). Up until Holzhey-Kunz (2014), for instance, daseinsanalytic writers have almost entirely ignored contemporary developments in the psychoanalytic field, where there is a much greater appreciation of intersubjective being. While some daseinsanalysts, then, are still disputing old deterministic concepts like transference and countertransference, psychoanalysts have become increas-ingly open to immediacy, purposefulness and co-constitutionality (Craig, 1988a). Moreover, by concentrating much of their energy on repeatedly set-ting up and knocking down a psychoanalytic Aunt Sally, daseinsanalysts may have failed to fully actualise their own approach to psychotherapy. As Craig (1988a: 229) states: 'Today it seems important for daseinsanalysts to move away from *reactive* argumentation with psychoanalysis and, instead, move steadily towards *proactive* research of its own, drawing on the richness of their own investigative methods.' The work of Holzhey-Kunz (2014) is a good example of the latter, where new understandings of the aetiology of psycho-logical distress have begun to emerge (see Box 3.1).

Boss's unerring loyalty towards Heidegger – the man who brought phenom-enology to 'its perfection' (Boss & Kenny, 1987: 187) – also gives daseinsana-lysis a somewhat conservative feel. While Heidegger is undoubtedly one of the great philosophers of the twentieth century, to tie a therapeutic approach to one particular philosopher makes it very difficult for that approach to develop and grow – particularly once that philosopher has died. Moreover, classical daseinsanalysis' rigid adherence to a Heideggerian framework has meant that some of its most innovative ideas – such as Binswanger's work on the 'dual mode of love' – have remained relatively undeveloped.

Another criticism of daseinsanalysis is that, while it claims to work in a phenomenological way – bracketing assumptions and engaging with the client's actual lived-existence – there are many assumptions that seem to find their way back in. In daseinsanalytic dream analysis, for instance, the daseins-analyst will often comment on the meaning or significance of a dream entity without recourse to clients themselves. To a client who has dreamt about running away from a horrible-looking giant, for instance, Boss suggests inquiring about his relationship to adult manhood. There is no reason, however, why a giant should be interpreted in this way. As Eugene Gendlin (1977: 57) writes, 'Boss imposes his scheme of ideas and also his personal values onto a dream with as little justification as is done in the methods of interpretation he attacks.' Boss's dream analysis, then, has not entirely overcome the symbolism of its Freudian and Jungian roots.

Such a criticism relates to a point made by British existential therapist Daren Wolf (2000), which is relevant to many of the different existential therapies discussed in this book. Wolf argues that any therapeutic approach that tries to take the writings of a philosopher as a guide-book for living will inevitably contain prescriptive elements: squeezing and pushing the client's experiences into a particular framework. For Wolf, the value of Heidegger's writings lies not in their ability to guide the client, nor in the nuggets of wisdom that they contain and which can be mined for the therapeutic encounter, but in the therapist's ability to directly engage with the texts – learning to see the world in a new way. 'In this way philosophical theory becomes something like an existential therapy training, with the aim of changing us into the sort of people who might be able to be philosophical or existential therapists' (Wolf, 2000: 61).

Finally, it should be noted that there is very little empirical evidence – aside from the daseinsanalysts' own case reports – to indicate that this approach does, indeed, help clients in the way that it is intended to. In fact, our comprehensive reviews of the evidence for existential therapies did not find a single study assessing the outcomes of this approach (Craig, Vos, Cooper, & Correia, 2016; Vos et al., 2014). Fazekas (personal communication, 10 February 2016) reports that there are current studies ongoing, but at present we need to be cautious in assuming that daseinsanalysis will be of benefit to clients, as its authors claim.

Conclusion

Paradoxically, while daseinsanalysis advocates openness and flexibility, it has its own tendencies towards dogmatism and closedness. Perhaps this is part of the reason why Boss never achieved the revolution in psychoanalytic thinking that he hoped for. Nevertheless, Fazekas (personal communication, 9 February 2016) suggests that the contemporary daseinsanalytic field is beginning to abandon a dogmatic adherence to Heidegger, giving way to 'a restored daseinsanalytic approach with a refreshing touch'. Here, suggests Fazekas (personal communication, 31 January 2016), daseinsanalysts will begin to address such contemporary issues as gender, migration and virtuality, and other topics that, to date, have remained 'taboo' within the daseinsanalytic field.

Whatever its future, daseinsanalysis – as the first comprehensive, systematic approach to understanding the human *as* human (E. Craig, personal communication, 8 February 2016) – will always provide some of the most incisive and comprehensive critiques of traditional psychoanalytic assumptions. And, although many contemporary psychoanalysts have moved on from this worldview; the mechanistic, deterministic, it-ifying assumptions spawned by classical psychoanalysis remain dominant in the therapy world today. In this respect, daseinsanalysis offers therapists of all persuasions an opportunity to reflect on, and reconsider, some of our most cherished beliefs.

Through these critiques of classic psychoanalytic assumptions, daseinsanalytic writers have also laid the foundations for subsequent existential therapies. Indeed, Boss's (1963) *Psychoanalysis and Daseinsanalysis* is still one of the clearest articulations of how existential ideas can be transferred to the therapeutic plane. In addition, daseinsanalysis offers existential therapists a range of concepts and practices that they might find useful in their own work: in particular, an understanding of psychological distress in terms of closedness to the world, and a non-analytical way of working with dreams.

Most intriguingly, perhaps, what daseinsanalysis offers is a way of approaching clients that is rooted not in psychological or even philosophical assumptions, but in ontology. That is, it starts from the question of 'What is Being?' and aims to work with clients in a way that brings this Being to light. This makes daseinsanalysis unique, even among the existential therapies, which tend to focus on specific existential themes or experiences, rather than Being *per se*. What does it mean, for you, to exist? What is the nature of your Being? What is the is-ness that you are? Daseinsanalysis holds open a clearing where clients, and the therapy world as a whole, can begin to address such questions.

Questions for reflection

- To what extent do you think your clients' difficulties can be understood in terms of closedness to their worlds?
- How different do you think a daseinsanalytic, descriptive approach to therapy is really likely to be from a psychoanalytic, interpretative one? What do you think the key differences might be, as experienced by clients?
- Based on the description given in this chapter, would *you* (as a client) want to see a daseinsanalyst? What are the reasons for your choice?

Recommended resources

Boss, M. (1963). *Psychoanalysis and daseinsanalysis* (L. B. Lefebre, Trans.). London: Basic Books.
Boss's finest English-language text, which provides a clear and comprehensive introduction to daseinsanalysis, exploring its similarities with, and differences from, Freudian psychoanalysis. Also provides an excellent introduction to Heidegger's later thinking.

Boss, M. (1979). *Existential foundations of medicine and psychology* (S. Conway & A. Cleaves, Trans.). London and New York: Jason Aronson.
The most influential of all texts on daseinsanalytic practice (Correia et al., 2016c), although, perhaps, less clear and engaging than Boss's 1963 text (above).

Craig, E. (Ed.) (in press). Daseinsanalysis. *World handbook of existential therapy*. London: Wiley. (Section 1.)
In-depth series of chapters on the key ideas and practices of the daseinsanalytic approach.

Heidegger, M. (2001). *Zollikon seminars: Protocols–conversations–letters* (F. Mayr & R. Askay, Trans.). Evanston, IL: Northwestern University Press.
Collection of lectures, notes and letters from Heidegger to Boss and his colleagues, outlining key aspects of Heidegger's thinking and their challenge to a psychiatric, medical worldview. The second most influential of daseinsanalytic texts (Correia et al., 2016c).

Holzhey-Kunz, A. (2014). *Daseinsanalysis* (S. Leighton, Trans.). London: Free Association.
Contemporary – albeit strongly interpretative – perspective on daseinsanalytic theory and practice.

Holzhey-Kunz, A., & Fazekas, T. (2012). Daseinsanalysis: A dialogue. In L. Barnett & G. Madison (Eds.), *Existential psychotherapy: Vibrancy, legacy and dialogue* (pp. 35–51). London: Routledge.
Brief, accessible, contemporary introduction to daseinsanalysis.

International Federation of Daseinsanalysis (IFDA): i-f-da.org.
Website of the international daseinsanalytic association and portal to other societies and sites.

4

MEANING–CENTRED THERAPIES: DISCOVERING MEANING AND PURPOSE IN LIFE

This chapter discusses:

- The history and development of Viktor Frankl's logotherapy and the meaning-centred approaches.
- Key influences on the approaches.
- Evidence in support of the meaning-centred therapies.
- The core meaning-centred assumption: that human beings need meaning, and experience psychological distress when it is absent.
- Frankl's logotherapeutic approach.
- Existential analysis, as developed by Alfried Längle and colleagues.
- Paul Wong's meaning-centred counselling.
- Meaning-centred therapies for people with chronic or life-threatening diseases.
- Criticisms of the meaning-centred approaches.

What gives you a sense of meaning and purpose in your life? Is it contributing to the wellbeing of others, experiencing happiness, or feeling that you are living life authentically? As we have seen in Chapter 2 (this volume), this question of what our existences *mean* – and the purposes we strive towards – is of fundamental importance to existential philosophers. Research indicates that it is of fundamental importance to many clients too (Vos, 2016b). The meaning-centred approaches are forms of existential therapy that specifically aim to help people find purpose and meaning in their lives.

The meaning-centred approaches to therapy are based in the work of Viktor Frankl (1905–1997), a Viennese psychiatrist. Frankl developed his therapeutic approach around 1929 (Klingberg, 1995), and termed it *logotherapy* (*logos* being the Greek term for 'meaning' (Frankl, 1984)), or *existential analysis*. Frankl's work is still the most important influence on meaning-centred practices today (Correia et al., 2016c) and, indeed, on the existential field as a whole (Correia et al., 2014a). In fact, Frankl's work has probably reached further into the public consciousness than any other form of existential therapy. Frankl's most popular book, *Man's Search for Meaning* (1984), has sold over ten million copies, and is still rated as one of the top ten books to make a difference to the lives of Americans (Schulenberg, Hutzell, Nassif, & Rogina, 2008).

Over the course of the twentieth century, Frankl and his followers (e.g., Fabry, Bulka, & Sahakian, 1979), articulated his logotherapeutic approach, most notably in Frankl's (1986) *The Doctor and the Soul*. His work also spread into other areas of healthcare, such as nursing (Starck, 1993). Frankl's 'classical' logo-therapeutic approach continues to be practised, developed and researched today, led by such psychotherapists as Elisabeth Lukas and Alexander Batthyány at the Viktor Frankl Institute in Vienna (details below). In addition, in the 1990s, a broader form of meaning-centred therapy split from the logotherapeu-tic movement through the leadership of another Austrian psychiatrist, Alfried Längle (1951–). Längle (2012) refers to his approach as *existential analysis* (rather than logotherapy), or the *Viennese school of existential analysis*. Today, research suggests that Längle is the second most influential author on meaning-centred practice (Correia et al., 2016c). His school of existential analysis is also one of the largest in the existential field, with around 1,200 society members, pri-marily in the German-speaking countries and Russia (A. Längle, personal com-munication, 29 January 2016).

In recent decades, further forms of meaning-centred therapies have emerged in other regions of the world, most notably in North America. This includes *meaning-centred counselling*, developed by the Canadian clinical psychologist and pastor, Paul Wong (2013), and Jim Lantz's (Lantz & Walsh, 2007) *short-term existential intervention*. A range of meaning-centred therapies have also been developed for people with chronic or life-threatening diseases, such as William Breitbart's *meaning-centred group psychotherapy* for patients with advanced cancer (Breitbart et al., 2010), and Virginia Lee's (2008) *meaning-making intervention*.

Today, there are as many as 28 different forms of therapy specifically addressing meaning in life to some degree (Vos, 2016b), and meaning-centred therapies, overall, are among the most widely delivered forms of existential practice (Correia et al., 2014b). Over 80 institutions exist worldwide, mainly in Europe (particularly in the German-speaking countries) and Latin America (Correia et al., 2014b). In addition, the meaning-centred interventions that have evolved over the past two decades are now 'commonly embedded in multi-modal supportive care interventions for cancer patients' (Lee, 2008: 781). Since the turn of the millennium, Vos (2016a) reports an 'exponential increase in research into meaning-centred interventions for individuals with chronic or life-threatening physical diseases', and this suggests that meaning-centred practices may be a major area for future expansion of the existential approach (see Chapter 9, this volume).

Influences

In contrast to daseinsanalysis, meaning-centred writings draw less explicitly from the works of existential philosophers. A key exception to this, however, is Frankl's indebtedness to the work of the German phenomenologist Max Scheler (1874–1928). Indeed, Frankl (1988: 10) specifically proposes that while

'Binswanger's work boils down to an application of Heideggerian concepts to psychiatry ... logotherapy is the result of an application of Max Scheler's concepts to psychotherapy.' Two aspects of Scheler's work were of particular importance to Frankl (Tengan, 1999). First was the idea that values are intuitively experienced qualities of things, such that people can discover the true meaning of a situation. Second was the idea that human reality could be stratified into body, mind and spirit, and that the latter could stand apart from, and even oppose, the physical and psychological planes.

As with most forms of existential therapy, logotherapy was also influenced by developments in psychoanalysis. Frankl grew up in Vienna, home of Sigmund Freud, and corresponded with him while still a teenager. Later, he went on to join Alfred Adler's 'second Viennese school of psychotherapy' – 'Individual Psychology' – before being expelled for criticising Adler (Frankl, 2000). In contrast to the daseinsanalytic approach, however, Frankl did not adopt Freud's psychoanalytic techniques. Instead, what he took from both psychoanalysis and individual psychology was the assumption that there was one driving force behind all human thought, feelings and behaviour. For Freud, this was the pleasure principle; for Adler, it was the will to power; and for Frankl (2000: 64), in developing 'the third Viennese school of psychotherapy', it was the will to meaning. Elements of this *teleological* assumption (i.e., that people's present lives are shaped by their perceived futures), however, can already be found in Adler's work.

Another important influence on the development of logotherapy was the religious background of its founder. Both of Frankl's parents were devout Jews, and although Frankl himself did not admit to being religious – fearing that people would say, '"Oh well, he's that religious psychologist. Take the book away!"' (Frankl, in Scully, 1995: 43) – his approach was clearly underpinned by theological assumptions (Tengan, 1999). In particular, there are echoes of Jewish, Talmudic thought throughout logotherapy: that human beings should live according to externally-given values; that each human being is called to a particular task in their life; and that suffering, guilt and anxiety have a positive role to play in life (Bulka, 1982; Gould, 1993). Many of the contemporary meaning-centred therapists, such as Wong (2013), also have a strong spiritual dimension to their work.

There is the influence too on logotherapy of Frankl's own personal history. It is well known that, during the Second World War, Frankl was interned for two-and-a-half years in a range of concentration camps, including Auschwitz, and that his parents, brother and first wife were exterminated in the Nazi genocide. It would be a mistake to assume, however, that Frankl's meaning-centred approach arose primarily as a response to these experiences. By the age of four, Frankl was already beginning to ask himself whether life had any meaning, and his internment in the concentration camps occurred over ten years after the establishment of his therapy. A more significant personal factor in the development of logotherapy, then, may have been the intense 'hell of despair' that he went through, as a young man, over the apparent meaninglessness of life. Having experienced a 'total and ultimate nihilism' (Frankl, 1988: 166), Frankl found a means of inoculating himself against this 'disease'. It was probably his desire to help others overcome such despair – particularly the self-harming and suicidal clients that he worked with throughout his life – that played the largest part in motivating him to develop his particular brand of therapeutic practice (Frankl, 2000).

Nevertheless, there is no doubt that the concentration camps provided Frankl with a testing ground for his theory. He wrote: 'Life in a concentration camp tore open the human soul and exposed its depths' (Frankl, 2000: 108). There, he observed how those who were able to transcend their immediate circumstances and hold on to something meaningful – for instance, by focusing on a reunion with a loved one – were more likely to survive than those who saw their situation as hopeless and futile (Frankl, 2000). In the concentration camps, Frankl also found support for the existential belief that human beings can always choose how to respond to their circumstances, however restrictive these circumstances might be. 'In this living laboratory,' he wrote, 'we watched and witnessed some of our comrades behave like swine while others behaved like saints. Man has both potentialities within himself: which one is actualised depends on decisions' (Frankl, 1984: 157). Equally significantly, Frankl saw the Holocaust as the logical end-point of a nihilistic worldview; and it reinforced his belief that the 'scourge' of nihilism and cynicism must be fought against at every opportunity.

The work of contemporary meaning-centred therapists continues to be strongly grounded in Frankl's ideas (e.g., Breitbart et al., 2010). However, aside from the classical logotherapists, there is a general opening-up to a wider diversity of ideas and practices from across the therapeutic orientations. Längle (2012), for instance, draws on person-centred and phenomenological practices, while Wong (2013), explicitly describing his approach as 'integrative', incorporates methods from CBT, solution-focused therapy, positive psychology and the wider psychological field. In terms of structure and formating, the meaning-centred interventions for individuals with chronic and life-threatening diseases also draw broadly from CBT techniques and programmes, and Kissane and colleagues (2004) have specifically developed a 'cognitive-existential' group intervention.

Empirical support

As will become evident in this chapter, meaning-centred therapies are one of the few forms of existential practice that, on average, have been shown through rigorous research to make positive differences to clients' lives. Drawing together evidence from 3,775 participants in 44 controlled studies, Vos and Vitali (2016) found that meaning-centred therapies brought about large improvements in quality of life and large reductions in psychological stress, both in the short term (within two months of the sessions) and the long term (within one year of the sessions). Furthermore, analyses indicated that improvements on such outcomes as depression and self-efficacy were specifically mediated by increased feelings of meaning in life. Combined with evidence on the relationship between meaning and wellbeing (see below), this provides powerful support for the hypothesis that meaning-centred interventions can help clients to experience greater meaning, and thereby greater wellbeing.

In addition, meaning-centred academics and practitioners have been very active in developing research and clinical measures to assess their key constructs. The first of these was the Purpose in Life (PIL) test, which is a psychometrically robust measure of the degree to which people experience a sense of personal life meaning (Crumbaugh & Maholick, 1964). The Seeking of Noetic Goals (SONG) test, also developed by Crumbaugh (1977), assesses motivation to find meaning. More recently, Steger, Frazier, Oishi, and Kaler (2006) have developed the Meaning in Life questionnaire, which assesses both the presence and search for meaning in life in a single, brief and very well-validated questionnaire. More broadly, Längle and colleagues (Längle, Orgler, & Kundi, 2003), from an existential analysis standpoint, have developed the Existence Scale, which aims to assess personal existential fulfilment along four dimensions: self-distancing, self-transcendence, freedom and responsibility (though see Brouwers & Tomic, 2016, for a critique of this measure).

The meaning of meaning

Meaning can be understood as the 'web of connections, understandings, and interpretations' that help us comprehend our lives (Steger, 2013: 165). One aspect of this is our *purposes*: the future-orientated directions that we set for ourselves to actualise our meanings, and to which we devote time and energy (Tengan, 1999). Research suggests that people may have a range of meanings in their lives, rather than one single 'super-meaning' (Baumeister, 1991).

For Frankl (1986), meanings are not something that reside 'within' us. Rather, as with Heidegger (Chapter 2, this volume) and the daseinsanalysts (Chapter 3, this volume), Frankl understands human Being as fundamentally in-the-world. Hence, for him, meanings arise at the interface between people and their contexts. That is, it is not that we 'have' meanings, but that the situations we encounter in life call on us to actualise meanings in a particular way.

Frankl (1986) suggests there are three types of values that may lie dormant in any situation, and which the individual can meaningfully actualise. The first is creative values, which can be actualised through work or artistic activity. For instance, losing one's job may present an individual with the opportunity to discover a new career path. The second type is 'experiential' values, which can be actualised through an increased receptivity to one's world, and particularly through love (cf. daseinsanalysis, Chapter 3, this volume). Most importantly for logotherapy, however, is the third type of values, which may lie dormant in a situation: 'attitudinal' values, which can be actualised through changing one's attitude to a situation. Hence, as logotherapists argue, even when there are no creative or experiential meanings to be actualised in a situation – for instance, when experiencing a financial disaster, losing a loved one, or, of course, being imprisoned in a death-camp – there are still attitudinal values that can be discovered and responded to.

Vos (2016b), in a more contemporary analysis of the literature, presents a somewhat different taxonomy. He suggests that meanings can take four main forms. First, there are *material and hedonistic* meanings, such as financial security, career success, or pleasure. Second, there are *self-orientated* meanings, such as self-acceptance, resilience or creative self-expression. Third, there are *social* meanings, such as service to others, feeling part of a community, or achieving depth in our interpersonal relationships. Finally, there are *transcending* meanings, which come from something 'larger' than ourselves or our relationships. This might be a spiritual belief, or a commitment to a value such as justice.

The need for meaning

For Frankl (1984, 1986), the most basic human need and motivation is to establish such meanings in our lives. Consistent with this, research has shown that many people do seek meaning and purpose in their lives (Vos, 2016a). This may be particularly true for people who are in crisis and/or experiencing severe illness (LeMay & Wilson, 2008; Vos, 2016a), where their assumptions about the meaningfulness and benevolence of the world may be shattered (Janoff-Bulman, 1997). In support of this hypothesis, a review of the data suggests that more than half of all clients with a chronic or life-threatening disease may start to ask questions about meaning, and that these concerns are one of the main reasons why such people seek professional psychological support (Vos, 2016a).

From a meaning-centred perspective, the corollary of this need for meaning is that, when it is absent, people may experience profound psychological distress. They may feel, for instance, hopeless, empty, depressed or even suicidal (Frankl, 1984, 1986). Moreover, Frankl suggests that the experiencing of such an *existential vacuum* can lead people to develop more serious and chronic *existential neuroses*. This is where they try to fill their existential void by such self-destructive behaviours as addictions, compulsions or phobias: that is, *purpose substitutes*, as opposed to *authentic purposes* (Keshen, 2006). For instance, a few sessions on in the work with Siân, it transpires that her liaisons with Rachel may be a means of dealing with the sense of emptiness in her life. 'Rachel's like an over-excited puppy – used to drive me crazy,' Siân says:

> But she does – when I'm sitting at my desk and bored and … . I *do* start yearning after her. It's the warmth, the cuddles, and I love she's just – it *is* great sex. *So* gentle. It takes me away from everything. At least for a bit. And then I – I do hate the lying to Hanako. I hate

myself. It definitely makes me more distant from her. But ... it's a ... treat, I guess, and, I dunno ... what would it be like if that went?

Here, as Frankl suggests, Siân's attempts to suppress her feelings of meaninglessness may lead to behaviour that only serve to increase her problems.

The hypothesis that psychological distress is associated with a lack of meaning is one of the best evidenced of all existential claims. As Steger (2013: 172) states, there are 'abundant links between meaning in life and a very wide range of other indicators of well-being'. People with lower levels of meaning in life, for instance, have greater levels of psychological distress, more substance-related problems, and more disruptive behaviour. They also have lower levels of life satisfaction, self-esteem, positive affect, and physical functioning (Batthyány, 2016; King & Hicks, 2013; Park, Park, & Peterson, 2010; Steger, 2013; Vos, 2016a). The correlational nature of these findings means that they do not *prove* that meaninglessness *causes* distress (King & Hicks, 2013). It may be, for instance, that people experience a sense of meaningless *because* they experience such little pleasure in their lives; and, indeed, research does show that people experience lower levels of meaning after negative life events (Vos, 2016b). However, combined with the evidence on the effectiveness of the meaning-centred approaches, these findings generally provide strong support for the hypothesis that a perceived lack of meaning may be a key factor in the aetiology of psychological distress.

This hypothesised relationship between the lack of meaning and distress has also been argued on evolutionary grounds. Writes Klinger (2013: 31):

> The human brain cannot sustain purposeless living. It is not designed for that. Its systems are designed for purposive action. When that is blocked, its systems deteriorate, and the emotional feedback from idling these systems signals extreme discomfort and motivates the search for renewed purpose, renewed meaning.

The aim of the meaning-centred therapies, then, is to help people out of their existential vacuums, and find this renewed meaning and purpose. However, for most meaning-centred therapists (e.g., Frankl, 1986; Vos, 2015), this meaning is not something to be created, but to be *discovered*. That is, it is assumed that each person has things in their lives that feel intrinsically meaningful to them – often at an unconscious level – and the role of therapy is to help them uncover these feelings. When Siân, for instance, talks about playing in bands at college, she describes a deep sense of attunement and 'rightness' with the world. 'It wasn't about being famous and a rock star,' she says, 'but about being – playing with others and being part of a – this amazing, beautiful, chaotic *flow* that just carries you down its river.' Siân also says that, when she watches Kai or spends time with other young children, her feelings of meaninglessness tend to evaporate. '*That's* when I feel I am doing something worthwhile,' she says.

Moreover, as we have seen, for Frankl, it is not that meanings reside 'within' us, but that they are an actualisation of values that lie dormant within our worlds. And because our circumstances always contain some form of values – even if it is only attitudinal ones – then there are always meanings to be found in our lives, however dire our circumstances. So although Siân might experience her web design work as meaningless, a meaning-centred therapist would hold that there remain meanings there that can be actualised. For instance, from this work she might learn the value of patience and forbearance; or it might be a means of helping her discern more clearly what it is that she wants to do with her life.

In addition, from a meaning-centred standpoint, human beings have the capacity to find meanings in the face of 'internally'-determined limitations, as well as externally-determined ones. For Frankl (1998), the human 'spirit' has the capacity to transcend – and defy – both physiological experiences (for instance, bodily pain) and psychological ones (for instance, inherited disposition, instincts, psychological mechanisms, and neuroses). Hence, from this perspective, it may be that Siân can never fully overcome her periods of depression; and Frankl (1986), in contrast to Laing (see Chapter 6, this volume), believed that many forms of mental misery were biologically-determined. However, she might still be able to change her attitude towards them. For instance, she might see these episodes as 'resources' by which she can better understand the experiences of other depressed individuals. According to Frankl (1986), such a choice – finding meaning in one's psychological suffering – is much less likely to compound the original suffering. This is because it avoids a vicious cycle whereby the person feels bad about feeling bad, which then leads them to feel even worse.

Logotherapy

Therapeutic practices that follow the traditional Franklian model can be described as *logotherapy*. As with all the meaning-centred therapies, the approach is quite distinct from daseinsanalysis and other existential therapies (Correia et al., 2016c). Here, therapists tend to adopt a more directive, structured and didactic approach, using a range of specific meaning-centred techniques. In logotherapy and other meaning-centred approaches, the therapy may also involve a considerable element of psycho-education. Here, the client will be taught the main principles of meaning-centred thinking – such as the importance of meaning in people's lives, and the different sources of meaning – and will be encouraged to engage with these ideas (Vos, 2016b).

As with other meaning-centred therapies, there is excellent evidence – qualitative (see Craig et al., 2016) as well as quantitative – to suggest that logotherapy is an effective intervention, with large effects on a range of existential, psychological and physical outcomes (see Batthyány, 2016, for an excellent review). Three of the most common therapeutic techniques are Socratic dialogue, paradoxical intention, and dereflection (Correia, 2015).

Socratic dialogue

Socratic dialogue is a logotherapeutic method that also features heavily in CBT (Dryden, 1999). Here, the therapist enters into a dialogue and debate with the client, and 'poses questions in such a way that patients become aware of their unconscious decisions, their repressed hopes, and their unadmitted self-knowledge' (Fabry, 1980: 135). As an example, Frankl (1988) presents the case of a young man, suffering from states of anxiety, who was 'caught and crippled' by feelings of meaninglessness and doubt. Frankl asked him what he did in response to these feelings, to which the young man – not unlike Siân – replied that he sometimes listened to music. Frankl then asked the young man whether, when the music touched him down to the depths of his being, he still doubted the meaning of his life. The young man replied that he did not. Frankl (1988: 93) responds:

> But isn't it conceivable that precisely at such moments, when you get in immediate touch with ultimate beauty, you have found the meaning of life, found it on emotional grounds without having sought for it on intellectual ones? At such moments we do not ask ourselves whether life has a meaning or not. But if we did, we could not but shout out of the depth of our existence a triumphant 'yes' to being.

In working with Siân, then, a logotherapist might pick up on her statement that 'everything feels so pointless', and instead encourage her to reflect on what does feel purposeful. What are the things in her life that give her a sense of meaning: for instance, her time with Kai, or her music? From this Socratic questioning, the logotherapist might then help her to think about ways in which she might more fully actualise these potentials. Could she, for instance, find ways of making music more central to her life, or perhaps take a larger proportion of the childcare role? And are there ways in which she might find greater meaning and purpose in her website design work? Here, we can see quite a strong contrast to a daseinsanalytic approach to working with Siân (Chapter 3, this volume), in which the therapist gave Siân much more space to explore her own experiences in her own way. In daseinsanalysis, Siân's sense of meaninglessness would certainly have been explored if Siân had raised it as a particular issue or concern. But in logotherapy, the therapist would be likely to specifically focus on this issue, whether or not Siân raised it herself, because of an *a priori* assumption that a sense of meaning would be integral to her wellbeing.

Paradoxical intention

Paradoxical intention is based on the assumption (see above) that individuals can choose the stance they take towards their psychological difficulties, and that the more they become afraid or saddened by their psychological symptoms, and draw attention to them, the more those symptoms are likely to be exacerbated. Hence, paradoxical intention involves encouraging a client to stop fighting against their difficulties and, instead, 'to evoke in his mind a strong wish and intention to do, or to experience, just what is most terrifying and embarrassing to him' (Frankl, 1965: 364). A man with a fear of sweating, for example, was advised to deliberately show people how much he could really sweat (Frankl, 1986). In a review of the evidence, Ascher and Pollard (1983) suggest that paradoxical intention has received preliminary empirical support. Indeed, it can be seen as one form of *exposure therapy* (behavioural techniques in which anxiety is purposefully evoked by confrontation with a fear-inducing situation) – among the best-evidenced forms of psychological interventions (Emmelkemp, 2013). However, Ascher and Pollard warn that paradoxical intervention should not be used without proper assessment, and also Frankl is particularly concerned to stress that it is absolutely contraindicated where clients are threatening suicide.

Dereflection

Dereflection is based on the existential-logotherapeutic assumption that human beings, in their natural, spontaneous state, are fundamentally in-the-world (see above) (Frankl, 1986). According to logotherapy, however, in some cases of neurosis and psychosis, individuals become so preoccupied with themselves and their internal processes – a state of *hyper-reflection* (Frankl, 1986) – that they forget this basic external-orientation. A man suffering from impotence, for instance, may become so focused on his sexual difficulties that he loses connection with the person he is in bed with, and consequently has less chance of becoming sexually aroused. In these situations, Frankl (1986) suggests that dereflection may be appropriate, which essentially involves encouraging clients to ignore their symptoms – to stop reflecting on themselves – and instead to orientate their attention to the world around them. The man suffering from impotence, then, might be encouraged to stop focusing on his state of arousal when he tries to make love, and instead to keep his attention on his partner. Similarly, a client who has a fear of being sick in public might be encouraged to focus on the people and events around her, instead of her feelings of nausea.

Box 4.1   Creative logotherapeutic techniques

In addition to the main logotherapeutic methods, a range of lesser-known methods have been developed by Frankl and contemporary logotherapeutic writers (e.g., Schulenberg et al., 2008). These are often of a creative or metaphorical nature.

- *The mountain range exercise.* To help clients clarify their positive qualities, values and purposes, they are asked to draw a mountain range, and put people of importance to them on different peaks. They are then asked to look at what they share with these people, as well as the peaks they would like to be part of.
- *The movies exercise.* To help clients reflect on their lives and future meanings, they are asked to develop a film of their lives up until the present time, and then from the present into the future. Clients can be asked questions like, 'Who would play you?' and 'What would the ending be like?' to help deepen their self-understandings.
- *The family shoebox game.* Clients are asked to stick magazine pictures onto a shoebox, to represent the values and meanings in their family. Images on the outside can be used to represent those values presented to the external world; images on the inside can represent those of particular importance to the family. Although proposed for use within family therapy, this may also be a useful exercise as part of a one-to-one intervention.
- *The value auction.* Here, clients are 'invited to consider various values that are auctioned off and how much they wish to "bid" on them from their limited pool of "funds"' (Schulenberg et al., 2008: 454).

In addition to these specific exercises, logotherapy writers have described a range of questions that may help clients to develop a deeper sense of their life meaning and purpose. For instance:

- Select one word which best expresses the meaning you would *like* life to have.
- Write the epitaph which you would prefer for yourself.
- If a murderer offered to let you live provided you could give him one good reason why you *should* live, what reason would you have? (Crumbaugh, 1979)

Alfried Längle's existential analysis

Although Längle's existential analysis is descended from Frankl's logotherapy, it is somewhat anomalous to consider it in a chapter on meaning-centred therapies. This is because, by its very nature, it is an attempt to broaden out an understanding of client distress and intervention from meaning alone (Längle, 2015). Indeed, Längle (personal communication, 30 January 2016) suggests that a focus on meaning makes up just a quarter or so of the basic theory, and less than a tenth of the actual clinical work. (For a range of practical case illustrations from an existential analysis perspective, see S. Längle & Wurm, 2016.)

Längle's (2003a, 2012; von Kirchbach, 2003) starting point is that there are four 'basic motivations' (including, but not limited to, the desire for meaning) that build cumulatively on each other and which, when frustrated or disturbed, may lead to psychological difficulties. First, there is the striving to feel that we exist. Without this, suggests Längle, the person may experience profound anxiety or even psychosis. Second, according to Längle, is the desire to relate positively to one's life: to feel that life is good and of value. Without this, it is hypothesised that the person may experience depression. Third, according to Längle, is the desire to be oneself: to be distinctive, unique and authentic in encounter with others. Without this, it is argued that the person may experience personality and 'hysteric' difficulties. Finally, as with classical logotherapy, there is the desire to live a meaningful life; and Längle hypothesises that the absence of this may lead the person to become dependent on others or feel suicidal. For Längle, the aim of existential analysis is to help clients say 'yes' to all these layers of their being – 'Yes, I exist, my life is good, I can be myself, and I can see for myself a positive future' – and he terms this 'living with *inner consent*'.

Although controlled studies have not been conducted on Längle's existential analytic approach, a number of pre- to post-therapy evaluations and retrospective studies suggest that it is associated with large improvements in existential and psychological wellbeing (e.g., Vos, 2016b).

As a therapeutic practice, Längle (2012) describes his approach as more dialogical and client-directed than classical logotherapy, and strictly phenomenological (A. Längle, personal communication, 1 February 2016). Indeed, he likens it to Rogerian person-centred therapy (though with a more action-orientated focus), and he considers acceptance by others to be critical in developing our own inner consent. However, Längle has also articulated a number of therapeutic strategies to help clients acknowledge and affirm the layers of their existences (Box 4.2).

The most commonly used of these methods (Correia, 2015), and the 'core' of Längle's existential analysis (S. Längle, 2003), is *personal existential analysis* (PEA) (Kwee & Längle, 2013; Längle, 2003b; S. Längle, 2003). This is a four-step, relatively generic, therapeutic process, which aims to help clients engage with the issues of concern to them and find ways forward. First is the stage of *description*, in which clients are invited to describe the external 'facts' associated with their concern. For instance, Siân might be invited to describe how often she meets her lover Rachel, and where. Second is the stage of *phenomenological analysis*, in which clients are invited to go more deeply into their experiencing of the phenomena. How does Siân feel, for example, when she is with Rachel, and what is she trying to communicate to her? Here, clients are also encouraged to accept their feelings and sensations. Third is the stage of *inner positioning*, in which clients are invited to understand their feelings and to come to a personal position regarding what they intend to do. How does Siân, for instance, make sense of her feelings towards Rachel? Is she acting according to her own deep sensing of Rachel? And is this relationship one that she wishes to continue? Finally, there is the stage of the *responding performance (act)*, in which clients are invited to consider how they can effectively realise what they want to do. Siân might decide, for instance, that she needs to tell Hanako about the relationship with Rachel, and make plans for how she will do this.

Box 4.2   Existential analysis methods

As with other meaning-centred therapists, Längle (2012, 2015; S. Längle, 2003) has articulated a number of therapeutic techniques and methods – generally of a step-wise nature. Some of the key ones are presented below, in approximately descending order of prevalence within Längle's existential analysis (Correia, 2015).

- *Personal existential analysis (PEA)*. See text above.
- *Method of personal positioning*. Clients are invited to articulate their position in relation to specific problems, their inner capabilities to respond, and their positive choices for moving forward.
- *Meaning-finding method*. Clients are encouraged to make sense of their present situation, evaluate the possibilities, and choose according to their personal feelings.
- *Attitude change method*. A step-wise process in which clients are invited to make conscious their attitudes and life positions, deepen their awareness of these and gain some distance from them, consider new life positions, and explore the consequences – and means towards – these new attitudes.
- *Biographical existential analysis*. Clients are invited to identify biographically relevant contents, integrate their experiencing of it, and consider how they want to deal with it in the present.
- *Will-strengthening method*. Clients are invited to explore the positive and negative aspects of their desired futures, as well as the obstacles to – and losses associated with – those possibilities. Feelings and decisions around positive intentions are then intensified.
- *Gates-of-death method*. Phenomenological process of confronting clients' fears: looking at where and how they experience anxiety, what they would really do if their feared future happened, and how it would be for them if they lost the things they deeply valued or even died.
- *Value-orientated imagery*. Clients are invited to have an imaginary experience that is then analysed.

Paul Wong's meaning-centred counselling

Wong's (2013) *meaning-centred counselling*, or *meaning therapy*, is a pragmatic, action-orientated, short-term therapeutic approach. Wong advocates the integration of a wide range of methods and exercises, based around his *ABCDE* intervention model: acceptance, belief and affirmation, commitment to specific actions, discovering meaning and significance, and evaluation of actions. Although there is limited evidence of effectiveness for his approach, it provides a useful framework for conceptualising – and practising – meaning-centred therapies more broadly (Wong, 2013; Wong & Wong, 2013):

- **A**cceptance of life might be facilitated through inviting clients to phenomenologically describe their 'negative' experiences, encouraging them to reflect on what can and cannot be changed, and teaching mindfulness meditation.
- **B**elief that positive change is possible might be facilitated through exploring with clients possibilities and opportunities, validating positive beliefs, and helping them identify their strengths.
- **C**ommitment to actions might be facilitated through a range of methods, such as helping clients to develop plans of action, and teaching them to monitor their progress on a daily basis.
- **D**iscovering hidden meanings, according to Wong, can be facilitated by paying particular attention to particular moments of 'awakening' in clients: for instance, when they have a feeling of awe during everyday activities.
- **E**valuating and enjoying changes might be facilitated through encouraging clients to reflect on their progress through therapy.

As part of this process, Wong (1998) suggests a number of specific methods that may help clients to discover what is meaningful to them, and to believe in positive possibilities. In *fast-forwarding*, clients are encouraged to imagine the kinds of scenario that are likely to follow a particular choice. Through being asked such questions as 'Where will it get you?', 'What differences will it make to your life?' and 'Are you sure this is what you really want to do?', clients can be helped to identify their most fundamental goals, and also to take responsibility for the consequence of their decisions. Another technique suggested by Wong is to ask clients 'miracle questions' (cf. Brief Solution-Focused Therapy). Wong suggests three:

- If you were free to do whatever you want and money is not an issue, what would you like to do on a daily basis right now?
- If God would grant you any three wishes, what would be your top three wishes?
- If you were able to decide your future, what would be an ideal life situation for you three or five years down the road?

Box 4.3   Jim Lantz's short-term existential intervention

Lantz, a logotherapy-trained professor at the Ohio State University's College of Social Work who died in 2003, developed and delivered a short-term existential intervention from the 1990s (Lantz, 1993; Lantz & Walsh, 2007). He was prolific in writing about and evaluating his meaning-centred approach. Lantz's therapy was particularly orientated towards crisis work – for instance, men who had suffered a heart attack (Lantz & Gregoire, 2003b) or Vietnam veterans (Lantz & Gregoire, 2000) – and it was often delivered in a family or couples context. Here, his emphasis was on helping the couple, or the family as a whole, to actualise and experience meanings in their lives (Lantz & Gregoire, 1996).

Lantz (Lantz & Walsh, 2007: 30) wrote about helping clients to 'hold', 'tell', 'master' and 'honour' their emotional pain, and to notice and actualise the meaning potentials that were hidden within the crises. Controlled evidence for the effectiveness of his approach was not generated, but through a series of case studies and pre- to post-therapy evaluations, Lantz showed that his short-term meaning-centred intervention was associated with significant improvements for a wide range of client groups (Lantz & Gregoire, 2003a; Vos, 2016b).

Meaning-centred therapies for people with chronic or life-threatening diseases

Like most contemporary meaning-centred approaches, meaning-centred therapies for people with physical illnesses tend to be relatively focused, directive and inclusive of a wide range of therapeutic techniques. Usually, however, they are delivered in a group – rather than an individual – format, though this is not always the case (e.g., Henry et al., 2010). These groups also tend to work with patients who have a similar diagnosis, such as early-stage breast cancer (Kissane et al., 2000) or advanced ovarian cancer (Henry et al., 2010). In recent years, this structured meaning-centred approach has also been extended out to other groups of clients, such as palliative care nurses (Fillion et al., 2009) and bereaved individuals (MacKinnon et al., 2014).

An example of a meaning-centred programme for physically ill individuals is Vos's (2015) *meaning-centred therapy in groups*. Vos's programme consists of nine weekly sessions, each approximately two hours in length. The programme aims to help clients experience greater meaning, hope and wellbeing in their lives, despite their physical illness. The initial sessions focus on introducing the programme, the concept of meaning, and resilience; and subsequent sessions then go on to consider each of the different kinds of meaning: material, self-orientated, social and transcending (see above). The penultimate session focuses on developing an action plan to actualise the meanings identified, before an ending session. With respect to content, each of the sessions combines psycho-educational input, discussion, reflective experiential exercises, and homework. For instance, Session 6, on social sources of meaning, begins with time for the group participants to 'check in': reflecting on any issues that have arisen in the previous week or from the previous session. They are then introduced to the idea that meanings can come from social sources; and a range of possibilities – such as feeling socially connected, altruism and feeling socially accepted – are presented. Participants are given some time to discuss this, and are then taken through a guided relaxation exercise in which they are asked to consider examples of social meanings in their own lives. They are invited to write these down, and then to discuss and share them with other group members. Next, participants are asked to complete a handout in which they are invited to identify the most significant meanings that have emerged from that session for them, and any corresponding changes they would like to make in their lives. This is, again, shared with the other participants, and then the group is brought to a close. At this point, participants are also asked to complete a handout prior to the next session, which invites them to start reflecting on the topic for Session 7: transcendent sources of meaning.

Lee's (2008; Lee, Cohen, Edgar, Laizner, & Gagnon, 2006) meaning-making intervention is another example of a structured meaning-centred intervention for people with serious physical illnesses, such as breast or colorectal cancer. The therapeutic programme is delivered on an individual basis, and consists of up to four sessions of about two hours each. The programme is based around the development of a *lifeline*, in which patients are presented with a blank piece of paper with a horizontal line, and asked to indicate on it their birth (at the left of the line), the end of their physical life (at the right end of the line), and where they see themselves now with their cancer diagnosis (as a large circle). The programme then consists of three tasks: helping clients to tell their story from diagnosis to the present so that they can come to terms with their illness; encouraging clients to describe life-turning events in their past so that they can identify their strengths and coping strategies; and then helping them to think about how they might live life as fully as possible for the future – re-establishing 'a sense of commitment towards meeting attainable goals in the context of one's mortality' (Lee et al., 2006: 3138).

Meaning-centred therapies for people with chronic or life-threatening diseases are, almost certainly, the form of existential therapy with the best evidence of making a positive difference to people's lives (Vos, 2016b; Vos et al., 2014). A review of 24 rigorously controlled studies with clients experiencing cancer and other physical illnesses found moderate to large effects on a range of existential, psychological and physical health indicators (Vos, 2016b). Most strikingly, and contrary to the *dodo bird hypothesis* (that different therapies are about equivalent in effectiveness; Wampold & Imel, 2015), the positive effects found in meaning-centred interventions were not found in alternative therapeutic interventions for physically ill patients, such as existentially-informed supportive-expressive therapeutic groups (Vos et al., 2014). Direct comparisons between these two therapies have also shown better outcomes for the meaning-centred approaches (Breitbart et al., 2010), though the meaning-centred allegiances of the researchers needs to be taken into account.

Critical perspectives

From an existential standpoint, perhaps the strongest criticism of the meaning-centred approaches – particularly in their more traditional forms – is that they can have distinctly authoritarian overtones (May, 1978; Yalom, 1980). Indeed, in relation to classical logotherapy, van Deurzen asks 'whether such a directive approach can be seen to be at all existential or whether it is more a kind of pastoral counselling and didactic behavioural method' (personal communication, 2001). Of course, meaning-centred therapists would not impose on their clients particular meanings to their lives, and clients in any meaning-centred therapy would be encouraged to actively engage with the therapeutic process. Nevertheless, by definition, meaning-centred therapists work from the assumption that meanings in life are good to have and are there to be found; and clients are encouraged – through psycho-education or Socratic dialogue – to also view the world in this way. Hence, it might be argued that meaning-centred therapies can tend to reinforce in clients a belief that others 'know best', potentially taking them further from their own authentic beliefs and values.

In response to this critique, it might be argued that it is legitimate to teach meaning-centred assumptions because there is good evidence for the claim that greater meaning leads to greater wellbeing in life. And, indeed, as we have seen above, this is generally true. However, the assertion that every situation we encounter has meanings to be actualised has yet to be substantiated and, in fact, is probably unsubstantiable. Indeed, from the position of Sartre (1958) or Camus (1955), this could be considered an example of bad faith: an attempt to deny the fundamental meaninglessness and absurdity of the human condition. Certainly, there is evidence to suggest that people will grasp at any meaning they can find to fill the vacuum of meaninglessness (Baumeister, 1991). In this respect, then, meaning-centred therapies may be of limited value to clients who are genuinely questioning of the meaning of existence and believe that it is quite legitimate to see the universe in this way.

Another problematic assumption within some parts of the meaning-centred field is that human beings' most fundamental need is for meaning. Again, there is no evidence on which to base this claim, and it may be a very culturally-determined viewpoint. Yalom (1980: 470), for instance, writes, 'The belief that life is incomplete without goal fulfilment is not so much a tragic existential fact of life as it is a Western myth, a cultural artifact. The Eastern world never assumes that there is a "point" to life, or that it is a problem to be solved; instead, life is a mystery to be lived.' However, within the meaning-centred field, there is an increasing recognition that finding meanings in life may be more or less important for different clients at different points in their lives (Vos, 2016b). That is, not everyone who is experiencing psychological distress is experiencing a lack of meaning. But for those who are, a meaning-centred approach may be particularly beneficial.

In terms of practice, the meaning-centred approaches might also be challenged for being so technique-based that they betray the very foundations of an existential stance. For Buber, for instance, such a technical approach might be seen as the epitome of an I–It relationship (see Chapter 2, this volume), where therapists are striving to 'do' something to clients, and putting their agendas and programmes of activities before the clients' distinctive preferences, needs and responses. Furthermore, in some instances, meaning-centred authors seem to be 'taxonomising' practices that, to a great extent, are perhaps just part of everyday therapeutic activities. For instance, it could be argued that the stages of personal existential analysis (see above) are simply things that nearly all therapists would do to help clients find better ways of acting.

Conclusion

In 1998, Wong wrote that logotherapy needed 'fresh ideas, rigorous debate, and systematic research, without which new developments in logotherapy are unlikely' (1998: 400). Today, Wong's prayers seem to have been answered. The meaning-centred therapies are now among the most vibrant, forward-thinking and creative approaches within the existential field, and have achieved a significant foothold within established healthcare settings. To some, the didactic, structured and systematised nature of the meaning-centred approaches may put them outside the existential fold; yet there is much that existential therapists of all orientations may be able to learn from them (see Chapter 9, this volume). This is the centrality of meaning and purpose to wellbeing; and the capacity of therapeutic interventions to help clients – even in the most distressing circumstances – to achieve greater hope and orientation in their lives.

Questions for reflection

- Do you think a meaning-centred intervention would be of benefit to Siân? If so, in what ways do you think it might help her?
- What kinds of clients do you think would benefit most, and least, from a meaning-centred intervention?
- How legitimate do you think it is for existential therapists to take a psycho-educational stance in their work, for instance, teaching, clients about different kinds of meanings?

Recommended resources

General

Frankl, V. (1946/1984). *Man's search for meaning*. London: Washington Square Press.
Bestselling account of Frankl's experiences in the death-camps, arguing that meaning,

freedom and dignity can still be found in the midst of the most horrendous suffering. Includes a concise introduction to meaning-centred principles and practice.

Längle, A. (Ed.) (in press). Logotherapy and existential analysis. *World handbook of existential therapy*. London: Wiley. (Section 4.)
In-depth series of chapters on the key ideas and practices of the meaning-centred approaches.

Vos, J. (2016). Working with meaning in life in mental health care: A systematic literature review and meta-analyses of the practices and effectiveness of meaning-centered therapies. In P. Russo-Netzer, S. E. Schulenberg & A. Batthyány (Eds.), *To thrive, to cope, to understand: Meaning in positive and existential psychotherapy*. New York: Springer.
Valuable overview of the evidence on meaning-centred therapy.

The psychology and philosophy of meaning

Klemke, E. D., & Cahn, S. M. (Eds.). (2008). *The meaning of life: A reader* (3rd ed.). New York: Oxford University Press.
Stimulating collection of reflections on meaning in life, from both theistic and atheistic perspectives.

Wong, P. T. (2013). *The human quest for meaning: Theories, research, and applications* (2nd ed.). New York: Routledge.
An invaluable, albeit academic, collection of chapters on all aspects of meaning, including its relationship to wellbeing. Steger's chapter provides a particularly illuminating account of the meaning–wellbeing relationship.

Logotherapy

Frankl, V. E. (1986). *The doctor and the soul: From psychotherapy to logotherapy* (3rd ed.). New York: Vintage Books.
Clearest, most comprehensive, and most detailed presentation of logotherapeutic principles and practice.

Schulenberg, S. E., Hutzell, R. R., Nassif, C., & Rogina, J. M. (2008). Logotherapy for clinical practice. *Psychotherapy: Theory, Research, Practice, Training, 45*(4), 447–463.
Valuable contemporary review of logotherapeutic theory, practice and evaluation.

Tengan, A. (1999). *Search for meaning as the basic human motivation*. Frankfurt am Main: Peter Lang.
One of the few books that provides a critically detailed examination of logotherapy. See also Gould (1993).

Viktor Frankl Institute of Logotherapy: logotherapyinstitute.org.
Site of the principal logotherapeutic institute, including information about journal *The International Forum of Logotherapy.*

(Continued)

(Continued)

Längle's existential analysis

Längle, A. (2012). The Viennese School of Existential Analysis: The search for meaning and affirmation in life. In L. Barnett & G. Madison (Eds.), *Existential psychotherapy: Vibrancy, legacy and dialogue* (pp. 159–170). London: Routledge.
Probably the clearest and most accessible summary of Längle's ideas and practices to date.

Alfried Längle home page: laengle.info.
Free download available of Längle's English-language publications.

International Society for Logotherapy and Existential Analysis (GLE-International): existential-analysis.org.
Web hub for Längle's existential analysis.

Meaning-centred counselling

Wong, P. T. P. (2013). From logotherapy to meaning-centred counselling and therapy. In P. T. P. Wong (Ed.), *The human quest for meaning: Theories, research, and applications* (2nd ed., pp. 619–647). New York: Routledge.
Succinct review of Wong's meaning-centred framework. See also Wong (2010) for a closely related review.

International Journal of Existential Psychology and Psychotherapy:
www.existentialpsychology.org/
Intermittent, freely available web-based journal of existential therapy, edited by Wong.

Meaning-centred therapies for people with chronic or life-threatening diseases

LeMay, K., & Wilson, K. G. (2008). Treatment of existential distress in life-threatening illness: A review of manualized interventions. *Clinical Psychology Review, 28*(3), 472–493.
Brief and succinct review of the different existentially-informed interventions for people with cancer and other life-limiting illnesses.

Vos, J. (2016). Working with meaning in life in chronic or life-threatening disease: A review of its relevance and effectiveness of meaning-centred therapies. In P. Russo-Netzer, S. E. Schulenberg & A. Batthyány (Eds.), *To thrive, to cope, to understand: Meaning in positive and existential psychotherapy*. New York: Springer.
Comprehensive and invaluable review of the evidence on, and practice of, meaning-centred therapies for physically ill clients.

5

EXISTENTIAL–HUMANISTIC THERAPY: OVERCOMING A RESISTANCE TO LIFE

This chapter discusses:

- The history and development of the existential-humanistic approach.
- Key influences on the approach.
- The core existential-humanistic assumption: that we resist, and repress, an awareness of our human condition.
- Presence and co-presence as therapeutic stances.
- The theory and practice of helping clients to face key existential givens: death, freedom, isolation, meaninglessness and embodiment.
- Criticisms of the existential-humanistic approach.

To introduce the existential-humanistic approach to therapy, let's go back to Siân, frustrated and berating herself as she talks about her experiences with Hanako and Kai in the doctor's waiting room (see page 47). As we have seen, from a daseinsanalytic perspective (Chapter 3, this volume), our inclination might have been to focus on Siân's openness or closedness towards her world. For instance, we might say, 'Siân, I get a really strong sense of how much you feel the anger of others towards you ... but, I wonder, is it more difficult to experience Hanako's concern for you?' From a meaning-centred perspective (Chapter 4), on the other hand, we might want to help Siân think about her meanings and purposes for the future: for instance, 'Siân, how would you like things to be with Hanako? What's important to you there?' An existential-humanistic approach contrasts with these previous perspectives in two main ways. First, it tends to focus more on the clients' experiencing of the here-and-now, immediate therapeutic relationship: for instance, 'Siân, what's it like for you sitting there telling me how much you hate yourself? How does it feel for you?' Second, the existential-humanistic approach puts particular emphasis on identifying the existential concerns 'underlying' clients' presenting problems: for instance, 'Siân, you're so angry with and blaming Hanako and yourself, but I just wonder if, in some ways, that might be a way of not talking about other things: like having to make choices about who you are going to be in your life.'

Existential-humanistic therapy emerged in the United States, and can be traced back to 1958 and the publication of *Existence: A New Dimension in Psychiatry and Psychology* by Rollo May (1909–1994) and colleagues. Through the publication of this book, the ideas and writings of European existential psychiatrists were brought to America for the first time. Rollo May, who initially trained as a minister but then went on to be a clinical psychologist, is generally considered the 'father of existential psychology in America' (Hoeller, 1999). Alongside co-editing *Existence*, he wrote a number of popular books, most notably *Man's Search for Himself* (1953) and *Love and Will* (1969a), which analysed such contemporary issues as sex, violence and the abuse of power from an existential perspective. May remains one of the most influential authors on contemporary existential-humanistic practice, and it was three of his protégés who went on to become the other most important authors in this approach (alongside Frankl; see Correia et al., 2016c). The first of these, James Bugental (1915–2008), was the most explicitly humanistic of May's mentees, and has presented and illustrated the existential-humanistic approach to therapy through numerous publications and workshops. The second, Irvin Yalom (1931–), is probably the best-known advocate of existential therapy in America – if not in the world – and is the most influential author on existential-humanistic practice overall (Correia et al., 2014a). Third, over the last two decades, Kirk Schneider (1956–) has taken a leading role in the development of existential-humanistic therapy, including authoring and editing key texts in the field (e.g., Schneider, 2008; Schneider & Krug, 2010).

As Schneider and Krug (2010: 9) suggest, the existential-humanistic approach, itself, falls roughly into 'two distinct camps'. The first of these, an *existential analytic* approach, tends to be more verbal and interpretative, drawing particularly from psychodynamic and interpersonal thinking and practice. The key figure here is Yalom, who has himself described his approach as 'existential psychodynamics'. The second camp, and the principal thrust within the existential-humanistic field today, adopts a more experiential approach, focusing particularly on bodily and affective experiences. This approach is strongly informed by humanistic thinking and practice, and has primarily been developed by Bugental and Schneider. For the purposes of this chapter, the ideas and practices of both camps will be drawn on. The second part of the chapter (on the existential givens) draws primarily from Yalom's existential analytical approach, while the first part draws more from the latter, experiential camp.

In addition, Schneider (2008, 2016) has articulated an *existential-integrative* approach to therapy which he sees as becoming increasingly prevalent in the existential-humanistic field (personal communication, 5 December 2015). This can be understood as a framework for coordinating a variety of therapeutic orientations within an overarching existential context. Here, a therapist might draw on such therapeutic approaches as behavioural interventions, eye movement desensitisation and reprocessing (EMDR), or acceptance and commitment therapy (ACT) to achieve the overall aim of 'setting people free' (Schneider, 2008; Schneider & Krug, 2010).

Today, in terms of practitioners and training institutes, the existential-humanistic approach is one of the smaller branches of existential therapy (Correia et al., 2014b). It is still primarily located in North America, with Schneider and colleagues' Existential-Humanistic Institute based in San Francisco and the International Institute for Humanistic Studies based in Petaluma, California. However, recent years have seen a growing dialogue between existential-humanistic therapists and psychologists in China, including a series of inter-national conferences on existential psychology held in Chinese cities (Hoffman et al., 2009; see Box 5.1). Alongside this, there has been a drive within the contemporary existential-humanistic field to engage with – and represent – voices across cultures (Hoffman, 2016; Hoffman, Cleare-Hoffman, & Jackson, 2014; Shapiro, 2016). Indeed, as Hoffman (personal communication, 3 February 2016) states, 'the multicultural dialogues are some of the most important con-versations occurring in existential-humanistic psychology today'. Existential-humanistic therapy has also been discussed specifically in relation to Latino (Comas-Diaz, 2008), African American (Rice, 2008), and lesbian and gay clients (Monheit, 2008).

Box 5.1   *Zhi mian*: Directly facing reality

'The real warrior dares to face life as it is, no matter how gloomy it might be; and to look unflinchingly at the scene, no matter how blood drenched it might be.' This description of *zhi mian*, or 'directly facing reality', comes from Lu Xun, a leading figure of modern Chinese literature (Wang, 2016). The concept has been adopted by Xuefu Wang, a Nanjing-based psychotherapist, and colleagues at the Zhi Mian International Institute of Existential-Humanistic Psychology, as a means of developing an indigenous Chinese therapy that has many links to the existential-humanistic field (Hoffman, 2009; Wang, 2011). *Zhi mian* therapy draws on the work of Lu Xun, and aims to help clients face their reality and to get to know the 'truth' of life (cf. van Deurzen, Chapter 7, this volume). It encourages clients to be authentic and to fiercely resist those forces that obstruct their growth, yet at the same time to develop their gentle, loving capabilities.

Lu Xun gives the analogy of an iron house to describe those social systems that claim to provide meaning for people, but are actually their shackles (cf. Heidegger's the One, discussed on p. 30): 'Imagine an iron house having not a single window and virtually indestructible, with all its inmates asleep and about to die of suffoca-tion. Dying in their sleep, they won't feel the pain of death' (cited in Wang, 2009: 153–154). But he goes on to ask, 'Now if you raise a shout to wake a few of the lighter sleepers, making these unfortunate few suffer the agony of irrevocable death, do you really think you are doing them a good turn? But if a few wake up, you can't say there is no hope of destroying the iron house.' Lu Xun was determined to shout and bang on the outside of the house; and although, here, he was referring to an awakening of the Chinese people from a perceived cultural slumber, the same analogy could be used for the role of the existential therapist; that is, that our clients, in the fallenness of their everyday lives, are entrapped in the iron house and slowly suffocating to death. To awaken them to their existential condition will, by no means, feel comforting for them, but it calls them back to reality, and provides them with an opportunity to make the most of their lives.

The existential-humanistic approach also remains hugely influential on the therapy world, as a whole, through the writings of Irvin Yalom. His much-loved books and novels, including *Love's Executioner* (1989), *When Nietzsche Wept* (1992), and *The Gift of Therapy* (2001), have transcended traditional boundaries between orientations. Indeed, they have reached far beyond the therapy world to achieve mass appeal.

Influences

In contrast to the daseinsanalysts, but like the meaning-centred therapists, existential-humanistic therapists have not tended to immerse themselves in – or tie themselves to – specific existential philosophical texts. Indeed, many of them openly admit that they find these writings abstruse and impenetrable (DeCarvalho, 1996; Schneider, 1990). Nevertheless, existential-humanistic therapists have been influenced by the writings of the existential philosophers through the teachings of Rollo May's mentor, Paul Tillich (2000), and they have also shown some interest in the works of Kierkegaard (Schneider & May, 1995c) and Nietzsche (Yalom, 1992). In contrast to the daseinsanalysts, then, existential-humanistic therapists, particularly the earlier writers such as Bugental, have tended to draw from the more individualistic elements of existential philosophy: those that emphasise the need for the human being to stand alone, and courageously face the anxiety of existence. From Tillich, there is also the notion that neurotic anxiety emerges when existential anxiety is denied (Chapter 2, this volume), and that human beings face a particular set of core concerns.

As the name suggests, the existential-humanistic approach has also been strongly influenced by the humanistic psychotherapy and psychology movement, which originated in the 1940s (Cain, 2002) and reached its zenith in the 1960s on the west coast of America. Indeed, to a large extent, the two approaches have grown up side-by-side, and have always been closely interrelated (Bugental, for instance, was the first president of the Association for Humanistic Psychology, while Carl Rogers and Abraham Maslow, two key figures in the humanistic psychology movement, contributed chapters to May's (1969b) *Existential Psychology*). As a reaction to the dominant, dehumanising psychologies of its day – behaviourism and psychoanalysis – humanistic psychology drew on many key existential premises: that human beings should be conceptualised as freely-choosing, self-aware, unique, meaning-orientated and fundamentally whole beings (Cain, 2002). In contrast to much existential philosophising, however, humanistic psychologists such as Maslow (1968) and Rogers (1959) placed particular emphasis on the sovereignty of individual, subjective experiences, and the need for human beings to be true to their own needs, rather than conforming to the needs of others. Maslow and Rogers also tend to downplay the tragic dimensions of existence, arguing instead that human beings have an innate tendency to actualise their potential and to grow. Hence, in drawing on these humanistic assumptions, the existential-humanistic approach tends to be the most individualistic and optimistic of the existential therapies. In addition, the existential-humanistic approach has drawn on many specific humanistic practices, such as Gendlin's (1996) focusing technique, gestalt therapy's two-chair work (Perls, Hefferline, & Goodman, 1951), and Rogers' (1957) core conditions.

Like daseinsanalysis and logotherapy, the existential-humanistic approach – particularly at the existential-analytical end of the spectrum – also draws widely from psychodynamic theory and practice. Indeed, because it places less emphasis on the in-the-world nature of human being, intrapsychic concepts such as resistance (or 'self-protection'), transference and unconscious processes form a relatively central element of existential-humanistic theory and practice. The existential-humanistic emphasis on choice and will also draws heavily from some of the more humanistically-inclined psychodynamic therapists, such as Alfred Adler, Otto Rank, Erich Fromm, Frieda Fromm-Reichmann and Leslie Farber. In addition, existential-humanistic therapists, most notably Yalom, are indebted to the 'interpersonal psychiatry' of Harry Stack Sullivan (1953), which understands mental misery in terms of an individual's problematic interactions with others.

As an American approach to existential therapy, the existential-humanistic approach is also infused with the spirit of pragmatism, as developed by such US philosophers as William James. Existential-humanistic therapists, then, may be open to using a wide range of methods (Correia et al., 2016c) as suits a particular client at a particular point in time, and they 'value a pluralistic understanding of human nature, psychotherapeutic integration, and complementariness among therapeutic approaches' (Schneider & Krug, 2010: 10). In this respect, role-plays, cognitive restructuring techniques, and behavioural interventions may all be part of an existential-humanistic psychotherapist's 'grab-bag' of approaches (Yalom & Elkin, 1974).

Box 5.2   Betty Cannon's Applied Existential Psychotherapy™

Applied Existential Psychotherapy (AEP) is a form of existential practice developed in the United States by Betty Cannon (1991, 2012), somewhat independently of the wider existential-humanistic movement. AEP is primarily rooted in Sartrean ideas, and is based on the assumption that we are 'free without excuses'. AEP draws on a range of experiential, gestalt therapy, body-orientated and psychodynamic methods to help clients focus on the 'nothingness' and anxiety of the immediate moment, to understand where their decisions (or lack of them) come from, and to experiment with new choices and ways of being in the world. For instance, if a client is struggling with procrastination, an applied existential psychotherapist might invite them to try out

(Continued)

(Continued)

'two-chair work' (from gestalt therapy), in which they would be asked to sit in a chair and speak from their 'procrastinating self'. Such an exercise might help them understand more about this voice and where it comes from – for instance, it might be a part of them that still feels like a scared child – and then to look at ways of 'standing back' from this voice so that they can choose to do things differently.

Resistance is futile

The aim of the existential-humanistic approach is to help clients become more 'present' to themselves and others: more 'fully and subjectively alive' (Schneider & Krug, 2010). Indeed, Schneider (2008) writes about the potential that we have to rediscover *awe* in our lives: humility and wonder, thrill and anxiety, towards the mystery of being.

So what is it that, from an existential-humanistic perspective, stops this happening? At the heart of the existential-humanistic enterprise lies an essentially psychodynamic reading of existential – particularly Kierkegaardian and Nietzschean – themes. For Freud, the eruption of sexual or aggressive drives from the depth of the unconscious creates a sense of anxiety, which the individual then attempts to quell through defence mechanisms such as denial and introjection (Yalom, 1980). Existential-humanists like Yalom (1980) agree with Freud that much human energy is dissipated in an attempt to ward off anxiety; and they also agree with Freud that much of this process goes on outside consciousness. Unlike Freud, however, they argue that the root of human anxiety is not sexual and aggressive impulses, but an awareness of the reality of existence (see Chapter 2, this volume). That is, existence – with all its uncertainty, pain, freedom and death – may be so threatening to the individual that they attempt to deny or distort this reality through such defensive mechanisms as compulsive behaviours or projection. An example of this is in the first meeting with Siân (see page 6), when she talks about sitting on the window ledge – a very serious brush with death – in a relatively light-hearted way. Here, from an existential-humanistic standpoint, we might hypothesise that Siân's 'playfulness' as she describes this event is a way of avoiding the anxiety-evoking reality that she came face to face with her annihilation. We might also hypothesise that her child-like demeanour – as well as, perhaps, her self-criticism – are means of denying the fact that she *is* an adult woman with freedom and responsibilities. That is, it is easier for Siân to say to herself, 'I'm such an idiot for messing things up' or 'I'm just a kid really', than it is to say, 'I'm a grown-up with the ability to do things differently'. In this respect, then, the psychoanalytic formula of

$$\text{DRIVE} \Rightarrow \text{ANXIETY} \Rightarrow \text{DEFENCE MECHANISM}$$

is replaced with

REALITY OF EXISTENCE ⇒ ANXIETY ⇒ DEFENCE MECHANISMS

(based on Yalom, 1980: 9–10)

From an existential-humanistic perspective, this denial of existential reality then brings with it all the problems described in Chapter 2 of this book. We become less capable of meeting the actual challenges facing us, neurotic anxieties emerge, and we end up living a shrunken and imprisoned life: devoid of passion, vibrancy and the full spectrum of emotions. As Bugental (1978: 126) puts it: 'Emotions are not so many packages of breakfast food lined up on the shelf, separate and unitary. *Emotionality is a unitary dimension of being:* one suppresses one aspect at the cost of crippling all.'

Bugental (1981) – along with contemporary existential-humanistic therapists (e.g., Hoffman, 2009; Shapiro, 2016) – refers to the ways in which clients seeks to avoid existential anxiety as *resistances*. Here, the term is being used in the broadest possible sense, to refer to those 'blockages' to reality that an individual erects: both outside and inside a therapeutic relationship. The fundamental project of existential-humanistic therapy, then, is to help clients identify and overcome their resistances: to unmask their self-deceptions, and meet the anxiety of existence with an attitude of commitment, decisiveness, courage, resolve (May, 1958) and *zhi mian* (see Box 5.1). In the case of Siân, for instance, it could mean both encouraging her to consider if her playfulness is a 'cover' for a deeper existential fear of having to choose, and helping her to meet life head on. Through such a process, it is proposed that clients can overcome their neurotic anxieties, live in harmony with the basic conditions of being human (Bugental, 1987), and reconnect with their potentiality for growth.

From an existential-humanistic perspective, however, the overcoming of these resistances will by no means be easy. Drawing on psychodynamic thinking – and in contrast to a daseinsanalytic approach – existential-humanistic therapists like Bugental (1981), Schneider and Krug (2010), and Yalom (1980) assert that an individual's resistances are likely to be deeply entrenched, and frequently subconscious. Hence, for Bugental (1978: 8) the process of tackling layer upon layer of resistance – which he likens to peeling an onion – will be 'an agonizing and conflictful struggle, for as the resistances are exposed and begin to be loosened, the threatening material which they covered press into consciousness'. Here, the client may be 'flooded with feelings of fright, pain, guilt, shame, dread and futility, and these may mount to a point at which the client feels unable to endure letting go of the ways which for so long gave a measure of protection'.

Because resistances are understood in this way, existential-humanistic therapists may adopt a relatively challenging stance towards their clients: encouraging them to face their fears and overcome their hurdles to reality. Existential-humanistic therapists also make it clear, however, that the aim of this process is to facilitate the client's own recognising and releasing of resistances (Bugental, 1978), and to empower clients, rather than to impose an external authority on them (Schneider & May, 1995c). Schneider (2003; Schneider & Krug, 2010), like other contemporary existential-humanistic therapists (e.g., Hoffman, 2009), also puts particular emphasis on relating to clients' resistances in a non-pathologising way: acknowledging that they may be clients' ways of protecting themselves and feeling safe and on familiar ground.

Facilitating an 'inner search'

From an existential-humanistic perspective – and, again, very much in contrast to a daseinsanalytic viewpoint (Chapter 3, this volume) – this facing-up to existence begins with an acknowledgement of our 'inner world of subjective experience' (Bugental, 1978): the kinaesthetic-affective realm of body, imagination, fantasy life, and intuition (Schneider & May, 1995c). For Bugental (1978), this private realm is our 'homeland' – the centre of our being (May, 1953) – but a homeland that many of us are exiles from.

Some of the most characteristic methods of existential-humanistic practice (Correia et al., 2016c), therefore, focus on helping clients become aware of their actual, in-the-moment experiences (Bugental, 1999). Bugental (1981) refers to this process as *inward searching* 'in which the awareness is tuned into one's own subjective experiencing in the moment and given free rein to move as it will' (Bugental, 1978: 52). To begin this process, existential-humanistic therapists may invite their clients to focus on their concerns (Schneider & May, 1995b), and to free-associate: following wherever their sense of concern may lead (Bugental, 1978). Bugental (1981: 107) sometimes gives the following directions to clients, if they inquire as to what they should talk about:

> Tell me what is of concern to you, what matters to you in your life today, right now as you lie here. What is it that you want to think through? What is it in your living that you want to make different? As you talk to me about your concern let yourself be open to mention any other awarenesses that come in whether or not they seem pertinent to what we are talking about. Sometimes these other awarenesses will be memories, sometimes physical sensations, sometimes emotions. Whatever they may be, let yourself mention them and then continue with what you were telling me about, or follow whatever you find is of concern to you at that point. Talk to me about what concerns you in your life.

Along similar lines, Schneider and Krug (2010: 114) describe a process of *invoking the actual*, in which clients are invited to focus on whatever is 'palpably relevant or charged' to them at that moment in time.

To facilitate this process, existential-humanistic therapists may use a range of strategies:

- Asking clients direct questions like: 'What does your inner experience tell you?' or 'How does it *feel* when you say that?'

- Inviting clients to be as detailed as possible in describing their experiences.
- Encouraging clients to slow down and 'stay with' their feelings.
- Inviting clients to express how they feel in the immediate moment, and in relation to their therapist.
- Encouraging clients to re-tell their experiences – on the principle that a human being 'almost literally cannot tell the same story twice in identical terms' (Bugental, 1978: 54).
- Encouraging clients to speak in the present tense and use the pronoun 'I' when discussing themselves.
- Helping clients to label, and differentiate between, different emotions.
- Inviting clients to visualise a particular scenario, role-play it, or actually try it out in the therapeutic meeting – for instance, making a dreaded phone call or expressing anger – and then reflecting on how that experience felt.
- Encouraging clients to develop the skill of self-awareness outside the therapeutic encounter as well as inside it. (Bugental, 1999; Schneider & Krug, 2010; Schneider & May, 1995b; Yalom, 1989; Yalom & Elkin, 1974)

In addition, from an existential-humanistic perspective, it is important that therapists:

- Provide clients with sufficient time to talk: Bugental (1981) suggests a ratio of client-talk to therapist-talk of approximately 19:1, respectively.
- Listen out for the dominant emotional theme that emerges in clients' narratives: the *red thread*.
- Pay attention to their own feelings, and use this as a guide to what clients might be experiencing.
- Trust that clients' experiences of pain and/or hurt will eventually transform, and assist clients to acquire that trust. (Bugental, 1981; Schneider & May, 1995b)

So what might this look like in actual practice? To illustrate this existential-humanistic approach, let's go back to the session (page 49) in which Siân is describing how quiet she feels: 'Just don't – feel like there's not much to say right now. Everything feels – it's all very flat' [one minute pause].

Therapist: So what's going on for you right now, Siân?
Siân: It's hard to – I can't really describe it …
Therapist: … Like in your body. Can you focus on what's going on inside? Maybe … Take a few moments to breathe in to it and see.
Siân: [Takes a few deep breaths] I can't …
Therapist: Just take your time, Siân. It's OK. Just …
Siân: There's – it's like butterflies in my stomach. Something really jangling about. Hard metal. Cold. It's really cold.
Therapist: Just stay with that coldness, Siân. Is there – can you say more?
Siân: It's cold. Frosty. Like I don't … Don't give a fuck. Some kind of tank. Like a big Russian tank all snowed in … in the middle of winter. Like some kind of – 'Stalingrad in my soul' [laughs].

Here, in contrast to a daseinsanalytic or meaning-centred approach, there is a particular focus on Siân's kinaesthetic experiencing: what she feels in her body. In such work, clients might be asked questions like 'How do you feel physically right now?' (Bugental, 1981: 239), or 'What's going on inside you?'

They may also be invited to place their hands on areas of their bodies that are noted or feel blocked. In addition, therapists may comment upon non-verbal aspects of their clients' being: for instance, their body postures, breathing patterns, or vocal fluctuations (Schneider & May, 1995b). Schneider and Krug (2010) describe this concerted attention to the physical dimension as *embodied meditation*. It has many similarities to the existentially-informed practice of *focusing* (Madison & Gendlin, 2012), in which clients are encouraged to focus in on – and allow to unfurl – their 'felt senses'. Here, one can also see resonances with mindfulness practices (see Nanda, 2010).

From an existential-humanistic perspective, such a process of inward searching can help clients to become more in touch with their subjective reality. As they do so, however, it is assumed that they will inevitably experience the anxiety of authenticity, and attempt to resist their inner search: through blocking, deflecting or distorting their awareness (Bugental, 1978). According to existential-humanistic therapists (Bugental, 1978; Schneider & May, 1995b), clients may:

- Start to change the topic.
- Become distracted.
- Talk about trivialities.
- Talk in clichéd, polite, formal, abstract or disinterested ways.
- Talk so quickly that they cannot 'hear' themselves.
- Start to intellectualise, rationalise, analyse or try to solve their concern.
- Distance themselves from their experiences and talk about themselves as if they are a different person.

Hence, in facilitating a client's inward search, a key role for therapists is to help clients notice when they are resisting the process. Schneider (2003) identifies two basic forms of *resistance work* – *vivification* and *confrontation*. Vivification involves heightening the client's awareness of how they block or limit themselves, and consists of 'noting' the client's initial resistances: for instance, 'You seem to change the topic every time I ask you about your illness.' This can then be pointed out every time this resistance is repeated (*tagging*). Confrontation is a more direct and amplified form of vivification, pressing – gently or otherwise – clients to overcome their blocks. Hence, while vivifying is intended to *alert* the client to their resistances, confronting is intended to *alarm* them about it (K. Schneider, personal communication, 27 December 2015). Hoffman (2009: 40) adds to this that sometimes *stark statements* can be helpful: 'short comments that jar the client into awareness'. An example of this, in the dialogue above, might be: 'Wow, Siân, you're just so struggling to stay with your feelings. You find it almost impossible.'

For Bugental (1987), it can be useful to both teach clients the negative effects of resisting their inner search, and help them to see that this is not merely an arbitrary or careless behaviour, but a motivated attempt at blocking an inner awareness. Schneider and Krug (2010) add that clients can be encouraged to *trace out* their resistances: to look at what the consequences of such actions would be.

Siân's laughter as she describes the 'Stalingrad in [her] soul' could be seen as one example of resistance: a means of avoiding going more deeply into her here-and-now experience. In this instance, an example of resistance work might be as follows:

Therapist: Siân, I notice that you laugh as you talk about that cold and frosty place. Is it hard to stay with? [Vivification]

Siân: It's pretty horrible. It's not – it's not much fun – what I like to be.

Therapist: So try staying with it Siân. Can you open it out more? Just be – be there with that hard metal in your stomach.

Siân: It's – it's such a funny – stupid saying: 'Stalingrad in my soul' [Siân looks up and smiles]. So cold and wintry. I guess at least all that cold freezes the elephant shit on my head! [Siân laughs].

Therapist: [Therapist smiles too] Siân, that does make me smile but … you know, I sense you're going away from it again [tagging]. I think – sometimes, Siân, I get a sense that you use – you laugh or you smile at me as a way of pacifying me, or you put yourself down. Siân, it feels really important to stay with what you're feeling inside, right now. Just try and stay with it [confrontation].

Siân: I [pause] … It's – there's something really cold down there and locked in. A big metal frozen box. And … I know – it's … just rage, I think, just rage trying to smash out. Great big red ball of fire burning inside the tank. Destroy everything.

Therapist: Stay with it Siân. See if you can really go into it.

Interpersonal presence

From an existential-humanistic perspective, an individual's authenticity is defined not only in terms of their willingness to know themselves, but also in terms of their willingness to be known by others (Bugental, 1978). This is defined as *presence*: being 'as aware and as participative as one is able to be at that time and in those circumstances' (Bugental, 1978: 36). As well as facilitating a client's inner search, then, existential-humanistic therapists will also try to facilitate a client's presence to another: their ability to communicate and express their authentic, in-the-moment experiencing (Bugental, 1999). In this respect, Yalom, Bugental and contemporary existential-humanistic practitioners place considerable emphasis on encouraging clients to articulate how they are feeling in the 'living moment' of the immediate therapeutic encounter, and particularly how they are feeling towards the therapist. Indeed, Yalom (2001: 72) writes that, 'I make an effort to inquire about the here-and-now at each session even if it has been productive and nonproblematic.' This might involve asking questions like: 'How are you and I doing today?' or 'How are you experiencing the space between us today?' Consistent with this, research indicates that existential-humanistic therapists are among the most relationally focused of all existential practitioners (Correia et al., 2016c; Norcross, 1987).

A good example of this here-and-now relational focus comes from Yalom's work with Ginny Elkin, which both therapist and client describe in *Every Day Gets a Little Closer* (Yalom & Elkin, 1974). Here, Yalom relentlessly inquires into Ginny's feelings towards him, and what her ways of behaving in the sessions might reveal. Why, for instance, does she not ask him any questions? Disagree with him? Or tell him that she cares about him? As outlined in *The Gift of Therapy*, Yalom (2001) consistently strives to bring the client's narrative back to the immediate encounter. When, for instance, Ginny says that she feels strangled by a friend, Yalom wonders whether she also might be feeling strangled by him. Similarly, he 'hones in very hard' on Ginny's feelings about alterations in the therapeutic frame. Having cancelled a session with Ginny, for instance, Yalom suggests to her that she may well be feeling angry or depressed about this.

As with presence to one's self, existential-humanistic therapists assume that this process of being fully present and open to an other can be highly anxiety-creating (May, 1958). Much of the existential-humanistic work around presence, then, involves vivifying and challenging clients' resistances to fully engaging with the therapist. In his case of the 'Fat Lady', for instance, Yalom (1989: 97–98) points out to his client, Betty, that the way she presents herself does not seem to reflect her real feelings and concerns.

Yalom:	… I think you are determined, absolutely committed, to be jolly with me.
Betty:	Hmmm, interesting theory, Dr Watson.
Yalom:	You've done this since our first meeting. You tell me about a life that is full of despair, but you do it in a bouncy-bouncy 'Aren't-we-having-a-good-time?' way.
Betty:	That's the way I am.
Yalom:	When you stay jolly like that, I lose sight of how much pain you're having.
Betty:	That's better than wallowing in it.
Therapist:	But you come here for help. Why is it so necessary for you to entertain me?

With Betty, Yalom (1989) also uses his feelings of boredom and disinterest as an indication that she is not fully present. He does not say this directly to her but, recognising that it is because she does not reveal anything intimate about herself, encourages her to try to be more disclosing.

Expressing one's authentic being, however, is only one side of the presence coin. The other, 'input' side is what Bugental (1978: 37) terms *accessibility*: 'having the intention to allow what happens in a situation to matter'. Being fully present, then, is as much about being open to the authentic being of others as it is about expressing one's own authenticity; and existential-humanistic therapists like Yalom will readily challenge clients to acknowledge the existence of another human being in the room with them. When Ginny, for instance, says that she cannot even look at him, Yalom challenges her to do so, and he fixes her gaze for a length of time (Yalom & Elkin, 1974). Construing presence in terms of accessibility as well as expressiveness also means that, from an existential-humanistic perspective, 'transference' is one particular form of resistance to presence. It is the client's 'unconscious attempt to re-establish an earlier, symbiotic relationship with a person important in his life' (Bugental, 1981: 137), and by so doing avoid the anxiety of being fully present to a unique, unfamiliar and unpredictable other. 'Analysing the transference', therefore, can be an important element of existential-humanistic psychotherapy (Bugental, 1981). By helping clients to see how, and from what source, they mis-perceive their therapists – and by extension other people in their lives – they can be helped to relate to others in a more authentic way.

From an existential-humanistic perspective, however, such a process can only be facilitated if therapists are also genuinely present to their clients (Bugental, 1978). Without this happening, therapists and clients would have no way of knowing the ways in which clients constrict their perceptions of real others, nor would clients be able to learn to develop fully authentic relationships. Furthermore, according to Schneider and May (1995b), therapists' presence creates a sense of safety in which clients' problems can be confronted, and also deepens clients' capacities to constructively act upon their discoveries. As Yalom (2008) puts it, it is the therapists' sheer presence that can help clients face such givens of existence as death. A final reason for the vital importance of therapists' presence is that it can create for clients a model of authentic living. Despite the many different techniques and interpretative formulations developed within the existential-humanistic approach, then, all this is considered secondary to the development of an authentic, genuine relationship between therapists and clients (Bugental, 1978). As Yalom's (1989: 91) 'personal mantra' puts it: 'It's the relationship that heals, the relationship that heals, the relationship that heals.' Almost 20 years later, he continues to write, 'In my work with clients, I strive for connectedness above all else' (Yalom, 2008: 206).

With respect to the accessibility side of the presence coin, therapist presence means that existential-humanistic therapists must be sensitive and open to the full scope of their clients' being. With Betty, for instance, Yalom (1989) comes to see that his disgust of obesity stops him from being fully attentive and caring towards her. With respect to the expressive side of the presence coin, it means that a therapist should be open and willing to self-disclose to her client, rather than remaining opaque and aloof (Yalom, 2001). Yalom suggests that therapists should always answer their clients' questions, and outlines three particular areas in which he feels therapists should be transparent. First, is the mechanism of therapy, such as the assumptions and rationale behind the process, and the ways in which clients might be most able to maximise their progress. Second are therapists' feelings towards their clients in the immediate here-and-now: whether tenderness, disinterest or an uncertainty about how to progress. Third, and perhaps most controversially, Yalom suggests that therapists should also be willing to be honest about their own lives, such as whether or not they are in a relationship, what their sexuality is, or what kind of films they like. Yalom (2001: 90) makes it clear that this needs to be done tactfully, and that therapists should also try to explore the process of the client's personal inquiries, but concludes that 'I have always facilitated therapy when I have shared some facet of myself'. Research goes some way to supporting this claim, though it also suggests that therapists' self-disclosures are most helpful when they are relatively infrequent, not too personal, and positive rather than critical of clients (Hill & Knox, 2002).

Addressing the existential givens

To this point, the existential-humanistic approach shares many similarities with other forms of contemporary humanistic practice, such as person-centred therapy (Murphy & Joseph, 2016), gestalt therapy (Brownell, 2016), and focusing-orientated psychotherapy (Krycka & Ikemi, 2016). In drawing on existential philosophy, however, the existential-humanistic approach goes beyond an exploration of the subjective, intersubjective and kinaesthetic realms to suggest that there are certain givens, or *ultimate concerns* (Yalom, 1980), that all individuals face (see Chapter 2, this volume). From an existential-humanistic perspective, these are the concerns that are at the fount of all our anxieties: the terrors of existence that become revealed once all the layers of resistance are peeled away (Bugental, 1978). According to Bugental, many clients will eventually come face to face with these terrors, and he calls this 'dark night' of the therapeutic journey the 'existential crisis'. Yalom (1980), on the other hand, takes a less linear perspective, suggesting that individuals at any point in their growth may face *boundary situations*: 'an event, an urgent experience, that propels one into a confrontation with one's existential "situation" in the world' (Yalom, 1980: 159). Working with these themes, then, is one of the most characteristic practices of existential-humanistic therapists (Correia et al., 2016c).

Bugental (1981) and Yalom (1980) also differ in their classification of these ultimate concerns. Yalom outlines four: death, freedom, isolation and meaninglessness; while Bugental outlines six: finiteness, potential to act, choice, embodiedness, awareness and separateness (this last given was subsequently revised to separate-but-related (Bugental & Sterling, 1995)). For the purposes of this chapter, Yalom's somewhat more concise schema will be used – though Bugental's concerns will be examined where relevant.

Confronting freedom

Facing up to our freedom and responsibility is a theme that runs throughout existential philosophy, and is the given that existential-humanistic therapists themselves see as most frequently helping clients to address (Correia et al., 2016c). May (1969a: 218), in *Love and Will*, usefully breaks this concept down into a number of constituent parts. At the root of human freedom, he suggests, is *intentionality*: the basic human tendency to 'stretch' towards something. *Wish* – '*the imaginative playing with the possibility* of some act or state occurring', lies on top of this. And on top of the wish lies *will*: '*the capacity to organise one's self* so that movement in a certain direction or towards a certain goal may take place'. Drawing on the writings of the American psychotherapist Leslie Farber (2000), May also distinguishes between effortful will – as in the Victorian notion of 'will-power' – and the more spontaneous, automatic and unconscious will by which many of our actions take place. For May, the significance of this distinction is that we may be making choices even when we do not experience ourselves as consciously, wilfully choosing. In other words, freedom is not limited to those moments of deliberate decision-making, but is an all-pervasive component of human experiencing.

As existential philosophers have pointed out (Chapter 2, this volume), however, this freedom to wish, will and choose can be profoundly unsettling. Hence, existential-humanistic psychotherapists have identified numerous ways in which individuals may try to defend themselves against the anxiety of freedom. To avoid having to make choices, for instance, people may procrastinate; become apathetic; act on whims and impulses; or behave in fixed, compulsive, obsessive or phobic ways (May, 1953; Yalom, 1980). One example of the latter is agoraphobia, which Wolfe (2008: 207) argues is a defence against the dizziness of freedom and space. Delegating one's choices to other people, institutions, deities or things may also be a means of trying to disencumber oneself of freedom (Yalom, 1980). Rebellion is a further strategy by which individuals may try to avoid choosing. Although this may have a semblance of freedom, by simply doing the opposite of what they are told or expected to do, rebels – as much as conformists – can avoid having to really think and choose for themselves (May, 1953).

Human beings may use similar strategies to avoid taking *responsibility* for the choices that they have made in the past. One of the most common means of defending themselves against the threat of guilt and blame is by displacing the responsibility for their actions onto something external. Individuals, for instance, may hold other people – including their therapists – responsible for the choices that they have made (May, 1969a), concomitantly construing themselves as the innocent victims of other people's actions (Yalom, 1980). Individuals may also hold social institutions responsible for their choices, or displace their responsibility onto such transpersonal forces as 'karma'. As part of this displacement of responsibility, individuals may feel that they have a 'divine right' to be taken care of (May, 1953): that the world owes them a living, rather than them having the responsibility for creating their own lives. Human beings, however, may also try to divest themselves of their responsibility by attributing their choices to uncontrollable internal factors, such as their personality, genes, mental illness, childhood or unconscious. Alternatively, clients might claim that 'I just lost control', 'I don't know what came over me', or 'I was out of my mind' (Yalom, 1980). Individuals may also try to defend themselves against the guilt and regret of responsibility by revising their view of the alternatives they needed to choose between. For instance, they may devalue the un-chosen alternative – a process that social psychologists refer to as *self-justification* (Aronson, Wilson, & Akert, 1999) – such that the feelings of loss and remorse can be attenuated (Yalom, 1980). A client, for example, who has chosen to stay in a loveless relationship, may then try to reassure themselves that they would have 'fallen apart' had they chosen to leave, such that they feel less regretful about their choice.

As existential philosophers have argued, however, the consequences of such defences against the dizziness of freedom can be severe (Chapter 2, this volume). By denying their ability to choose, human beings undermine their ability to act in ways that feel meaningful and right for them, and are left with a sense of powerlessness, hopelessness and futility. In the case of Siân, for instance, we could hypothesise that she does gain some comfort from putting herself in the position of 'playful child', but the cost of this is that she does not pursue her dreams and passions, and make of her life what she wants it to be. By failing to fulfil their potential, clients also increase their sense of existential guilt (Yalom, 1980). This is illustrated, again, in the case of Siân. She knows that she is not doing what she really wants to be doing; she knows that time is moving relentlessly forward; and she knows that, at some level, she has the capacity to make things different. Moreover, the defence against existential anxiety becomes a breeding ground for neurotic anxiety. People may, for instance, develop obsessive feelings of hatred and anger towards those who they perceive as restricting their freedom (May, 1953), or become trapped in a vicious circle of apathy and powerlessness. Furthermore, because they cannot entirely deny that they are making choices – even if the choice is not to choose – then they continue to be haunted by the threat of blame (Bugental, 1981) and the call of their conscience.

Hence, a central aim of the existential-humanistic approach is to help clients discover, establish and use their freedom (May, 1981). Indeed, Yalom (1980) writes that therapy is effective to the extent that it influences and mobilises patients' wills. This means that an important aspect of the existential-humanistic approach is helping clients to recognise points at which they could – or can – make choices, and encouraging them to act in wilful (rather than compulsive) ways (Bugental, 1981), both inside and outside the therapeutic relationship. Here, clients may be encouraged to consider the alternative paths of action that they can take (Yalom, 1980). They may also be encouraged to 'slow down', so that they have 'the power to stand outside the rigid chain of stimulus and response, to pause, and by this pause to throw some weight on either side, to cast some decision about what the response will be' (May, 1953: 161). From an existential-humanistic perspective, helping clients to become more aware of their feelings and in-the-moment experiences should help them to become more aware too of their deeper wishes (May, 1953; Schneider & May, 1995b; Yalom, 1980). If, for instance, our client Siân could be helped to recognise that she may be feeling angry when she goes quiet, then this might help her express her dissatisfaction with what is going on and her desire for change.

Yalom may also use a more didactic approach to help clients recognise the 'intrauterine kicks of their inborn will' (Yalom & Elkin, 1974: 226). During one session with his Ginny, for instance, Yalom tries to make her realise that her situation is not out of control, as she imagines it to be, and that she retains freedom of choice in each instant. She can, he says, take each of her problems one by one, and think of correct moves. In helping clients acknowledge their freedom and possibilities, he suggests that four insights, in particular, may be useful for the therapist to convey to their client:

- Only I can change the world I have created;
- There is no danger in change;
- To get what I really want, I must change;
- I have the power to change. (Yalom, 1980: 340–341).

Challenging clients' resistances to making choices and taking control of their lives is also a central aspect of the existential-humanistic therapeutic process. Clients, for instance, may be encouraged to replace words like 'can't' with 'won't' (May & Yalom, 1989). Through observation or interpretation, therapists may also point out to their clients ways in which they seem to divest themselves of power and act in non-assertive ways (Yalom & Elkin, 1974). In working with Siân, for instance, an existential-humanistic therapist might say something like this:

I get a sense – Siân, you know, when I look at your life I get a sense that it's hard for you to take control of things. You're – you talk as if Hanako's in charge, and then you – it's as if you're too little. But, Siân, you know, I just wonder if it's hard for you to make the choices here, like who you want to be. Who do you want to be, Siân?

Encouraging clients to see how they divest themselves of power within the therapeutic relationship may be a particularly immediate and direct means of helping clients to see their resistances to choice in everyday life. Do they, for instance: Look to their therapist to make something happen (Yalom, 1980)? Believe that their therapist is a 'God' who knows how the therapeutic work should progress (May, 1953)? Or expect their therapist to dictate the process of therapy (Bugental, 1981) and then 'rebel' against every suggestion that they make? Some years back, for instance, I worked with a female client who would come to each session saying that she didn't know what to talk about, and asking me for some suggestions. Every time I reluctantly suggested a particular line of exploration for her, however, she would sooner or later find fault with it: that she'd already talked about this before, or that she really couldn't see the point in talking about this. When I fed back to her my perception of this process, we came to see that she felt much safer saying 'nay' or 'yay' to my choices than making choices of her own. Furthermore, she realised that this was a dynamic that occurred in many other areas of her life. We also came to see that, while she felt less exposed and open to criticism by reacting against the choices of other, it meant too that she rarely got to do what she wanted, and she was often left feeling angry that others had not made the right choices for her.

To challenge clients' resistances against taking control within the therapeutic relationship, it can also be very useful for therapists to ask and re-ask their clients what they want from the therapeutic process (Yalom & Elkin, 1974), or 'why they have come today' (May, 1969a). This may force the client out of the passive, yet potentially comforting, stance that the therapeutic healing will simply *happen* to them if they turn up on a weekly basis – like turning up for a dental appointment – and into an acknowledgement that they are responsible for making the therapeutic changes occur.

Existential-humanistic therapists may also be keen to point out to their clients that not choosing is a choice in itself. In the following exchange, for instance, Bugental (1981: 346) encourages a mother, Thelma, to see that she is making numerous choices about her daughter's relationship with a boy of 'ill repute':

Thelma:	I can't do a thing, she's going to go, and that's it.
Bugental:	So you decided to let her go with John?
Thelma:	I haven't decided. She's the one who decided.
Bugental:	No, you've decided too. You've chosen to let her go with John.
Thelma:	I don't see how you can say that. She's insisting.
Bugental:	That's what she's doing; what you're doing is accepting her insistence.
Thelma:	Well then I won't let her go. But she'll be unhappy and make life hell for me for a while.
Bugental:	So you've decided to forbid her to go with John.
Thelma:	Well, isn't that what you wanted? What you said I should do?
Bugental:	I didn't say that you should do anything. You have a choice here, but you seem to be insisting that either your daughter is making a choice or that I am.
Thelma:	Well, I don't know what to do.
Bugental:	It's a hard choice.

Confronting death

For Yalom (2008: 202), death is the most prominent and bedevilling of the ultimate concerns. He writes that it is 'ubiquitous and of such magnitude that a considerable portion of one's life energy is consumed in the denial of death' (1980: 41). Bugental (1981) construes this given of existence in slightly wider terms, as 'finiteness', and suggests that an awareness of the limits of our existence brings us face to face with uncertainty, and evokes an anxiety of fate as well as death. Along similar lines, the clinical psychologist Barry Wolfe (2008: 205) has written that, 'The fear of dying is the most common root fear in anxiety disorders that I have encountered in my clinical work.' He gives the example of a patient with severe bridge phobia, whose underlying anxiety was that he would 'hurl himself over the bridge once he reached the top of its height' (Wolfe, 2008: 206). In other words, behind many apparently ontic-level anxieties – such as a fear of needles or panic attacks (Randall, 2001) – may be an ontological fear of our own annihilation.

In support of these assumptions, contemporary research in the field of 'terror management theory' shows that mortality is a 'hot button' within people's cognitive networks. That is, it is a concern that is relatively easy to 'light up', and one that people have developed a range of strategies to keep at bay (Arndt, Cook, & Routledge, 2004). A robust body of psychological research, for instance, shows that people will tend to cling more tightly to cultural world-views when their awareness of death (*mortality salience*) is increased, and will also strive to bolster their self-esteem to ameliorate their death-related anxieties (Pyszczynski, Greenberg, & Koole, 2004).

Yalom (1980) suggests two particular strategies by which individuals may attempt to defend themselves from an awareness of their demise. The first of these is a belief in one's own *specialness*. Here, individuals ward off an awareness of their own finitude by convincing themselves that they are unique and 'different', such that, while mortality may apply to other people, they are exempt from this natural law. Such a resistance is hypothesised to take a number of forms. Through compulsive risk-taking, for instance, individuals may attempt to prove to themselves that they are uniquely invulnerable to the threat of death. Aggressive and controlling behaviours may also be ways in which individuals attempt to prove their superiority over others, and hence their uniqueness. According to Yalom, another manifestation of the 'I'm special' defence may be workaholism, in which individuals strive to achieve a unique position in the workplace hierarchy, and thereby stand far above the yawning chasm of mortality. Individuals who adopt the 'I'm special' defence may also manifest many narcissistic traits: an intense self-focus, the expectation that they should be loved and admired for whatever behaviours they emit, and a diminished recognition of the rights and needs of the other. The second defensive strategy identified by Yalom is that of *the ultimate rescuer*: a belief that some being – a god, a parent, a doctor, or even one's therapist – will somehow rescue them from the jaws of infinite non-existence.

Existential-humanistic psychotherapists have identified numerous other strategies by which individuals may attempt to ward off an awareness of their own mortality. Through the clamour of compulsive sexual activity, for instance, individuals may attempt to drown out the ever-waiting presence of death, and reassure themselves of their vitality and youthfulness (May, 1969a). As with workaholism, social activism, or a desperate desire for children, this compulsive sexual activity may also be an attempt to 'leap-frog' death by leaving some kind of legacy behind. Yalom (1980) refers to such defence mechanisms as *immortality projects*. Defences against death may be highly personal too. In Yalom's (1989) case of the 'Fat Lady', for instance, Betty's experience of seeing her father wither away from cancer was interpreted as the reason why she strived, albeit 'unconsciously', to maintain her body fat, lest she should die too.

Yalom (1980, 2008) suggests that a defence against the reality of one's own death, to some extent, may serve an important self-protective function. As La Rochefoucauld observes: 'One cannot look directly at either the sun or death' (quoted in Yalom, 1980: 103). Like all defences against reality, however, at more developed levels this may become highly dysfunctional. Indeed, Yalom states that, as death is the primordial source of anxiety, it is also the primary fount of psychopathology. Individuals who doggedly try to assert their own specialness, for instance, may find it difficult to form mutual and intimate relationships, or may risk their lives in 'death-defying' activities. Similarly, individuals who adopt the ultimate-rescuer defence may suffer from 'self-effacement, fear of withdrawal of love, passivity, dependence, self-immolation, refusal to accept adulthood, and depression at collapse of the belief system' (Yalom, 1980: 134). Furthermore, as Heidegger argues, by not facing up to their own finitude, individuals are not able to make the most of the life that they do have. In the words of Otto Rank, the neurotic refuses the loan of life to escape the debt of death (quoted in Yalom, 1980: 147). Here, existential-humanistic writers agree with existential philosophers that facing up to the reality of death can shock people into taking the present seriously and making the most of their own, individual lives (May, 1953). This hypothesis is supported by empirical research, which shows that an increased awareness of death leads people to become more focused on their own, individuated goals and values, and away from culturally conditioned standards (Martin, Campbell, & Henry, 2004). Such an awareness of death may also give them a sense of fellowship with other human beings who are 'in the same boat' (May, 1999).

For Yalom, then, helping clients to face up to the reality of their inevitable demise is an important part of the therapeutic work. Indeed, Yalom (1980: 194) writes that, 'any long-term intensive therapy will be incomplete without working through awareness and fear of death' (although, interestingly, only a small proportion of contemporary existential-humanistic therapists see working with being-towards-death as a central characteristic of their practice (Correia et al., 2016c). Yalom does not suggest, however, that therapists should specifically confront clients with the fact that they are going to die. Rather, in instances where clients are temporarily divested of their defences against death – for instance, when they realise they are less special than they thought, lose their parental ultimate rescuer, or pass through such milestones as birthdays and anniversaries – therapists should try to 'nurse the shudder rather than to anesthetize it' (Yalom, 1980: 166). At the most basic level, this may simply involve encouraging clients to talk about their death anxieties rather than blandly reassuring them that they've got years to go, or interpreting the death anxiety as a product of non-death-related fears. It may also mean being open and responsive to the possibility that, behind clients'

apparently ontic-level anxieties, lie deeper ontological fears. Another implica-
tion of this analysis is that therapists, themselves, should explore their own
attitudes and anxieties towards death (see Box 5.3).

Box 5.3   Artificial aids to increase death awareness

For therapists to work effectively with clients' anxieties about death, they too will
need to face up to their own demise. Yalom (1980) outlines a number of exercises
that may be useful for this purpose:

- Write your own obituary or epitaph. You may want to try writing this both as you
  think it will be and how you would ideally like it to be.
- Close your eyes and try to visualise your own death: Where do you imagine it will
  occur? When? How? What would your funeral be like?
- On a blank sheet of paper, draw a line, with one end representing your birth and
  one end representing your death. Draw a cross to represent where you are now,
  and spend some time meditating on this image.
- In small groups, write all the names of group members on slips of paper, and then
  place them in a bowl. Begin a conversation about any topic, and at some point,
  pick – or have a facilitator pick – one of the names from the bowl. The person
  picked should then stop talking and turn their back to the others. After some
  minutes, discuss your experience of the exercise. What was it like to be picked?
  What was it like to have someone 'taken away' from you? And what was it like to
  experience the arbitrariness of the choosing?

For Yalom (2008: 78), however, 'death concerns are not conscious to most
individuals but must be inferred by disguised manifestations'. Hence, Yalom
(1989) may interpret a client's dreams, feelings or experiences in terms of an
underlying anxiety about – and defence towards – death. Yalom suggests to a
client who has advanced cancer, for instance, that his attempts to convince
himself that he is tantalisingly close to being loved by beautiful women is a
way of buttressing his belief that he is no different from anyone else, and
thereby not mortally ill. In another example, he suggests that a woman's anxieties towards her son's addiction are actually about her own ageing process
(Yalom, 2008). Similarly, for Yalom, a client's refusals to acknowledge the ending of the therapeutic relationship may say something about his attitude
towards human finiteness. For Yalom, analysing the transference may also be
an important way of helping clients to uncover their defences against death.
If, for instance, a client relates to their therapist as if they are the one person
who can save them from destruction, then – in the right circumstances – it
may be appropriate to suggest that this is a means of protecting themselves
from an awareness of their own mortality. In exploring death and finitude,
Yalom may take an even more didactic stance: reminding clients that the life

they are leading is their one and only life and not a rehearsal, with no 'rain-checks', replays or possibilities of postponement (Yalom & Elkin, 1974).

Helping clients explore their anxieties, defences and attitudes towards death may be particularly important when they are in the boundary situations of serious or terminal illness. Here, writes Yalom (1980), the defences erected against death invariably falter, and individuals are faced with the reality that they are not special and exempt, and that there are no ultimate rescuers waiting in the wings. In the face of such realisations, Yalom suggests that terminally ill clients can feel betrayed: as if their very foundations have been kicked away from underneath them. However, for Yalom, the breaking-down of such defences against death can also act as a catalyst towards significant personal change, particularly if the awareness of death is fostered, rather than countered, by a therapist. Yalom reports that such squaring-up to death can help clients live more fully in the present and overcome the tendency to 'postpone existence'; appreciate more deeply the positive aspects of their lives; and dis-identify with the more superficial aspects of themselves, including their pre-illness worries and neuroses. In his later work, Yalom (2008: 83) also suggests that clients can be helped to overcome the dread of death by recognising the *rippling effect* of their own lives. This 'refers to the fact that each of us creates – often without our conscious intent or knowledge – concentric circles of influence that may affect others for years, even generations'.

Confronting isolation

For both Yalom (1980) and Bugental (1981) – though less so for some contemporary existential-humanistic practitioners (Schneider, 2008) – a third given of existence is that 'the individual is inexorably alone' (Yalom, 1980: 353). Yalom (1980: 355) writes that there exists 'an unbridgeable gulf between oneself and any other being', as well as an unbridgeable gap between the individual and their world. For Bugental (1981), an awareness of this fundamental separateness evokes an anxiety of loneliness and isolation in people, as well as an anxiety that no one really cares about them or is thinking about them, and that they do not really matter to other people. One could also include here the anxiety that they are unloved by others, and that no one could really love them if they knew who they were.

As with the other givens of existence, Yalom (1980) and Bugental (1981) argue that, at an unconscious level, human beings develop numerous defensive strategies to protect themselves against an awareness of their fundamental isolation. For instance, they may constantly strive to be noticed and affirmed in the eyes of others, like a little child shouting 'Look at me! Look at me!' (Yalom, 1980). Individuals who have a desperate desire to be famous, or who behave in attention-seeking or overly-dramatic ways, may have adopted this line of defence. Another defence may be to try to fuse with others (Yalom, 1980): to soften one's ego-boundaries and to try to become part of another person, group or thing. For instance, people may sacrifice their individuality in relationships: obsequiously following the dictates and behaviours of others, or unquestioningly conform to a culture's values, norms and ways of behaving. Not expressing one's anger or disagreeable feelings towards others – as with Siân – could be part of this struggle to merge too (Yalom & Elkin, 1974), as could the desire to take on a nurturing or 'rescuing' role. Sexual obsessiveness may be another manifestation of the desire to merge with another (Yalom, 1980). According to May (1953), individuals may also try to protect themselves against an awareness of their isolation through religion: by believing in a 'cosmic papa'-like God who is always by their side.

Paradoxically, however, such defences against existential isolation may lead individuals to become more isolated in their lives rather than less. 'If', as Yalom (1980: 363) writes, 'we are overcome with dread before the abyss of loneliness, we will not reach out towards others but instead will flail at them in order not to drown in the sea of our existence.' In these instances, he goes on to write: 'We behave toward other beings as toward tools or equipment. The other, now no longer an "other" but an "it," is placed there, within one's circle of world, for a *function*' (1980: 363). Hence, rather than individuals developing mutual, I–Thou love, they develop 'use and be used' relationships, in which elements of true connectivity and intimacy are rare. Furthermore, potential mates are likely to find such neediness – whether in terms of a need to be dominated, or a need to be nurtured – unattractive, and consequently push the person further away. Another reason why defences against isolation may lead to further isolation is because they are likely to engender neurotic anxiety: feelings which individuals may defend themselves against by withdrawing further from relationships. An individual, for instance, who desperately desires to merge with another may fear tremendously that this desire will be rejected. Consequently, they may defend themselves against their neurotic anxiety by withdrawing from intimate relationships altogether. Finally, because, of course, the anxiety of existential isolation does not go away, individuals who defend themselves against it will constantly worry that they will one day be left on their own. From this existential perspective, then, it is only by acknowledging their true isolation and individuality that individuals can come together with another, and love and be loved in a mature and need-free way (see Fromm's *The Art of Loving* (1963)). From an existential-humanistic perspective, such an acknowledgement also allows individuals to actualise their own unique potential – free of the desire to conform and be approved of by others.

Alongside helping clients face up to their death and freedom, then, existential-humanistic psychotherapists may also be concerned with helping their clients face up to their fundamental aloneness (Yalom, 1980). Clients may be encouraged to plunge into their feelings of lostness and loneliness, and, during the course of the therapy, may even be advised to have periods of self-enforced isolation. Clients may also be challenged to look at the ways in which they attempt to defend themselves against their fundamental aloneness; and, as with the other existential givens, may be particularly encouraged to look at the ways they try to defend themselves against this anxiety within the therapeutic relationship itself. Indeed, Yalom (1980: 393) writes: 'The characteristics of a need-free relationship provide the therapist with an ideal or a horizon against which the patient's interpersonal pathology is starkly illuminated.' Therapist and client, for instance, can look at whether the client tends to constantly seek affirmation from their therapist, or whether the client maintains a stance of detachment and disinterest. Through the challenging of such resistances, the client can then begin to experience the depths of aloneness in the thera-peutic relationship and, with it, their ability to relate to their therapist in an independent, need-free way. While such a relationship may be temporary, what remains with the client is their knowledge that they have the potential for this kind of relationship.

To illustrate how such work might look, let's go back to Siân as she's invited to stay with the image of the great big red ball of fire, burning inside the tank.

Siân:	It's such a hot, angry … irritated feeling. Waiting to – to explode. Shatter the tank.
Therapist:	Can you let it shatter?
Siân:	[Pause] No. I feel so … shut down. Constipated. It's such a strong metal case. Shiny.
Therapist:	And what – What's your … your fear if it did shatter?
Siân:	[Quietly] Shrapnel. Destroying you. Everyone. Just exploding and destroying everyone around me.
Therapist:	So you feel like, if you did connect with that rage, that red fire, you'd – it would destroy everyone?
Siân:	Mm … You'd all – couldn't bear it. You, Hana, Kai, my dad …
Therapist:	And – so, can I ask – I mean, if that did happen, what then? I mean, how would that be for you?
Siân:	Just this – big, massive expanse. Everyone going away from me. Siberian-plains kind of stuff again. Everyone – not destroyed, but walking away.
Therapist:	And it's just you there …
Siân:	… Hated by everyone.
Therapist:	And can you just stay there? In that place? With everyone's back to you?
Siân:	[Pause] It's really hard …. Disconnected. All gone. And … [Pause]. Kind of quiet as well. Quite quiet. Peaceful. Something quite calm …

In this example, Siân is invited to go more deeply into her fears, and what she touches on is a profound anxiety of being abandoned and alone. Here, from an existential-humanistic standpoint, the therapist encourages Siân to stay with these feelings, and to come to see that, although they are painful, they are also bearable. In doing so, the hope is that Siân will come to see that she does not need to invest so much energy in entertaining others and being play-ful, as a means of trying to avoid her feared future.

Confronting meaninglessness

A fourth existential given identified by Yalom (1980) and Bugental (1981) is that of meaninglessness. Yalom, drawing heavily from the work of Frankl (see Chapter 4), argues that human beings are fundamentally meaning-seeking creatures. In contrast to Frankl, however, both he and Bugental – though not all existential-humanistic practitioners (L. Hoffman, personal communication, 3 February 2016) – hold that human beings must face up to the ultimate meaningless of their existence: 'that there exists no "meaning", no grand design in the universe, no guidelines for living other than those the individual creates' (Yalom, 1980: 423). On this basis, then, an existential-humanistic approach to meaninglessness might highlight the way in which individuals tend to defend themselves against an awareness of this given – for instance, by throwing themselves into mindless pursuits or crusading for a cause – and how these defences fail to really stem the sense of nihilism, absurdity and despair (Bugental, 1981). It might also argue that if human beings can face up to the meaninglessness of their existence, they can confront it directly, and find ways of carving out their own, personal meaning in life: for instance, through altruistic acts, dedication (to a cause), creativity or hedonism (Yalom, 1980). From this standpoint, the role of therapists would be to help clients identify their defences against the anxiety of meaninglessness, and to encourage them to 'stay with' the awareness that there is no given meaning to their lives. Helping clients to identify the ways in which they deny meaninglessness in the therapeutic relationship – for instance, by assuming that the therapist knows what the ultimate value of therapy is – would also be an intrinsic part of this process.

Interestingly, however – and, again, in direct contrast to Frankl – Yalom suggests that the anxiety of meaninglessness may not be a primary anxiety, but a '"stand-in" for anxiety associated with death, groundlessness and isolation' (1980: 470). From this perspective, people who desperately want to find some meaning in their lives may be seen as trying to find a way of transcending their deaths by leaving a legacy behind. Similarly, people may be seen as feeling that life is intrinsically meaningless because they are defended against close, loving relationships that nothing provides them with any sense of pleasure. On this basis, Yalom (1980: 462) suggests that therapists should not take clients' statements that 'life has no meaning' at face value, but should 'rigorously examine the legitimacy of the complaint', and help clients to examine the other concerns and anxieties on which such statements may be based. Furthermore, based on the analysis that a sense of meaninglessness often comes from a lack of engagement with the world, Yalom suggests that therapists should pursue the question of meaning obliquely, helping clients to re-engage with their world and immerse themselves in the river of life.

Confronting embodiedness

A fifth given of existence outlined by Bugental (1981: 443) is that of 'embodiedness': 'Our bodies are the always-present condition of our conscious experience [see Chapter 2, this volume], so that the fact of embodiedness permeates all phases of our living.' As with the other existential givens, however, Bugental argues that an awareness of our embodied being evokes anxiety – specifically the anxieties of pain and destruction – such that we tend to repress this awareness, through such strategies as dissociation and depersonalisation. But the consequences of such denial are that individuals feel a deadened, joyless existence within their body. Hence, the more that therapy can help clients to reconnect with their physical being – through such strategies as embodied visualisations – the more clients can experience the fullness of an embodied life.

May (1969a: 123) focuses on one very specific aspect of this embodied, biological being: what he calls 'the daimonic'. By this, he means '*any natural function which has the power to take over the whole person*'. This is not unlike Freud's id, and consists of all those untamed energies that reside 'deep' within the individual's being: for instance, sex and eros, anger and rage, and the craving for power. Like Freud, May (1969a: 145) sees these energies as having a very destructive potential; and, in contrast to humanists like Rogers, believes that 'We humans carry within us the seeds of our own destruction .... We must hate as well as love.' At the same time, he sees them as a source of great potential personal power, creativity and connection to others. According to May (1969a), for instance, the daimonic eros is a yearning to transcend ourselves and bind with others, to achieve a greater state of wholeness. Similarly, while daimonic rage has the potential to be highly destructive, it is also a means by which we can assert and affirm our being.

As with the other givens of existence, May (1969a) argues that, within our culture, we tend to repress an awareness of such uncontrollable, animal-like, and potentially overwhelming forces. The result of this, however, is an increasing feeling of apathy and lifelessness. May, for instance, argues that the contemporary obsession with the technicalities of sex – with its emphasis on performance, length and the acquisition of new techniques – is a consequence of the loss of eros from the sexual arena. Sex today, states May, is about sensation rather than passion: it has lost its intimacy, spontaneity and abandon in an effort to eliminate anxiety from the sexual act. Furthermore, where individuals repress their daimonic energies, there is always the danger that those energies will finally erupt in uncontrollable and highly destructive ways. For instance, individuals who do not allow themselves to experience their anger may finally get to a point where they explode in rage and violence (May, 1969a). To avoid such forms of 'daimonic possession', then, May suggests that individuals need to move beyond a stage in which the daimonic is a blind, impersonal push, and begin to own and integrate the daimonic in a personal way. By directing and channelling these powers, individuals can begin to transform their destructive side into constructive activities, and achieve a higher level of integrated consciousness.

In terms of therapeutic practice, then, existential-humanistic practitioners may try to help clients develop a greater awareness of this daimonic energy, and to come to accept and utilise this force within themselves (see S. A. Diamond, 1996). Many of the therapeutic strategies discussed earlier in this chapter may be used to facilitate this process. For instance, clients may be provided with space to express this energy; encouraged, directed or instructed to express such daimonic feelings as anger or sexuality (Yalom & Elkin, 1974); or helped to understand their feelings and behaviours in terms of the expression – or resistance towards – daimonic energies. Again, too, there may be an emphasis on looking at how these energies are manifested and resisted within the therapeutic relationship. Yalom, for instance, strongly encourages his client Ginny to explore any sexual feelings she may have towards him, and interprets some of her behaviour and verbalisations in terms of her sexual attraction towards him (Yalom & Elkin, 1974). He also suggests to Ginny that her timid, respectful and kind behaviour is perfectly explicable in terms of the murderous degree of rage she is harbouring and her fear that some of this will leak out (Yalom & Elkin, 1974). May (1972) takes this a step further and actually models the expression of anger for one of his clients: venting rage towards the client's mother so that the client can eventually acquire this mode of behaviour herself.

Critical perspectives

From a Heideggerian and philosophical position, the existential-humanistic approach has been criticised for lacking philosophical depth (Craig, 2015; van Deurzen-Smith, 1991). Certainly, within the writings of Bugental (1981) and May (1969a), there are some fairly significant misunderstandings of key existential ideas, many of them revolving around a tendency to reduce ontological concepts to the ontic level (Craig, 2015). Bugental, for instance, writes that presence is *dasein* 'in the purest sense' (1981: 383), as if an individual can be more or less 'there', while May (1958) equates being-in-the-world with the experience of community. Yalom, too, has been criticised for simplifying and misrepresenting complex theoretical issues: reducing fundamental ontological questions to everyday issues and personal concerns (Craig, 2015). Craig, a US-based authority on daseinsanalysis, describes Yalom's approach as an *existential thematic* stance, rather than a genuinely ontologically-orientated practice, and he sees it as a product of the Americanisation of existential therapy. He writes: 'the intellectual, philosophical, and, especially, linguistic challenges of ontological seriousness do not make for an easy partnership with America's deeply rooted preoccupations with materialism, optimism, pragmatism and individualism' (Craig, 2015: 80).

The existential-humanistic reading of existential themes – along with integration of ideas and practices from humanistic and other orientations – also means that, at times, the approach advocates understandings and methods that contradict a more established Heideggerian standpoint. First is the focus – particularly in earlier texts – on clients' 'inner' lives, which contradicts the existential tendency to see being as in-the-world (see Chapters 2 and 3, this volume). Second, and closely related to this, is the widespread use (particularly in the existential-analytic literature) of the concept of the 'unconscious'. This means that the existential-humanistic approach (and, again, particularly it's existential-analytic camp) can be very interpretative at times. We saw this, for instance, when Yalom interprets Ginny's feelings of strangulation by a friend as feeling strangulated by him. This would seem incompatible with a more phenomenological existentialism (see Chapters 2 and 3, this volume), which emphasises the value of description over interpretation, and assumes that the key elements of people's lives are accessible to consciousness.

Following on from this is the widespread use within the existential-humanistic literature of the concept of 'resistance'. This implies that clients are acting in ways towards their therapy that they are not aware of – and that their therapists need to help them recognise. It also suggests an *a priori* judgement: that clients' desires to keep themselves safe and protect themselves from the reality of their existences are, to some extent, less valid than their desires to emerge and grow. A consequence of this assumption is that existential-humanistic therapists may tend to point their clients in what they see as the 'right' direction. And, indeed, some existential-humanistic therapists, most notably Yalom, are not averse to coaxing, coercing, directing or instructing their clients to be more authentic and free (see Bugental, 1987; Yalom & Elkin, 1974). As discussed earlier, however, recent years have seen a softening of this position within the existential-humanistic field. Schneider, for instance, recommends that the term 'resistance' be replaced by 'self-protections'; and he encourages therapists to always approach resistance work from an 'invitational', rather than 'declarative', standpoint (personal communication, 27 December 2015).

A closely related problem is that what existential-humanistic writers define as 'authentic' may be more their own subjective views than any universal given of the human condition. This is of particular importance when we take into account cultural differences. Yalom (1980, 2008), for instance, works on the assumption that everyone fears death and that, therefore, clients who say they do not are resistant or in denial. Research shows, though, that the fear of death can be quite culturally-specific. For instance, Hindu Indians have been found to have lower levels of death anxiety than Christian Indians, possibly because they have the strongest belief in life after death (Gire, 2002). As discussed in the introduction to this chapter, however, it is important to note that the contemporary existential-humanistic community has been among the most active advocates of multicultural understandings within the existential field. And, indeed, this has included consideration of what existential givens might look like from a non-Western cultural perspective. Here, for instance, Chan (2014) has written about the givenness of social harmony and human connectedness, as viewed from an indigenous Chinese perspective.

Related to the above criticism is the issue that some existential-humanistic authors tends to present authenticity as a goal that clients can work towards – akin to the humanistic concept of 'self-actualisation' (Maslow, 1971) – rather than as a form of self-relating that is inherently transient (see Chapter 2, this volume). In this respect, existential-humanistic therapists (particularly Bugental) can tend to present the therapeutic process as one of linear, uni-directional growth – the peeling of the onion layers – rather than as an ongoing grappling with life. Again, however, there is a general softening here, with contemporary existential-humanistic writers moving towards an acknowledgement that clients will always live with paradoxes and contradic-tions in their lives, as opposed to achieving some rarefied form of authenticity (K. Schneider, personal communication, 27 December 2015).

A final criticism of the existential-humanistic approach is that it lacks spe-cific, robust empirical evidence to support its claims. To some extent, the emphasis on in-depth kinaesthetic and experiential processing is supported by research in the emotion-focused therapies field (Elliott, Greenberg, Watson, Timulak, & Freire, 2013), but it is not clear how much the latter findings can be transposed onto the former practice. Similarly, as Schneider and Krug (2010) argue, the relational emphasis of the approach is supported by the 'common factors' literature: in particular, that the quality of the therapeutic relationship is closely associated with therapeutic outcomes (see Norcross & Wampold, 2011). However, as these findings are correlational, they do not demonstrate that an existential-humanistic-type relationship *per se* can effect psychological change. And while Schneider and Krug (2010: 92) are right to say that the approach 'has produced some of the most eloquent case studies in the profes-sional literature', these are rarely conducted systematically or independently, and therefore may be very open to the authors' own biases. In our own review of the research (Craig et al., 2016), we found very few studies that rigorously tested the effects of an existential-humanistic intervention. And, in fact, the overall effects of those that did – mainly focused on a Yalom-based therapy for people with cancer, *supportive-expressive group therapy* (e.g., Spiegel, Bloom, & Yalom, 1981) – were small, albeit significant. In these respects, while Schneider and Krug claim that empirical research on the existential-humanistic approach is at a 'nascent but promising stage' (2010: 94), considerably more research is needed to demonstrate that it can bring about change in the way it intends to.

Conclusion

There is no doubt that the existential-humanistic approach has produced some of the richest and most engaging literature within the existential field – if not the therapeutic world, as a whole. Through the work of such forebears as May, Bugental and Yalom, it has lain bare the existential encounter at the heart of the therapeutic relationship, as well as the existential givens that human beings face. Today, under the guidance of Kirk Schneider – and with the emergence of new voices such as Louis Hoffman, Orah Krug, Xuefu Wang, and Sarah Kass (managing editor of the *New Existentialists* website) – the existential-humanistic approach is continuing to forge new ground for existential theory and practice. In particular, it is leading the way in broadening the focus of existential therapy to consider theory and practice across cultures and diversity. 'Less and less', write Schneider and Krug (2010: 10), 'is existential-humanistic practice confined to the rarefied environs of its psychoanalytic forebears or to upper class elites; it is opening out to the world within which most of us dwell.'

Questions for reflection

- What does 'presence' mean for you? In what ways can you facilitate it in your own practice?
- To what extent do you agree that Yalom's 'ultimate concerns' – freedom, death, isolation and meaninglessness – are issues of universal relevance? Are they true for you? What about your clients?
- Do you think that the concept of 'resistance' is a helpful one for existential practice?
- How do you think that existential therapy might need to be tailored to working with clients from different cultures?

Recommended resources

Contemporary sources

Hoffman, L. (2009). Introduction to existential psychology in a cross-cultural context: An east-west dialogue. In L. Hoffman, M. Yang & F. J. Kaklauskas (Eds.), *Existential psychology east-west* (pp. 1–67). Colorado Springs, CO: University of the Rockies.
Concise contemporary introduction to existential theory and practice from an existential-humanistic perspective.

Schneider, K. J. (2007). *Existential-humanistic therapy over time* [DVD]. Washington, DC: American Psychological Association.
A video demonstration by Schneider of his existential-humanistic approach, with commentary on practice. (www.apa.org/pubs/videos/4310756.aspx)

Schneider, K. J. (Ed.). (2008). *Existential-integrative psychotherapy: Guideposts to the core of practice*. New York: Routledge.
Wide range of chapters on all aspects of existential-integrative therapy, including work across diverse groups. Chapter 4 gives a particularly valuable summary of practice. See also the excellent chapter by Wolfe on anxiety disorders.

Schneider, K. (Ed.) (in press). Existential-humanistic and existential-integrative therapy. *World handbook of existential therapy*. London: Wiley. (Section 3.)
In-depth series of chapters on the key ideas and practices of the existential-humanistic approach.

Schneider, K. J., & Krug, O. T. (2010). *Existential-humanistic therapy*. Washington, DC: American Psychological Association.
Succinct and well-illustrated guide to contemporary existential-humanistic theory and practice.

Existential-Humanistic Institute: ehinstitute.org.
Training site and forum for the existential-humanistic approach.

The New Existentialists: saybrook.edu/newexistentialists.
Wide range of contemporary writings related to existential-humanistic practice.

Irvin Yalom

Yalom, I. D. (1980). *Existential psychotherapy*. New York: Basic Books.
Yalom's *magnum opus*, detailing the manifestations of, resistances to, research about, and therapeutic work with four 'ultimate concerns' of existence: death, freedom, isolation and meaninglessness. The second most influential text on existential-humanistic practice (Correia et al., 2016c) and essential reading for existential therapists of all persuasions.

Yalom, I. (1989). *Love's executioner and other tales of psychotherapy*. London: Penguin Books.
Hugely popular collection of case studies, which brings Yalom's existentially-informed therapy to life in a uniquely vibrant, humane and engrossing way. See, also, his 2015 collection, *Creatures of a Day*, and *Every Day Gets a Little Closer* (1974), which he co-authored with his client Ginny Elkin.

Yalom, I. (2001). *The gift of therapy: Reflections on being a therapist*. London: Piatkus.
Tips from the master, with a particular emphasis on the importance of being real with clients and working with the here-and-now relationship.

James Bugental

Bugental, J. F. T. (1981). *The search for authenticity: An existential-analytic approach to psychotherapy* (exp. ed.). New York: Irvington.
A forgotten classic in the existential-therapies world. Repetitive and rambling at times, but a uniquely comprehensive, detailed and in-depth presentation of an existential-humanistic approach. The most explicitly existential of Bugental's works.

Bugental, J. F. T. (1987). *The art of the psychotherapist: How to develop the skills that take psychotherapy beyond science*. New York: W. W. Norton and Co.
Step-by-step guide to Bugental's existential-humanistic therapy, illustrated with numerous examples of therapist–client dialogue.

(Continued)

(Continued)

Bugental, J. F. T. (1999). *Psychotherapy isn't what you think: Bringing the psychotherapeutic engagement into the living moment*. Phoenix, AZ: Zeig, Tucker and Co.
Extends and develops the ideas and practices presented in *The Art of the Psychotherapist*, placing particular emphasis on working with the immediate here-and-now moment. The third most influential text on existential-humanistic practice after Yalom and Frankl (Correia et al., 2016c).

Rollo May

May, R. (1969a). *Love and will*. New York: W. W. Norton and Co.
May's *magnum opus*, which critiques the apathy and emptiness of contemporary society, encouraging people to realise and recognise their will, their 'daimonic' urges, and their passion.

May, R. (1983). *The discovery of being*. New York: W. W. Norton and Co.
One of the most accessible, concise and comprehensive introductions to the principles that underlie existential therapeutic practice.

May, R., Angel, E., & Ellenberger, H. F. (Eds.). (1958). *Existence: A new dimension in psychiatry and psychology*. New York: Basic Books.
Classic text that kick-started existential therapy in the USA, with some of May's best writings on existential psychology and psychotherapy (includes Binswanger's case study of Ellen West).

6

R. D. LAING:
MEETING WITHOUT MASKS

This chapter discusses:

- R. D. Laing: the man, and his significance.
- Key influences on his approach.
- Laing's belief in the intelligibility of 'madness'.
- The concept of *ontological insecurity.*
- Laing's analysis of the social and interpersonal entanglements that could foster psychological distress.
- Laing's approach to therapeutic practice: a genuine, direct encounter.
- Contemporary developments in 'Laingian' thought and practice.
- Criticisms of Laing's approach.

The Scottish psychiatrist R. D. Laing (1927–1989) is one of the most infamous – yet most frequently misunderstood – existentially-informed therapists (see Box 6.1). At the height of his career, in the mid- to late 1960s, he 'was the most widely read psychiatrist in the world, reaching people across disciplinary boundaries and all walks of life' (Burston, 2000: 1). Today, more than 25 years after his death, Laing's ideas are still debated in books, journals and conferences; and a number of therapeutic communities in Britain and the United States continue to apply his ideas. Laing's work was also foundational for the development of the existential-phenomenological approach to existential therapy in the UK (Chapter 7, this volume), as well as other post-'Laingian' training programmes. Laing's most important influence, however, was probably on the wider world of health and social care for people with severe psychological distress. Although Laing was ultimately ostracised from the psychiatric community, his impassioned calls for the 'mentally ill' to be treated with care, respect and understanding may have played a critical role in the development of more humane attitudes towards sufferers of severe psychological distress. Indeed, it has been said that 'Laing did for the psychotic what Freud did for the neurotic' (Kirsner, 2015: 70): fostering a culture in which their experiences and behaviours are more likely to be listened to and treated with respect, rather than dismissed out of hand.

Laing's disposition has been variously described as mercurial, enigmatic, arrogant, iconoclastic, sceptical, bullying and brilliant; and his writings display many of these characteristics (for illuminating personal descriptions of

Laing, the man, see Mezan, 2015; Thompson, 2012). Of all the existential therapies examined in this book, Laing's approach is the most difficult to characterise. Laing never attempted to establish a 'Laingian' theory or school of therapy. He does not codify his way of working, gives virtually no examples of his practice, and changes his ideas quite substantially across time. Hence, it is only through brief passages in his writings and the accounts of his clients that one can begin to build up a picture of his work. To some extent, however, this is deliberate: Laing feared that any attempt to formalise his approach would be corrupted and misunderstood (Mullan, 1995), and would undermine the very principles of spontaneity that formed the core of his therapeutic outlook. Laing's primary concern with the aetiology and treatment of schizophrenia may also have meant that he focused less of his energies on outlining his broader therapeutic practice. Nevertheless, Laing's critique of contemporary psychiatric practice, his existential-phenomenological analysis of mental misery, and his interpersonal approach to therapeutic practice have a key place in the pantheon of existential therapies.

Box 6.1   R. D. Laing: Myth and reality

Myth: Laing romanticised and idealised schizophrenia.
Reality: Laing (1969: 74) did assert that, for *some* people, 'what we call psychosis may be sometimes a natural process of healing'. However, he never described the experience of the schizophrenic 'as anything but a mixture of chronic fear, confusion, isolation and despair, punctuated by relatively brief intervals of lucidity or ecstasy' (Burston, 2000: 70).

Myth: Laing rejected the theory that schizophrenia has a genetic, biological basis.
Reality: Laing believed that the case for biological determinants remained unproven, but he also acknowledged that biological factors could predispose an individual to psychosis (Resnick, 1997).

Myth: Laing founded the 'anti-psychiatry' movement.
Reality: The term 'anti-psychiatry' was developed by David Cooper – one of Laing's associates – and was explicitly rejected by Laing, who wanted to circumvent such partisan terms (Burston, 1996). For Laing, the issue was not one of pro- or anti-psychiatry, but the fact that psychiatric treatments could be imposed on a patient regardless of their will.

Influences

While Laing (1965a) acknowledged that his key work, *The Divided Self*, was not a direct application of any established existential philosophy, he goes on to state that his main intellectual indebtedness is to the existential tradition.

Laing read many of the key existential texts while still in his youth, and draws liberally from a range of existential-phenomenological thinkers, among them Kierkegaard, Nietzsche, Tillich, Heidegger, Jaspers, Merleau-Ponty and Husserl. In particular, Laing 'lifted' from Husserlian phenomenology the idea that to fully understand another's lived-experience, one must bracket off all attempts at categorising, labelling or diagnosing them, and should try, instead, to stay with that person's lived-experience at a purely descriptive level (Chapter 2, this volume). Perhaps the strongest existential influence on Laing, however, was Sartre, whose writings fascinated Laing from his youth (Kirsner, 2015). 'Laing's landscape was essentially Sartre's,' writes Kirsner (2015: 144), 'our essential freedom, self-deception, experience and its violation, the terror of the group, fear and intrusion of others, mystification, being for others as hostility and objectification.' At other times in his work, however, Laing takes a more optimistic view of human relationships and possibilities, and here he comes closer to Buber's (1958) notion of an I–Thou interpersonal stance (see Mullan, 1995). Indeed, Gans (2015) argues that Laing's teachings were ultimately about an 'awakening to love'.

To some extent, Laing's approach was also influenced by the work of those European psychiatrists who had attempted to formulate psychological difficulties in existential and phenomenological terms. Earliest among these was Karl Jaspers, whose *General Psychopathology* (1963, first published in 1913) attempted to move away from detached scientific observations and causal explanations of 'abnormal psychic phenomena' to describing these phenomena in terms of the patients' actual, meaning-orientated, conscious lived-experiences. Another European existential psychiatrist who had impressed Laing was Eugène Minkowski, who was particularly interested in the way that certain psychological problems were associated with particular experiences of time (Mullan, 1995). In addition, while Laing 'detested' Binswanger (see Chapter 3, this volume) for his lack of ethical consideration towards the severely mentally ill (M. Thompson, personal communication, 29 December 2015), there are many ways in which his account of schizophrenia parallels Binswanger's (1963). This includes the assertion that schizophrenics withdraw from independent autonomous selfhood, try to defend themselves against dissolution, and experience a sense of naked horror in the face of potential annihilation. Indeed, prior to Laing, Binswanger had argued that there is method and meaning – rather than pure chaos – in the alleged disorder of insanity; and that 'a person is judged "sick" wherever his social behaviour deviates from the respective norm of social behaviour and thus appears conspicuous or strange' (1958: 227).

Like the proponents of Daseinsanalysis, logotherapy and the existential-humanistic approach, Laing was also significantly influenced by psychoanalytic thinking (for an excellent review, see Thompson, 1996). In Laing's case, however, this was more the influence of the 'British school of object relations' and the 'middle group' of psychoanalysis, than of Freud directly. Having spent a number of years practising and researching at the Tavistock Institute – during which time he graduated as a qualified psychoanalyst – Laing rubbed shoulders with many of the British psychoanalytic greats, among them John Bowlby, D. W. Winnicott, Marion Milner (who acted as his supervisor), and Charles Rycroft (who acted as his therapist). The influence of British psychoanalytic thinking on Laing's work – particularly Winnicott – is particularly noticeable in his tendency to account for adult experiences and behaviour in terms of early childhood experiences, particularly the absence of love. Laing, in his earlier work, also drew heavily from psychoanalytic, Winnicottian concepts in his idea of the 'true' and 'false' selves. In practice, too, Laing owed a great deal to psychoanalysis. As with the daseinsanalysts (Chapter 3, this volume), Laing was thoroughly schooled in the psychoanalytic practice of free association, whereby clients are encouraged to utter out loud whatever comes into their minds, and this served as the basis to much of his clinical practice (Thompson, 1997). Indeed, for Laing, the practice of free association formed a bridge between psychoanalysis and the existential philosophical tradition, providing clients with the freedom to express themselves unencumbered by the expectations and assumptions of their therapists (M. Thompson, personal communication, 29 December, 2015). Laing also drew heavily from the psychoanalytic practice of interpreting the transference, whereby the client's displacement onto their therapist of feelings and ideas derived from previous figures in their lives is elucidated and expounded upon.

Like Yalom (1980), Laing was influenced too by the interpersonal psychiatry of Harry Stack Sullivan (see Mullan, 1995). In addition, from a more interpersonal and systemic perspective, he drew extensively from the ideas of the anthropologist Gregory Bateson and the 'Palo Alto' group (Bateson, Jackson, Haley, & Weakland, 1956), who argued that schizophrenia may emerge when a person is caught up in dysfunctional family patterns of communication.

A fifth important influence on Laing's work was a broadly socialist-humanist-libertarian standpoint. Laing rarely took an explicitly left-wing stance, but he had read Marx widely and was deeply committed to challenging injustices – a commitment that lay at the heart of his approach to mental misery. Like Marx, Laing also argued that a micro-context could not be understood without an understanding of the macro-context (Collier, 1977: x). That is, an individual could not be understood in isolation from their family system, and a family system could not be understood without an understanding of its wider social, cultural and political nexus. In addition, Laing's grounding in Marxism led him to question the assumption that what we take for normal is necessarily good. Rather, like Marx – as well as like Heidegger (1962) and other existential philosophers – he came to believe that 'normal' human beings are, in fact, hugely *alienated* from their own selves and potential: 'a shrivelled, desiccated fragment of what a person can be' (Laing, 1967: 22).

A final factor that almost certainly had a major influence on Laing's thinking and practice was his own childhood. Perhaps the single most important element here was the loveless, suffocating and confusing relationship that he had with his mother. From the biographical evidence, it seems that Laing was not wanted by his mother (Burston, 1996), and her antagonism towards him was manifested in many ways. She rarely cuddled or touched him; destroyed toys and musical instruments that he became attached to; and even, when he was older, stuck pins into a 'Ronald Doll' in the hope of giving him a heart attack! Just as significantly, however, Laing's mother consistently denied these hostile feelings, telling her son that she loved and cared for him, and acting towards him in overtly possessive and intrusive ways (for instance, not allowing him out of the house until his first day of school). It is perhaps no surprise, therefore, that much of Laing's writings are concerned with the way that children are subjected to rejection, mystification and emotional violence by their parents (particularly by their mothers), often under the guise of love. Indeed, a number of the examples of parental mistreatment in Laing's books are, in fact, directly from his own childhood.

Finding meaning in madness

As a trainee psychiatrist in the 1950s, Laing came to reject the general psychiatric worldview of his – and, to a large extent, our – day. This was for a number of reasons. First, he abhorred the 'unspeakable violence' of lobotomies, electro-convulsive therapies, and padded cells. Second, he felt that there was a complete breakdown of genuine, human relationships between psychiatrists and patients. Third, he felt that psychiatrists had an unparalleled degree of power over those in their charge. Fourth, he felt that the psychiatric system – by labelling, objectifying, 'thingifying' and dismissing certain people as 'mentally ill' and 'dysfunctional' – failed to acknowledge the sense and meaning behind these people's symptoms (Laing, 1965a). In contrast to this approach, then, Laing argued that psychiatrists and therapists should strive to enter their clients' phenomenologically lived world. Here, he argued, they would come to see a far greater meaning and purposiveness in their clients' thoughts, feelings and behaviours than they had initially imagined.

In this respect, Laing's work extends and radicalises the viewpoint of earlier existential and phenomenological psychiatrists. While Jaspers (1963: 110), for instance, described neurotic and psychotic experiences phenomenologically, he still retained the use of such terms as 'abnormal' and 'psychopathological', and distinguished between 'those affective states which *emerge in understandable fashion*' and those 'which defeat understanding'. Similarly, daseinsanalysts like Boss (1963) continued to talk about 'perversions' or 'obsessional neuroses', as if these ways of being were somehow less legitimate, valid or meaningful than more 'normal' ones. At its core, then, Laing's work can be seen as an attempt to extend the existential ethic of humanisation (see Chapter 2, this volume) to *all* human beings, however much distress and psychosis they are experiencing – that is, that schizophrenics, as much as anyone else, should be treated *as* human beings, and not as something other than human.

Hence, Laing wanted to show that even the most bizarre behaviours were intelligible from the sufferer's point of view. As an example, one of the young women in Laing and Esterson's (1964) series of case studies, *Sanity, Madness and the Family*, would sit or stand still for over an hour at a time. Psychiatrically, such behaviour could be diagnosed as 'catatonic immobility': typical symptoms of her schizophrenic illness that have no meaning other than to indicate her level of impairment. When Laing and Esterson (1964: 204) interviewed this young woman, however, 'putting entirely in parenthesis the validity of any attribution of illness', they found that the young woman's immobility was anything but meaningless. When asked, for instance, what she would do if her mother – an intrusive and infantilising woman – expressed an opinion that she disagreed with but subsequently saw to be right, the young woman replied that she would go rigid and stiff inside so that no one could 'get at her' and alter her opinion. Furthermore, she said that she held her breath – and displayed other symptoms of her 'schizophrenia', such as habitually sniffing and coughing – to protect herself from her mother's barrage of words. Unusual behaviours, perhaps, but the point was that there was an intelligibility behind this young woman's behaviours and 'symptoms': they were more than just random expressions of crazed activity.

For therapists, then, the Laingian edict is, perhaps, 'assume intelligibility unless proved otherwise', as opposed to 'assume unintelligibility unless proved otherwise'. In other words, therapists should try to engage with their clients, holding a basic *trust* that the client's behaviours and experiences are meaningful attempts to deal with their world, rather than pathological or irrational errors of functioning. Maintaining such a trust, however, is by no means easy, because the very foundations of therapy are based on the assumption that the client is getting something wrong.

As a personal example, I worked some years ago with a man in his mid-50s who, after many years of failing to find work, was finally offered an exciting opportunity at a new local firm. My initial assumption was that this client should have been delighted with this offer, and when he 'ummed' and 'ahhed' about the post – and seemed to fall into deeper depression – my instinctive response was to try to help him look at what was 'impeding' his growth. As we explored his situation further, however, it became increasingly apparent that there was a great deal more sense and intelligibility to his ambivalence. Suppose he did take this job. Suppose it was rewarding and enjoyable. What terrible, crushing regret he would then have to live with: that he hadn't managed to find such a job 20 years ago. In a way, it was less painful for him to forgo the job and maintain his belief that he simply wasn't employable. My initial tendency, then, was to look for what this client was doing *wrong*, and it was only by trying to bracket my assumptions that I could begin to understand the sense behind his behaviour and feelings. Indeed, I got to the point where I *genuinely* felt I did not know what was the best thing for him to do. This was a good indicator, perhaps, that I had truly entered his lived-world.

Ontological insecurity

In attempting to demonstrate that 'schizophrenia' may be the outcome of meaningful, intelligible acts, Laing describes a range of intrapsychic and inter-personal ways of being that may lead individuals to develop psychosis.

At the intrapsychic level, Laing (1965a: 39) suggests that schizoid-predisposed individuals may experience a fundamental sense of *ontological inse-curity*. This is where an individual has not developed a 'firm sense of his own and other people's reality and identity', and has not acquired any 'unquestion-able self-validating certainties'. Laing goes on to state that the ontologically insecure person:

> may feel more unreal than real; in a literal sense, more dead than alive; precariously dif-ferentiated from the rest of the world, so that his identity and autonomy are always in question. He may lack the experience of his own temporal continuity. He may not possess an over-riding sense of personal consistency or cohesiveness. He may feel more insubstan-tial than substantial, and unable to assume that the stuff he is made of is genuine, good, valuable. (1965a: 42)

Because people in a state of ontological insecurity feel that they cannot take their identity for granted, there is a constant fear that their very self will be annihilated. In particular, Laing talks about three fears that ontologically inse-cure people may have. First, there is a fear of *engulfment*, that their autonomy will be devoured and subsumed by the will of others. Second, they fear *implo-sion*, a terror that they will be obliterated by the 'real' world around them: 'as a gas will rush in and obliterate a vacuum' (Laing, 1965a). Here, one can include the fear of intrusion and invasion by others (Collier, 1977). Third, there is the fear of *petrification and depersonalisation*: the dread of being turned into an inanimate object – an 'it' – by the other (note the similarity here with Sartre's (1958) notion of 'the Look', Chapter 2, this volume).

How does ontological insecurity lead to 'schizophrenia'? Laing (1965a) sug-gests that the ontologically insecure person may attempt to deal with the per-ceived threats to their existence by 'splitting in two'. They may withdraw their *true self* from their body and retreat into an inner, private citadel of their mind, where they hope they will be safe from the threat of annihilation. What they leave behind is a depersonalised body: a *false self*, a shell that they hope will protect them against the threat of engulfment, implosion, petrification and depersonalisation. In a sense, the only way that the individual feels that they can preserve their sense of being is by sacrificing one component of it – a decoy that they throw to the outside world in the hope that their real being may be left alone. At this point, such an individual may be perceived by the external world as quite normal. Indeed, because they have foregone responsibility for their false, public self, they may willingly comply with the demands of those around them – even going so far as to imitate the personalities and behaviours of those they comply with. As the real self withdraws further and further inwards, however, so the sane schizoid individual may cross the boundary into psychosis. They are so withdrawn and alienated from their body that they feel others must be controlling their actions. They may try to overcome their sense of physical deadness through self-mutilation. They may be furious at those who demand their compliance (as well as the false part of themselves that complies with these demands) and hence grotesquely characterise and ridicule – rather than imitate – those they are complying with. And because, as the real self withdraws, it becomes less and less able to experience real relationships with (and confirmation through) others, so it loses what precarious sense of realness it has. Ultimately, the desperate battle to protect the self brings about its own annihilation: a descent into the gates of hell, wracked with despair, terror and a sense of dissolution (Laing, 1985). In the eyes of the world, then, the individual has moved from good to bad, to mad (Collier, 1977).

The social context of mental misery

For Laing, however, severe forms of mental misery, like schizophrenia, could not just be understood as private, individual, intra-psychic activities. Rather, Laing believed that schizophrenia was a particular strategy that individuals develop to try to survive in particular *social* situations (Laing, 1967). Like many intersubjective philosophers, Laing believed that human beings were essentially inter-relational beings, such that the experience and behaviours of one individual could not be understood without an understanding of the experiences and behaviours of those around them. Hence, where an individual develops such bizarre forms of behaviour and experiences as paranoia or psychosis, Laing believed that it was only through an understanding of the social context in which these responses arose that the true meaning and intelligibility of these ways of being could come to light.

For Laing, the family was the primary social context through which an individual might come to a state of severe mental misery. Laing (1967: 55–56), at his most rhetorical, described the family as a 'protection racket', which – as the primary agent of socialisation – beats its children into shape 'in the manner that beggars maim and mutilate their children to make them fit for their future situation in life'. For Laing, however, this beating was not carried our primarily physically, but through disturbed and disturbing means of relating and communicating.

Central to Laing's (1969) analysis of the family was his extension of the psychoanalytic concept of *phantasy* from the individual to the family as a whole.

Laing suggested that families, like all groups, develop *social phantasy systems*: shared sets of inferences and assumptions – frequently held non-consciously – about the way in which the family and its members experience their world. For the family (including, at least initially, the 'sick' individual) this phantasy system is the right way of seeing things, such that if individuals testify to experiences that lie outside these systems, or attempt to extricate themselves from them, their families will defend themselves against such threats. Here, Laing is extending the psychodynamic concept of defence mechanisms from the intrapersonal level to the transpersonal level.

Such transpersonal defences may involve a denial or invalidation of a family member's experiences. It may also involve their *mystification*: befuddling, clouding, obscuring or masking whatever the person is experiencing, to induce their compliance and preserve the social phantasy system (Laing, 1965b). There are numerous examples of these processes in Laing and Esterson's (1964) *Sanity, Madness and the Family*. One young woman, for instance, upon telling her parents that she masturbated and wondered about them having sex, was simply told that she did not. Another young woman, upon trying to challenge the family myth that she and her mother were entirely alike, was quickly misinterpreted into saying that she was the same as her mother. In attempting to maintain the social phantasy system, a young person's perception of what others are really up to may also be discounted or denied. For instance, when one of the young women in *Sanity, Madness and the Family*, left the room during an interview, her mother, father and brother began a furtive whispered exchange about her. When she re-entered the room and said uncertainly that she thought they had been talking about her, however, the family denied the accusation and looked at the researchers as if to say 'see how suspicious she is' (Laing & Esterson, 1964: 114).

Through such invalidations and mystifications of feelings, perceptions and desires, Laing (1969) suggests that individuals can come to mistrust the fabric of their own experiences, and lose any sense of self-assurance. Individuals no longer know what is right or not: Are people really talking about them? Are people meddling in their relationships? Are the people who are supposed to love them lying to them? Furthermore, if the individual's experiences are denied by others, and other experiences are imposed upon them, then they may be induced into what Laing termed a *false position*, in which they lose any real sense of their own experiences and actions. As Laing writes: 'I'm sure that truth deprivation can wreak as much havoc to some people as vitamin deprivation' (1976b: 136).

To further compound matters, the family system may not only deny individuals' experiences, but also deny that any denial is taking place – or even deny that a denial is being denied! Writes Laing: 'It is not enough to destroy one's own and other people's experiences. One must overlay this devastation by a false consciousness inured ... to its own falsity' (1967: 49). Laing (1967) believed that the emotional and communicational violence perpetrated in families was often conducted under the name of love, and perhaps there is no better example of this than in Laing's own family, where his mother's cold, rejecting attitude was covered up beneath a façade of care and concern. Through mystifications such as these – with their 'constant shifting of meaning and of position' (Laing & Esterson, 1964: 96) – Laing believed that young people may come to find their position not only false but also untenable. That is, they feel that there is no way for them to turn. They know that they are being lied to, but cannot acknowledge the lie; they know that they are living falsely, but cannot acknowledge the falsity of their position.

One untenable position that Laing was particularly interested in was that of the *double-bind* – a concept that Laing adopted from the American anthropologist Gregory Bateson and his team (Bateson et al., 1956). Such a situation is one in which an individual is told that they will be punished if they do one thing, but also told – often at a more covert, non-verbal level – that they will also be punished if they *don't* do that thing. Furthermore, there may also be a further injunction that they cannot leave the situation. For instance, one of the mothers in Laing and Esterson's (1964) *Sanity, Madness and the Family* expressed regret that her 'schizophrenic' daughter did not express herself more, but then, when the daughter did express herself, interrupted her, dismissed her, or criticised her for fussing. Here, where the individual feels that they 'cannot make a move without catastrophe' (Laing, 1969: 146), they may seek refuge in their own inner world. They may also lose their trust in others, or start to communicate at a more metaphorical and indirect level, as a means of communicating what they want to communicate, while protecting themselves from retaliation and attack (Bateson et al., 1956). What appears to be withdrawn, paranoid or bizarre behaviours, then, may be the individual's attempts to keep themselves sane in an insane world.

Over the course of the 1960s, however, Laing came to see that the kinds of social processes he was describing were not limited to the families of schizophrenics. Gans (2015: 107) reports:

> In order to convince scientific workers in their own research terms of the validity of his 'evidence' he had to demonstrate a difference between families of schizophrenics and normal families. The communication patterns and atmosphere in normal families unfortunately proved to be as or more stifling of love and truth in Ronnie's terms than the psychotogenic [i.e., psychosis-generating] families he had studied.

An example of the processes of mystification and invalidation in 'normal' families can be seen in Siân's early childhood experiences. Siân describes how, after her mother died, a 'social phantasy system' emerged which, at its core, held that 'father's wellbeing must be maintained at all costs'. Here, each family member came to be ascribed very specific roles. Siân's father became 'the sick one': preoccupied and withdrawn, curled up in his bedroom for days. Siân's younger brother became 'the carer' – the source of practical and emotional support for their father. And Siân became 'the fun one': sociable, entertaining, cheerleading – the beam of light in an otherwise darkened household. And, as with all social phantasy systems, experiences that did not fit into this narrative were denied. Siân describes how she hated school, for instance, because her classmates made 'jokes' about her mother's death, and she got into fights. However, her father and brother 'reframed' this as Siân being typically mischievous. She also reports that she was told she needed to calm down and stop messing about. But her own feelings of rage towards her classmates, and grief towards her mother, were never properly acknowledged. Worse, says Siân, was when her father invited her up to his room when she got home from school, to tell him about her day. 'It was the one time I could be close to dad', she says, 'but I couldn't be close because I couldn't be honest. I couldn't tell him the bad bits, about the fights. He couldn't hear that. I so wanted to be close to him … but it had to be as someone else. I became someone else for him and for – to keep the family together.'

Laing was not only interested, however, in the knots and tangles of family life, but also those of adult relationships. In his 1966 book *Interpersonal Perception* (written with H. Phillipson and A. R. Lee), Laing examines the realms of *metaperceptions*: 'What I think you think of me' and 'What you think I think of you' (for a more detailed discussion, see Cooper, 2015: Chapter 7). One of the basic premises in Laing's book was that the way we imagine other people see us (our *metaperceptions*) is often very different from the way they actually perceive us (their *perceptions*), and this can lead to some vicious and destructive spirals. For example, Siân's metaperception is that Hanako does not really take her seriously: that she sees her as a child and weak. But when she reports what Hanako has actually fed back to her in their arguments, it seems Hanako's real perception is very different: that she experiences Siân as distant, disinterested in her, and aggressive. Were Siân really able take this in, she might be able to address some of the problems in their relationship. But because Siân is responding to Hanako *as* she thinks she is seeing her (childish and weak), her tendency is to try to be forceful with Hanako, compounding Hanako's viewpoint, *ad nauseam*. Of course, the metaperceptual errors may also work the other way around: that Hanako thinks Siân is uninterested in her when, actually, she finds Hanako deeply fascinating. This may account for her coldness towards Siân. And, of course, the more that Siân and Hanako responded negatively towards the other, the more this might convince each one that their metaperceptions really are right – 'She *really* doesn't take me seriously', 'She *really* isn't interested in me' – leading to an ongoing downward spiral of conflict and miscommunication.

During his career, Laing (1970, 1976a) also published a number of poems and imaginary conversations that attempted to describe some of the entanglement, knots, conundrums, vicious circles and binds that can beset adult relationships. For instance:

JILL: You put me in the wrong
JACK: I am not putting you in the wrong
JILL: You put me in the wrong for thinking that you put me in the wrong
JACK: Forgive me
JILL: No
JACK: I'll never forgive you for not forgiving me (1970: 21)

Candid confrontation

So how did Laing set about helping his clients to untie the interpersonal and intrapsychic knots that they had tangled themselves up in? At the most basic level, Laing believed in the crucial importance of attending to his clients: a simple, focused listening in which clients had an opportunity to articulate, and connect with, their real experiences. From Laing's perspective, clients had withdrawn into the inner citadels of their mind to protect themselves from a demanding, intrusive world. Hence, a non-invasive, non-intrusive inter-personal connection was necessary to facilitate their self-recovery and re-integration: a journey that Laing referred to as *metanoia* (Burston, 1996). In this respect, it was not unusual for Laing to remain silent for whole sessions although, as former client Jan Resnick (1997) reports, such was his attentive-ness that he could repeat back to clients what they had said, word-for-word, in subsequent sessions. Furthermore, as with the daseinsanalytic approach, Laing's attentiveness went far beyond a detached, psychoanalytic 'neutrality'. Many of Laing's clients have described the intensity of his therapeutic engagement. Resnick (1997: 378), for instance, wrote that, 'The atmosphere was often electric, charged with the silent tension of a chess match. Deep concentration.'

As we have seen, however, Laing also believed that clients had become entangled due to deceptive, manipulative and indirect methods of rela-ting. Disentanglement and demystification, therefore, required honest, non-manipulative and direct I–Thou engagement. Laing (1967: 39) writes:

> Psychotherapy consists in the paring away of all that stands between us, the props, masks, roles, lies, defences, anxieties, projections and introjections, in short, all the carry-overs from the past, transference and counter-transference, that we use by habit and collusion, wittingly or unwittingly, as our currency for relationships.

Through such an authentic encounter, Laing believed that the client's capa-city for real relatedness to others could be restored, and with it their ability to meet their most basic 'existential needs': love, ontological security, freedom from deception, the ability to self-disclose, affirmation by others, and – of course – real human relatedness (Burston, 1996).

What seems to have been most fundamental to Laing's therapeutic app-roach, therefore, was that he was simply himself. Laing, as a therapist, wore no masks. He did not become another person when the therapeutic session commenced: he simply said what he thought, felt and perceived – drawing on all his insights into the human condition. Mina Semyon, one of Laing's long-term clients, describes him as having an 'intimate directness'. For instance, during their initial session, Semyon said to Laing that she wanted to do something with her life. Laing simply replied, 'Then do something.'

Semyon:	I don't know what.
Laing:	Then do nothing.
Semyon:	But I want to do something.
Laing:	Then do something.
Semyon:	[Tears welling in eyes – Laing smiles] I feel like I've made a deal with … I don't know whom … let nothing exceptionally good happen to me as long as nothing exceptionally bad happens either, and I made a promise I won't attempt to rise above mediocrity.
Laing:	Do you realise you'll have to give up the deal if you want to do something in life that is meaningful to you? Do you think you could? (Semyon, 1997: 187)

Semyon's (1997) account shows that Laing could be strikingly honest with his clients as to how he perceived them. He told Semyon that she was 'extraordinarily naïve'; and, when she complained that her husband saw her as critical and judgemental, Laing said that he agreed with her husband's perception. In another instance, when Semyon complained that people lost interest in her, Laing replied that she carried with her 'the gloom of the Russian steppes'. In letting his clients know how he perceived them, Laing also sometimes drew on psychoanalytic theory, or his own insights into the nature of human being: such as the tendency for people to withdraw into their own inner world. Laing suggested to one of his supervisees, for instance, that he might say something like the following to one of his clients, a woman who was highly distressed and seemingly incapable of speaking directly about anything personal:

I am about to make a remark to you which is not intended as a criticism …. I simply want to point out that in the past (however many number of) sessions after about 15 minutes you run away from me (in your own mind). You appear to be frightened about what might happen if you don't. You seem to go a long way into yourself to get a safe psychological distance from me …. Are you afraid of my feelings? my impulses? what I might do? Or afraid of your own feelings? what you might want to do? Could this be based on a memory? a fantasy? or some former catastrophe? What dreadful catastrophic possibility is evoked for you when you are here for over 15 minutes? You seem to be going into all of this (regressive behaviour) because *something might* happen that you feel the need to avoid … (Resnick, 1997: 389–390)

Resnick (1997: 390) reports that when he did 'parrot' something like this to his client, she 'came out of her fog', focused her eyes, and said, 'That's right. I am afraid that if I really show you how horrible I am inside that you won't be able to cope with it.' As a consequence of this 'distinctly Laingian brand of honesty' (1997: 390), Resnick reports that his client became more present in the therapeutic relationship, and more able to fully engage with him.

While Laing, therefore, believed that empathic attunement was essential to the therapeutic process, his realness meant that, at times, he could also be highly confrontational. In particular, Laing believed that it was essential that therapists did not collude with the phantasy system that clients would almost inevitably be projecting onto them – phantasy systems in which clients would often construe themselves as powerless, and 'the other' as responsible and in control. Laing was unequivocal that such invitations to collusion should be rejected; and not, in the psychodynamic manner, with tentative interpretations over a period of time, but with direct and honest challenge. Resnick (1997: 378) reports that a typical 'Laingian' 'construction' might be: 'You seem to feel that you are unhappy because I am not giving you what you want. But if you look closely at what leads you to this expectation I suspect you will find its origins entirely within yourself.' Laing, himself, puts it more bluntly: 'I might say "Do you realize that by virtue of what you've just said you are treating me like your father. Now I want to point out to you that I'm not your fucking father"' (Mullan, 1995: 319). Laing (1969) believed that such non-collusive therapy would almost certainly be experienced by the client as frustrating, but he felt that therapists needed to be able to tolerate a client's basic hatred as a way of evoking a more genuine human relatedness. However, he was also clear that candid confrontation could only be effective if it was preceded by a basic sense of communion and relatedness between client and therapist (Burston, 2000).

So what might a 'Laingian' approach to therapy look like in the work with Siân? Let's go back to the session (page 49) in which Siân has become very quiet. Here, both a daseinsanalytic and existential-humanistic therapist might encourage Siân to look at how she was feeling in the therapeutic relationship. However, a 'Laingian' style of therapy might take this a step further: strongly encouraging Siân to be 'real' with the therapist.

Therapist: Siân, I noticed you haven't said much this session.
Siân: It's ok. I'm just – I feel quiet at the moment. Just don't – feel like there's not much to say right now. Everything feels – it's all very flat. [One-minute pause. Siân looks up.]
Therapist: Siân, are you waiting for me to say something?
Siân: Not really. Are you – what were you going to say? [smiles].
Therapist: Siân, you're smiling and it's – it's kind of disarming. But I think there's more – it doesn't quite – Siân, what's going on for you now?
Siân: I just – I don't know … Just quiet.
Therapist: It feels like something more, Siân. I just don't – I think you smile at people and it's a way of – not saying what's really going on for you. It's like pacifying everything … trying to dampen down … but what's …. What do you feel towards me, Siân? No pat answers. Try and really sense it.
Siân: I just … irritated? angry? Feel like you're pushing me …
Therapist: I *am* pushing you because … I want to get a sense of what's really going on. There's something kind of – detached with you, Siân. It feels like … almost the silence is saying, 'I can't be bothered to be here.'
Siân: I guess – You know, as a kid, anger wasn't my thing. I was the happy one.

Therapist:	But, Siân, you're not a kid any more. You're an adult. And if you – if you feel angry with me you can say it.
Siân:	I guess I ... I show my anger by withdrawing. Pulling away.
Therapist:	I know you do Siân. You pull away from me ... from Hanako ... from your own life. But – and I guess that doesn't really show your anger, it just sends out ... confusion. How am I – Hana supposed to know what's going on if you just ... pull away? It feels like disinterest. Not anger.

In this vignette, the therapist challenges Siân to be honest, and takes the risk of being honest himself. Towards the end of the dialogue, he also suggests to Siân that her metaperception (that others can see her anger when she withdraws) is actually inaccurate. That is, that what they actually perceive at those times is someone withdrawn and detached.

Laing's genuineness in the therapeutic relationship also meant that he had little time for externally-imposed boundaries. His sessions would regularly run over 'the therapeutic hour'; he might go for walks with clients, accept cigarettes from them, or see them for longer periods of time if they were in crisis (Burston, 1996). More heretically, Laing might also meet clients outside the therapeutic relationship for discussion groups, yoga or partying; and he was well known for forming friendships with current (and ex-) clients. In the case of Mina Semyon, Laing went to court at her request, and even holidayed with her and her family. For Laing (1967), then, rules and guidelines were of far less therapeutic significance than the spontaneity and unpredictability of a genuine human encounter. Indeed, Laing believed that the decisive moments in therapy were often the ones that were unpredictable, unique, unforgettable, always unrepeatable and often indescribable – moments of I–Thou encounter, which, as Buber (1958) states, cannot be ordered or planned (Chapter 2, this volume). Laing gives the example of a seven-year-old girl who was brought to him by her father because she had stopped talking. Without any plan, Laing sat down on the floor in front of her and touched the tips of her fingers with his ...

And for something like forty minutes or so, nothing [happened] except a gradually developing movement/dance with the tips of her fingers .... After about forty minutes, I opened my eyes and as I opened my eyes I found her eyes opening just at the same moment, without a word having been spoken. So we withdrew our fingers from each other, and went back to my chair. I said to her, bring your dad along now if that's all right with you, and she nodded. (Quoted in Schneider, 2000: 596)

According to Laing, when the father subsequently asked the young girl what had gone on between her and Laing, she had replied 'It's none of your business!' – the first words she had spoken for approximately two months (in Schneider, 2000).

After Laing

While the existential elements of Laing's work were developed by Emmy van Deurzen and UK-based proponents of an 'existential-phenomenological' approach to existential therapy (see Chapter 7, this volume), other followers of Laing articulated and developed the more psychoanalytical elements of his writings (e.g., Thompson & Heaton, 2012). Many of these were grouped around the 'Philadelphia Association' (PA; R. Cooper et al., 1989). This was founded by Laing in 1965, and continues to run community households and training courses in existentially-informed therapy (see Box 6.2). Many of the leading members of the PA also drew on the work of such critical, contemporary philosophers and psychoanalysts as Levinas, Wittgenstein, Derrida and Lacan (see Gans, 1989). This means that, in some instances, there is a move away from Laing's attempts to establish a relationship of 'pure presence' (Oakley, 1989) – in which all the masks, defences and pretences have been stripped away – and instead there is an acknowledgement that all relationships are ultimately mediated through language, discourses and narratives. In this respect, these practitioners may be less concerned than Laing with getting to the 'real person' beneath the mask, and more accepting of the inevitable limitations and 'unknowns' in developing a close, therapeutically-healing relationship (Cooper et al., 1989).

Along these lines, Del Loewenthal (who trained at the PA) and colleagues at the University of Roehampton, London, have developed a *post-existential* approach (Loewenthal, 2010, 2011, 2016). This is described as a 'psychotherapy without foundations' – located between existentialism and postmodernism – in which practice is prioritised over theory, and where there is a particular acknowledgement of the unstable, ambiguous and temporary.

Box 6.2 'Laingian' community households

In the mid-1960s, Laing and his colleagues in the Philadelphia Association began to establish a series of community houses for people with severe mental distress, the most famous of which was Kingsley Hall in London. Consistent with Laing's theory of metanoia (see above), these households aimed to help severely distressed people 'live through their madness' and come out the other side (Thompson, 2015), by providing them with an environment of benign, non-intrusive care.

Thompson (2015) gives the example of a young man, Jerome, who had been diagnosed with catatonic schizophrenia having spent many years withdrawn from social contact by locking himself in his bedroom. On arrival at the community household, Jerome asked for a room of his own, and said that he wanted to stay in it until he was ready to come out. This was agreed to. Jerome stayed in his room for many months – hardly eating anything and becoming increasingly incontinent – until the rest of the community became so concerned about him that they felt it was essential to intervene. He was moved into a room with one of the therapists, and bathed, fed and massaged on a regular basis. However, Jerome's condition did not improve. Eventually, the community became resigned to Jerome's withdrawal and habits, and were shocked when, one evening almost a year later, a talkative and social Jerome sauntered down the stairs and said that he was famished. When they asked him what he had been up to all that time, Jerome explained that 'he had had to count to a million and then back to zero, uninterrupted, in order to finally achieve his freedom' (Thompson, 2015: 139). Why had it taken so long? According to Jerome, the various attempts by the community to engage with him had distracted him from his task, and meant that he had had to start counting all over again! Thompson writes that Jerome never had another psychotic experience, and 'proved to be an unremarkable person, really, ordinary in the extreme'. (For an in-depth account of life inside a Laingian community household, see Barnes and Berke, 1971.)

Although the community households aimed to provide peace and 'asylum' from any kind of interference, the reality seems to have been much more chaotic. Kirsner (2015: 142), for instance, writes that they were like the Freudian unconscious: 'anarchic, time-less, creative, unconventional and unpredictable though to some extent interpretable'. More critically, van Deurzen (personal communication, 7 December 2015) likens them to Dante's Inferno: 'grim, challenging and tortured'. She goes on to state, 'it was also extremely depressing, upsetting, wearing and maddening when it was not possible to save someone from self-destructive behaviour.' In this respect, the 'hands off' philoso-phy of care at the 'Laingian'-style community households seems to have been a double-edged sword: liberating for some, neglectful – however benignly – for others.

One of the most significant offshoots of Kingsley Hall was Soteria House. This was a community household established in California by the American psychiatrist Loren Mosher (Mosher & Hendrix, 2004). Mosher visited Kingsley Hall several times (Heaton, 2006), but aimed to circumvent some of the pitfalls he had seen there, including the atti-tude of neglect, the chaos, and the run-down state of the house. In addition, uniquely, Mosher established a series of rigorously controlled studies assessing the effectiveness of his approach. In an independent review of this data, covering 223 participants, Calton et al. (2008: 1) concluded that, 'the Soteria paradigm yields equal, and in certain spe-cific areas, better results in the treatment of people diagnosed with first- or second-episode schizophrenia spectrum disorders (achieving this with considerably lower use of medication) when compared with conventional, medication-based approaches.' Although the authors go on to state that there is insufficient evidence to recommend the Soteria paradigm as a standard treatment, these findings provide encouraging sup-port for a 'Laingian' approach to addressing severe psychological distress.

Critical perspectives

In terms of practice, there is no doubt that Laing's approach – or, at least, what is known about it – was refreshingly genuine. However, Laing's 'obses-sional tendency' to seek out authenticity in others meant that he could be bullying, arrogant and judgemental – a stance which fundamentally contra-dicted his commitment to seeing intelligibility in others (Thompson & Heaton, 2012). It is also ironic given that, as Thompson (personal communi-cation, 25 January 2016) states, Laing's essential message seems to be 'try to be kind and compassionate with the patients in your charge. They are more vulnerable than you imagine.' Moreover, from an evidence-based standpoint, contemporary research would suggest that therapists should be very cautious in disclosing to clients negative or critical perceptions (Cooper, 2008a). There is some evidence that clients do better in therapy when they perceive their therapists as genuine (Kolden, Klein, Wang, & Austin, 2011) and self-disclosing (Hill & Knox, 2002); but generally it is positive disclosures to clients (for instance, 'I think you are doing really well here'), rather than negative one (for instance, 'I think you are talking bullshit'), that seem to have the most positive benefits. Research also suggests that therapists should avoid highly intimate or personal self-disclosures (Hill & Knox, 2002).

It should also be noted that Laing's lack of attention to boundaries has the potential to raise a range of ethical concerns. However, in support of Laing, some research does suggest that a certain amount of flexibility around boundaries (for instance, the therapist visiting the client in hospital when they are sick), may be predictive of better outcomes (Jones, Botsko, & Gorman, 2003).

Theoretically, one of Laing's most enduring contributions to the fields of psychotherapy and psychology – if not psychiatry – has been his concept of ontological insecurity. Van Deurzen, however, argues that he failed to make explicit, or understand, that 'the ontological insecurity at the core of schizophrenia is essentially there in all of us' (1998: 10). For van Deurzen, what Laing was describing as ontological insecurity was 'pure existential anxiety': the dread of nothingness and a sense of not-at-home-ness at the heart of the human condition; and this, as existential philosophers have argued, is a universal human experience. From this perspective, then, Laing's attempts to cure his clients of their ontological insecurity are fundamentally misguided. Rather, therapists should be helping their clients find ways of courageously and constructively coming to terms with this given of existence. Van Deurzen-Smith (1997: 165) concludes, then, that Laing's work never fully overcame the medical model of illness and cure, and that 'Most of the concepts Laing contributed fit more naturally with Winnicottian analysis than with existential theory'.

Furthermore, there is no reason why the fears that Laing associated with ontological insecurity (i.e., engulfment, implosion and petrification), and the strategies that he suggested people develop to protect themselves against these fears (such as splitting and withdrawal), should be seen as being limited to severely distressed individuals. As Collier (1977) points out, for instance, many people describe themselves as having 'real' and 'false' selves, and Eleftheriadou (1997) draws some interesting parallels between the experiences of ethnic minority members and such fears as depersonalisation and engulfment. With respect to the fear of being petrified by another, it is also important to note that Sartre (1958) considered this a universal human concern, and not one limited to schizophrenically-predisposed individuals (Collier, 1977).

From a phenomenological standpoint, a further criticism of Laing's theory is that he tends towards reifying the notion of the self (Cohn, 1993; Heaton, 1991). That is, rather than seeing human existence as a verb-like flux of experiencing (Chapter 2, this volume), Laing (1965a) tended to talk about 'true' and 'false' selves, as if they were object-like entities. Moreover, Laing's (1965a: 77) suggestion that the schizoid individual 'retracts his lines of defence until he withdraws within a central citadel' suggests that this real self is located – or locatable – *within* the individual, rather than *between* the individual and their world. Despite Laing's commitment to an inter-relational understanding of human being, then, he has been accused of ultimately adopting a relatively individualistic and solipsistic perspective (Collier, 1977; Heaton, 1995).

Conclusion

To some extent, Laing's work deviates from an established existential position, and this is something that he acknowledges in the preface to *The Divided Self* (1965a). Nevertheless, his teachings are of considerable significance to the world of existential therapies and beyond. Laing challenged therapists to question their assumptions about normality and abnormality, and to look for the sense in even the most bizarre behaviour. Furthermore, he provided therapists with many different models and concepts – both intrapersonal and interpersonal – through which this understanding could be enhanced. Within Laing's work, there are also a whole host of ideas whose therapeutic and psychological potential has yet to be tapped: most notably, perhaps, his work on metaperceptions. In addition, Laing's actual therapeutic practice offers some important challenges to the practitioners of today. In particular, as Thompson (personal communication, 19 November 2015) summarises, Laing's message to therapists was: 'to do your own thing, be your own person, and never presume to know what is going on, but above all else, to be acutely sensitive to the vulnerability of each patient'.

Questions for reflection

- How 'real' are you with your clients? Would you be willing to say, for instance, the kinds of things that Laing said to his?
- Do you think that ontological insecurity is experienced by all people, or do you agree with Laing that there is a particular form of this insecurity experienced by people predisposed to psychosis?
- Think of a client, or someone else in your life, whose behaviour is difficult to understand. Are you able to think of ways in which that behaviour might, actually, be intelligible?
- Do you think that Siân would have benefited from a 'Laingian'-style directness in her therapy?

Recommended resources

Laing

Laing, R. D. (1965). *The divided self*. Harmondsworth: Penguin Books. (Originally published 1960).
Laing's best-known work: a brilliant existential-phenomenological exposition of the symptomatology and aetiology of schizophrenia.

(Continued)

(Continued)

Laing, R. D. (1967). *The politics of experience and the bird of paradise.* Harmondsworth: Penguin.
Laing at his most lucid, rhetorical and revolutionary. Argues that society, and particularly the family, serve to massively alienate people from their authentic possibilities and experiences, and that 'schizophrenia' is one strategy that some people invent to try to survive in this insane world.

Laing, R. D. (1969). *Self and others* (2nd ed.). Harmondsworth: Penguin.
Ground-breaking study of the relationship between one person's experiences and behaviours and those of another, and how certain ways of relating can lead to 'madness'. Possibly Laing's most difficult – and most rewarding – work.

Laing, R. & Esterson, A. (1964). *Sanity, madness and the family.* Harmondsworth: Penguin.
Fascinating and disturbing case studies of 11 young female 'schizophrenics' and their families, demonstrating the intelligibility of the women's symptoms within a contexts of deceit, double-binds and denial.

Commentaries on Laing

Burston, D. (2000). *The crucible of experience: R. D. Laing and the crisis of psychotherapy.* Cambridge, MA: Harvard University Press.
Detailed, critical examination of Laing's relationship to existential-phenomenological philosophy and psychology.

Laing, A. (1994). *R. D. Laing: A biography.* New York: Thunder's Mouth Press.
Accessible account of Laing's life and work that pulls no punches. Mullan's (1999) biography is more sympathetic to Laing, while Burston's (1996) has a more theoretical focus.

Mullan, B. (1995). *Mad to be normal: Conversations with R. D. Laing.* London: Free Association.
Over 250 pages of in-depth interviews with Laing on every area of his work and life, including his therapeutic approach and philosophical background.

Thompson, M. G. (Ed.). (2015). *The legacy of R. D. Laing: An appraisal of his contemporary relevance.* Hove: Routledge.
Rich, stimulating and informed collection of contemporary reflections on Laing, his ideas, and his practice.

Thompson, M. G., & Heaton, J. M. (2012). R. D. Laing revisited: A dialogue on his contribution to authenticity and the sceptic tradition. In L. Barnett & G. Madison (Eds.), *Existential psychotherapy: Vibrancy, legacy and dialogue* (pp. 109–125). London: Routledge.
Brief, stimulating and accessible introduction to Laing – the man, and his ideas. By two people who knew him well.

The Philadelphia Association: philadelphia-association.org.uk.
Training and therapy organisation that continues Laing's legacy.

The Society for Laingian Studies: laingsociety.org.
A range of scholarly resources on Laing.

7

EXISTENTIAL–PHENOMENOLOGICAL THERAPY: THE EXPLORATION OF EXISTENCE

This chapter discusses:

- The history and evolution of the existential-phenomenological approach, as developed within the UK.
- Key influences on the British tradition.
- Philosophical existential-phenomenological therapy, as developed by Emmy van Deurzen.
- Relational existential-phenomenological therapy, as developed by Ernesto Spinelli.
- Brief existential-phenomenological therapies.
- Existential-phenomenological therapy from a pluralistic perspective.

In 2003, the first edition of this book – like other writings of the time (e.g., Spinelli, 1997; van Deurzen & Adams, 2011) – wrote of a 'British school' of existential therapy (Chapter 7 of that edition), based on the existential training programmes at Regent's College and the New School in London. Today, with the growing geographical spread of this approach, it no longer seems appropriate to define this approach by one specific region (see Preface; Correia et al., 2016c). In addition, it is becoming increasingly evident that there are a number of other existential approaches around the globe (particularly Latin America, see Correia, Correia, Cooper, & Berdondini, 2014; Robles & Signorelli, 2015) that are similar in theory and practice to the British tradition, but have evolved independently. For instance, an existential movement started in Brazil in the 1970s, developed by such writers as Emílio Romero (2004) and Maria Feijoo (2010), which was deeply rooted in both phenomenology and existential philosophy. Today, the Brazilian Instituto de Psicologia Fenomenológico-Existencial do Rio de Janeiro (IFEN) has over 400 associated members (E. Correia, personal communication, 29 January 2016). The long-established 'Duquesne school' of psychology in Pittsburgh, USA – with its in-depth understanding of, and commitment to, phenomenology – also has many similarities in outlook to the British tradition, although its focus has primarily been on research methods, rather than psychotherapy *per se* (e.g., Giorgi, 1985). These existential approaches, as with the British tradition, emphasise a descriptive, non-diagnostic exploration of clients' lives and experiences. Hence, the umbrella term *existential-phenomenological* is increasingly being used to describe these approaches (Correia et al., 2016c; Craig et al., 2016; van Deurzen & Adams, 2016), and this is the term that will be used throughout this chapter.

As with the previous edition of this book, however, the primary focus of this chapter will be on the existential-phenomenological approach as developed within the UK, for two reasons. First, few of these other writings, as relevant to psychotherapy, have been translated into English. Second, the British tradition remains, probably, the largest, most dynamic and most influential of the existential-phenomenological approaches (Correia et al., 2014a, 2014b).

In the UK, the principal driving force behind the development of an existential-phenomenological approach has been Emmy van Deurzen (1951–) (formerly van Deurzen-Smith), who remains one of the main influences on existential-phenomenological practice (Correia et al., 2016c). Born in the Netherlands, van Deurzen worked as a therapist and trained as a clinical psychologist in France, before coming to the United Kingdom in 1977 to work in a 'Laingian' therapeutic community. In 1982, van Deurzen established her first UK-based training course and, from there, went on to develop a range of existential training programmes with colleagues: first, at the School of Psychotherapy and Counselling at Regent's College, London (formerly Antioch University); and, since 1996, at the London-based New School of Psychotherapy and Counselling and the Existential Academy.

In 1988, the UK-based Society for Existential Analysis was formed, which aimed to 'provide a forum for the expression of views and the exchange of ideas among those interested in the analysis of existence from philosophical and psychological perspectives' (journal *Existential Analysis*, back cover). This Society continues to be a focal point for the activities of existential-phenomenological therapists in the UK, organising regular discussion fora and conferences, and publishing an internationally-respected journal, *Existential Analysis*. In 1988, van Deurzen also published *Existential Counselling in Practice* (van Deurzen-Smith, 1988), a landmark text that presented a uniquely accessible, systematic and comprehensive account of existential therapeutic practice. Around the same time Ernesto Spinelli – who had been teaching phenomenological psychology at Richmond College, London – published *The Interpreted World* (1989, 2nd ed. 2005). This provided an accessible guide to phenomenology, including its use in psychotherapeutic practice. In 1989, Spinelli joined the team at Antioch University and, with van Deurzen and colleagues, worked on developing the Advanced Diploma in Existential Psychotherapy (ADEPT) programme.

A 'second phase' of this UK-based existential-phenomenological tradition emerged in the 1990s (Spinelli, 1997: viii), as van Deurzen, Spinelli and their colleagues began to clarify and develop their approach. Significant contributors during this phase included Hans Cohn, who detailed the Heideggerian foundations of existential-phenomenological practice (Cohn, 1997, 2002; see Cooper, 2003: 125–126); Freddie Strasser, who developed a time-limited approach to existential therapy with his daughter, Alison

(Strasser & Strasser, 1997); and Simon du Plock (1997), who edited a series of case studies on existential-phenomenological practice.

In the 2000s, a 'third phase' of this existential-phenomenological approach evolved, as trainees of van Deurzen, Spinelli and their colleagues began to develop their own ideas, writings and trainings. Key contributors here include Martin Adams (2013), Laura Barnett (2008; Barnett & Madison, 2012), Susan Iacovou (Iacovou & Weixel-Dixon, 2015), Darren Langdridge (2012), Greg Madison (2010, 2014), Martin Milton (2014; Milton, Charles, Judd, O'Brien, Tipney, & Turner, 2003) and, I would like to hope, myself (Cooper, 2003, 2012, 2015). This phase also saw a broadening-out of existential-phenomenological writings to such areas as work with children and young people (Gavin, 2013; Quinn, 2010; Scalzo, 2010), relationship therapy (van Deurzen & Iacovou, 2013), supervision (van Deurzen & Young, 2009), and coaching (Spinelli & Horner, 2007; van Deurzen & Hanaway, 2012). In addition, a number of contemporary existential-phenomenological writers have gone on to explore the links between existential perspectives and wider social, political and environmental issues (e.g., Cooper, 2015; Langdridge, 2012; Milton, 2010). Some of the most interesting work here has been in the field of sexuality and gender identity (see, in particular, Milton, 2014). Authors like Meg-John Barker (2014), for instance, have examined such contemporary issues as non-monogamies, and looked at the ways in which existential ideas and practices can inform therapeutic practices in these areas.

Today, the existential-phenomenological approach is one of the largest branches of existential therapy, with over 20 institutes worldwide (Correia et al., 2014b). The most sizeable of these is the UK-based Society of Existential Analysis, and a large proportion of existential-phenomenological therapists are located in the UK. However, with the attendance of international students at the London-based trainings, and with van Deurzen, Spinelli and colleagues developing trainings internationally, there has been a dissemination of ideas and practices from within the British tradition across the globe (see Box 7.1), particularly in Europe (including Belgium, Denmark, Greece, Lithuania, Portugal, Russia and Sweden), and in Israel, Australia and Mexico. In addition, as we have seen, independent traditions of existential-phenomenological thought and practice continue to thrive in Latin America and the USA.

Box 7.1   *Oistros*: Awakening a passion for life

With the dissemination of the British tradition of existential-phenomenological thought and practice across Europe, local groups are now beginning to develop their own unique take on existential therapy, flavoured by their national cultures and

(Continued)

(Continued)

traditions. An example of this is the concept of *oistros* (Dallas, Georganda, Harisiadis, & Zymnis-Georgalos, 2013), developed by the Hellenic Association for Existential Psychology (*Gignesthai*), which was founded in 2004 and is now certified as a training institute by the European Association for Psychotherapy (K. Zymnis, personal communication, 30 October 2015). In ancient Greece, *oistros* was a gadfly that stung animals and drove them to react, and Socrates used it to describe his ability to awaken people from their lethargy and laziness. As with *zhi mian* (see Box 5.1), *oistros* can be seen as a force that energises, inspires and focuses people: stimulating a sense of creative and passionate enthusiasm. Perhaps the clearest example of a person stung by *oistros* is 'Zorba the Greek' (Kazantzakis, 2008), who squeezed out each drop of life, living every moment to the full. For *Gignesthai*, the concept of *oistros* forms a link between their Greek heritage and the ideas and practices of existential-phenomenological therapists. But for the wider existential community, as with *zhi mian*, such concepts can also provide a rich source of cultural resources for widening and deepening the existential approach.

Of all the existential therapies discussed in this book, the existential-phenomenological approach (even just within the UK) is probably the most diverse. As van Deurzen (2012a: xi) writes: 'The movement has its own history of splitting and fighting and there is a healthy disagreement about what existential work should be.' In the British tradition of existential-phenomenological therapy, two broad strands have been identified (van Deurzen & Adams, 2011: 2) (although, perhaps, they are better conceptualised as two ends of a spectrum; see Chapter 8, this volume). The first can be termed *philosophical existential-phenomenological therapy*, and is based on the work of van Deurzen (2010, 2012a, 2015; van Deurzen & Adams, 2016). It is characterised by the use of existential philosophical ideas to try to support clients towards more engaged, inspired and meaningful ways of being. The second can be termed *relational existential-phenomenological therapy*, and is primarily based around the work of Spinelli (2006a, 2006b, 2015). In this approach, there is a particular emphasis on the therapeutic relationship, working descriptively, and conceptualising clients' experiences from an intersubjective standpoint. As these two strands form the strongest influences on existential-phenomenological practice globally (Correia et al., 2014a; Correia et al., 2016c), they will form the principal foci for the present chapter.

Influences

Given the diversity of interests and practices within the existential-phenomenological approach – both in the UK and globally – it should come as no surprise that it is influenced by a wide variety of existential philosophers.

Practitioners within the existential-phenomenological approach have drawn on such existential philosophers as Kierkegaard (van Deurzen, 2010), Nietzsche (van Deurzen, 2010), Sartre (Spinelli, 2006b), Jaspers (van Deurzen, 2010), Buber (Morgan-Williams, 1996), and Merleau-Ponty (N. Diamond, 1996).

As with the daseinsanalytic approach, however, Heidegger's writing – particularly *Being and Time* (Heidegger, 1962) – tends to be the key influence on existential-phenomenological thought and practice. Hence, for instance, there is an emphasis on the in-the-world-with-others nature of human existence, and a rejection of the individualism and subjectivism that is inherent in more humanistic approaches. British therapists like Spinelli (2006a) and Cohn (1997) have also joined with – and drawn on – Boss and Binswanger in critiquing many of the assumptions within traditional psychoanalytic thinking, such as the notion of an unconscious and intrapsychic dynamics. In contrast to many daseinsanalysts, however, few therapists within the existential-phenomenological approach see in Heidegger's writings the definitive version of human truth; and some, such as Spinelli (1996b), openly question the applicability of Heidegger's ideas to the therapeutic arena.

Existential-phenomenological therapists also tend to be strongly influenced by phenomenological ideas and practices (Correia et al., 2016c), particularly as articulated by Spinelli (2005). Here there is an emphasis on bracketing theories and assumptions, as well as working in a broadly descriptive way (see Chapter 2, this volume). Hence, while interpretations, explanations and diagnoses find their way back into daseinsanalytic, logotherapeutic, existential-humanistic and even Laingian ways of working, existential-phenomenological therapists tend to be particularly committed to 'staying with' the actuality of clients' lived-experiences.

This Husserlian influence, combined with its Laingian roots, means that the existential-phenomenological approach, of all the existential therapies, tends to most vigorously reject the medical model of mental health (van Deurzen, 2015). There is a strong commitment to dispensing with distinctions between 'healthy' and 'pathological' modes of functioning, and therapists tend not to view their clients through clinical categories and diagnoses (van Deurzen, 2010). Instead, clients are seen as having 'problems with living' (Spinelli, 1996a; van Deurzen, 2014b) – difficulties that all human beings, including their therapists, may face at some time in their lives. Hence, existential-phenomenological therapists, along Laingian lines, tend to reject the idea that clients should be helped towards some norm of mental health whereby they can slot back into society and the status quo (van Deurzen, 2015). Rather, clients are encouraged to find their own unique way of being. As a consequence of its Laingian roots, there is also a strong emphasis in the existential-phenomenological approach on a non-hierarchical, mutual relationship between therapists and clients (Spinelli, 2006a; van Deurzen, 2010).

As with all the existential therapies discussed in this book, there is no doubt that the existential-phenomenological approaches have also been influenced by the authors' own personal histories. In a very candid account, for instance, van Deurzen (2014a) describes some of the childhood experiences that came to shape her philosophy of therapy and of life. Through witnessing her father hiding from the Nazis in a freezing loft in The Hague, for instance, she developed a profound awareness of 'the fragility of life' (2014a: 7), while living in scarcity taught her to 'count her blessings' (2014a: 8). Later in her youth, having experienced the heartache of a lover 'abruptly and silently' disappearing from her life (2014a: 11), she writes that she learnt she was 'able to face whatever life threw at me', and 'decided to expect catastrophe and loneliness as predictable and standard'. Following this experience, she also writes that she was 'determined to help create a world in which people would be more able to communicate, be more genuine and love each other'.

Philosophical existential-phenomenological therapy – Emmy van Deurzen

The philosophical existential-phenomenological approach developed by van Deurzen can be seen as having two elements that are relatively unique among the existential therapies. First, there is a particular emphasis on informing the therapeutic dialogue with insights and understanding from philosophy. Indeed, for van Deurzen and Adams (2011: 9), 'Existential therapy is the practical application of philosophy to everyday life.' These insights are most likely to be from existential philosophers (see Chapter 2, this volume), but van Deurzen may also bring in ideas and understandings from other philosophers, as and where they may be seen as helping clients find better ways of living. Here, van Deurzen is not suggesting that therapists should start referencing or quoting specific existential writings: for instance, 'Siân, you know, on page 25 of *Being and Nothingness* Sartre says, "the essence of human being is suspended in his freedom" – what do you think of that?' Rather, it means drawing on ideas from philosophical traditions to help clients think about their lives: for instance, 'Siân, you feel that things are determined for you, but maybe you are discovering that you can change you situation and that you have a certain amount of choice and freedom to make something new of what is given to you.'

The second aspect of this philosophical existential-phenomenological approach that is relatively unique among the existential therapies is that it is primarily concerned with helping clients face up to the challenges of *everyday* life, rather than the more overarching and abstract givens of existence. That is, while existential psychotherapists, such as Yalom (1980; see Chapter 5, this volume), focus on such 'ultimate' existential concerns as freedom and meaninglessness, van Deurzen tends to focus more on the difficulties, limitations, and disappointments of day-to-day being. In relation to our client Siân, then, there would be no assumption from this perspective that she needs to look at such 'deeper' existential issues as death, meaningless or even freedom for her therapy to be of value – though if these issues emerged they would certainly be looked at. Rather, the work is likely to be more orientated towards how she deals with problems and obstacles in her everyday living (like her relationship with Hanako or her feelings of stagnation in her career) and how she strives to address them and learn from them.

Facing the daily struggle of human existence

For van Deurzen (2015: 181), 'life is an endless struggle, where moments of ease and blissful happiness are the exception rather than rule'. Life, she states, is hard, tough, rough and unfair – filled not only with joy and satisfaction, but also with crises, disappointments, injustices and failures (van Deurzen, 2009, 2012a). Moreover, she argues that human beings are unavoidably caught up in a web of tensions (van Deurzen, 2012a): pulled between different poles of a dilemma for which there are no resolutions. An individual, for instance, may want to be close to others, and they may also want to have their independence. For her, then, there is no possibility of attaining a perfect life: a paradise on earth. Even if, as she argues, a human being's external world was ideal, the fact that human beings are a nothingness or lacking (see Chapter 2, this volume) means that they will constantly be striving for something more.

As with other existential theorists, however, it is not, for van Deurzen, the existential reality that is the primary fount of our psychological difficulties. Rather, it is our attempts to evade this reality. She writes, 'one-third of suffering is ontological and the other two-thirds occur because we cannot accept the one-third' (van Deurzen & Adams, 2011: 91). For van Deurzen (2012a), an awareness of this existential reality inevitably creates anxiety. And, in an attempt to dispel this, we can end up fantasising about a perfect and problem-free life that is 'just around the corner' (van Deurzen-Smith, 1994: 41): 'If only I could have a child', for instance, or 'Once I sort out my marriage everything will be fine'. Alternatively, we may hold on to an assumption that there are easy answers to our problems – for instance, 'If I could just "work through" my childhood issues it'll all be OK' – rather than accepting the enigmatic, irresolvable nature of many of our difficulties. 'Most of us,' van Deurzen (2009: 77) writes, 'have secret fantasies about a state of safety and never-ending good experiences, in a place where resources do not run out and we get everything we need and want'. In other words, van Deurzen argues that we can be *reluctant* to face the reality of our existences: that life has been – and always will be – a struggle. Moreover, for van Deurzen, this tendency to shy away from the existential realities of life is not just something that happens at the individual level, but is perpetuated by cultural and social ideologies. In *Psychotherapy and the Quest for Happiness* (2009), she argues that contemporary Western society has become increasingly dominated by hedonistic values, aspirations and expectations. We are sold the myth that if we can have the latest car, or box set, or type of orgasm, then we can enter a 'brave new world of sublime and enduring well being' (van Deurzen, 2009: 71).

Van Deurzen (2009) argues that such individual and cultural self-deception may provide a modicum of comfort. However, given the actuality of human existence – in all its roughness, toughness and challenge – the more that we 'pipedream about the happiness we long for, the less we are prepared for the harshness of existence' (van Deurzen, 2009: 159). That is, when things go wrong – as van Deurzen (2012a) suggests they inevitably will do – then we can end up feeling that we have failed; or feel frustrated, disappointed and angry that we have been 'robbed' of the good life we feel entitled to.

Moreover, for van Deurzen (van Deurzen-Smith, 1995a), if we feel that life should be comfortable and challenge-free, then at these crisis points we may tend to retreat further and further from reality, rather than resolutely facing our problems. This, suggests van Deurzen (2012a: 54), can only bring 'doom and despair': 'Life has a way of exposing cracks in the most stubborn self-deceptions' (van Deurzen-Smith, 1997: 274), she writes. Like debtors who try to deal with their financial problems by refusing to open their bank statements, people who turn away from life's challenges only makes things worse for themselves. The problems build up, fester and reach a point where they feel insurmountable. For van Deurzen (2012a: 30), then, the psychologically distressed individual is not sick or ill, but 'clumsy at living'. In other words, their problems are not so much caused by deep-seated psychological injuries, as by a misguided philosophy of life, which lead them down a path of disillusionment, self-destruction and misery.

Hence, van Deurzen (2010) proposes that the aim of existential therapy is to help clients face up to the reality of their situation and to wake up from self-deception. It strives to help clients come to terms with life in all its contradictions: to immerse themselves in life rather than evading their troubles, and to creatively grapple with life's problems. Clients are encouraged to bravely face up to their predicaments and struggles, their trials and tribulations, their irresolvable tensions and dilemmas, and their inevitable failings and frailties; and they are also encouraged to discover the strengths and talents within them that can help them overcome these challenges. 'Truth and the good life', writes van Deurzen (2009: 29), 'are to be found not by avoiding life or by living in hiding, but rather by facing the daily struggle of human existence with courage and determination.' And instead of 'looking for happiness', clients are encouraged to 'learn to live instead' (van Deurzen, 2009: 79).

Given van Deurzen's (2009, 2010, 2012a, 2015) assertion that 'life is an endless struggle', it should come as no surprise that she does not see therapy as leading clients to some utopian state. For her, there are no instant gratifications, no dramatic results, and no cures at the end of the therapeutic road. Clients do not come out of the therapeutic process 'actualised', and she is critical of the 'happiness industry' that promises a cure for every psychological ailment. Rather, as with Camus' (1955) Sisyphus, she holds that clients will still be burdened with the reality of a challenging, rough and unfair existence. However, she does suggest that the therapeutic process can help clients to achieve a number of things. First, it can help them get back on top of their lives, take control, and have a sense of mastering their world rather than being at its mercy. Second, it can help them realise that they are able to take much hardship, and that they are stronger than they think. Third, it can help them to welcome, rather than fear, life's challenges: to take life's ups-and-downs more in their stride. Fourth, it can help them to respond to life's challenges as constructively as possible: summoning and harnessing all their resources to find the most satisfactory ways forward. Fifth, it can help clients to experience the whole spectrum of their ways of being, rather than being stuck in rigid patterns of behaviour. Sixth, it can help them rediscover a passion for life: an aliveness, enthusiasm and sense of adventure that comes from fully engaging with the world, and meeting the challenges of life. Finally, then, for van Deurzen, existential therapy can help clients move beyond a fear of life, to a discovery that life is full of promise and ultimately worth living.

In striving to enable clients to 'become truthful with themselves again' (van Deurzen-Smith, 1995a: 9), van Deurzen advocates a primarily descriptive approach to therapy, in which clients are encouraged to articulate, in increasing levels of detail, the actuality of their lived-world. Within this process, the existential therapist is a 'fellow investigator' or 'ally', who joins her clients on this journey of exploration. Van Deurzen (2012a) likens the existential therapist to an art tutor, who helps their students get a sense of perspective and build up an increasingly detailed picture of the world around them and their place within it. The therapeutic process described by van Deurzen (van Deurzen-Smith, 1995a) also has a relatively conversational and informal style, with therapists using any form of engagement that might help clients clarify their understandings of their lived-worlds. Therapists, for instance, might ask clients questions like, 'Can you tell me more about that experience?' or 'What does this mean to you?' They might also offer clients interpretations, in the sense of making explicit the implicit links, connections and themes in a client's worldview (van Deurzen, 2010). In phenomenological terms (Chapter 2, this volume), this might be understood as the process of *eidetic reduction* (seeking for the essence of something) and the process of *transcendental reduction* (finding the truth of something by keeping going with verification and 'universalisation' until it fits) (E. van Deurzen, personal communication, 30 December 2015).

The four worlds of existence

To some extent, this descriptive exploration of clients' lives and experiences is similar to the existential-humanistic inner search. Given her Heideggerian background, however, van Deurzen is less interested in an exploration of clients' subjective experiences *per se*, and more in an exploration of the different ways in which they relate to their world. More specifically, van Deurzen (2010, 2012a) – in one of her most influential contributions to the field (Correia, 2015) – outlines four different, though entirely interdependent and inter-linked, dimensions of worldly-being that clients can be encouraged to explore. These are the physical dimension, the social dimension, the personal dimension, and the spiritual dimension (see Table 7.1). The first three of these dimensions are drawn from Binswanger's work, but van Deurzen has added the fourth, spiritual dimension – the dimension of things that cannot be seen or proven – and emphasises these four dimension more strongly than contemporary daseinsanalysts. Van Deurzen and Arnold-Baker's *Existential Perspectives on Human Issues: A Handbook for Therapeutic Practice* (2005) provides a comprehensive and in-depth discussion of different elements of each of these four dimensions, such as procreation and eating (physical dimension) and language and families (social dimension).

Table 7.1   van Deurzen's (2010, 2012a) four dimensions of existence

Dimension	Physical (*umwelt*)	Social (*mitwelt*)	Personal (*eigenwelt*)	Spiritual (*überwelt*)
Relation to	Things	Others	Self	Life
World of ...	• natural environment, climate, etc. • physical environment • body • health • physical needs: e.g., hunger, thirst, warmth, comfort • leisure activities • material possessions	• interpersonal relationships • culture • race • class • family	• sense of 'me' • character/ disposition • intimate relationships	• values • meanings • faith • ideals • systems of belief • philosophical outlook
Polarities	• domination–acceptance • expansion–contraction • birth–death	• extroversion–introversion • egoism–altruism • intimacy–separation • trust–distrust • belonging–isolation • competition–cooperation • conformity–individualisation	• self-acceptance–self-development • authenticity–inauthenticity • integrity–disintegration • resolve–yielding	• meaning–meaninglessness • purpose–futility • good–evil • transcendence–mundanity

Van Deurzen (2012a: 75) argues that one of the central values of this four-fold map is that it can help both therapists and clients to stand back from clients' immediate concerns, and ensure 'that all different aspects of the client's reality are explored'. As van Deurzen (personal communication, 2002) states, clients' understandings of their worlds will inevitably be 'partial, deficient, full of holes and lacking in perspective'. Such a map, then, allows some of these gaps in awareness to be filled in. For instance, with our client Siân, we have developed a fairly good sense of her social world. But it is interesting to note that, to this point, we have little sense of her in the physical world. How does she feel, for instance, 'inside' her body, or in relation to her sexual desires? And we also have little sense of Siân's values and ideals in the spiritual world. What, for instance, is her moral code, and what is her political outlook? These might not be questions that we would directly ask Siân, but keeping this fourfold map in mind might be very useful in supervision, in helping us to build up a more comprehensive understanding of Siân's existence.

Tensions and paradoxes

Van Deurzen's (2010, 2012a) map of existence also helps to highlight some of the irresolvable tensions, dilemmas and polarities that clients face, which they can be encouraged to explore. For van Deurzen (2010: 138), 'we are involved in a four-dimensional forcefield at all times', pulled not only between the different dimensions, but within the dimensions themselves. Siân, for instance, has a tension between her desire to be close to Hanako (social dimension) and her desire to be independent (personal dimension); but she also has a tension, within the social dimension, between her desire to be close to Hanako and her desire to be intimate with Rachel.

Here, working descriptively, the therapist's role may be to help clients develop a deeper understanding of the dimensions across and along which they are pulled. Helping clients to recognise hidden, unacknowledged ends of these tensions may be particularly helpful in showing them how they may be better able to negotiate apparent contradictions. An illustration of this can be given in the work with Siân:

Siân: There's something – I don't know why but I feel – Just this incredible guilt. I *know* I should talk to Hanako about what's going on with Rachel but I – every time I get close to it I – something stops me.

Therapist: There's something that stops you …

Siân: I – I sit there … I write notes … I get all ready for it. I want – it's really important for me – I'm not someone who goes slinking around life, lying about stuff but I –

Therapist: So what is it that stops you? That pulls you the other way from being honest in – in the way you want?

Siân: It's … fear. I dunno. The thought of her – I just think about her being angry and – I can't …

Therapist: You're really scared of her being angry. Is that it?

Siân: It's crazy, I know. I'm … I'm almost 30. But the thought of her anger just paralyses me.

From a philosophical existential-phenomenological standpoint, however, the point here is not just to help clients understand their tensions better. It is also to help them accept the fundamentally tension-ridden nature of existence, and to live life *despite* these tensions, rather than hanging on for some perfect and pain-free solution. This is how the dialogue with Siân might continue, for instance:

Therapist: Siân, I really understand how frightening it feels – the idea of Hanako getting angry with you, but – I wonder if you're, sort of, expecting for some point when you can tell her and it won't be scary.

Siân: Yes, I guess that would be – that would be nice [smiles].

Therapist: And, I can understand you doing that and wanting that but …

Siân: … But is it going to happen? [smiles].

Therapist: Mm … Yup … You know, of *course* you don't want to upset her, of *course* you don't want her angry with you, but I just wonder – you could be waiting for years and it could – I don't even know how it would happen, Siân. Like's she never going to be particularly pleased – is she ever going to say, 'Great, Siân, that's great about Rachel!'

Siân: It *is* just so scary.

Therapist: It *is* Siân, I know. But you've got something to say to someone that, almost by definition, they're not going to like. It *is* scary, but the choice is – it's not about whether this is scary or not. The choice is whether you get on with it and take the risk and face it, or whether you – I dunno, just hang on and hope for some unimaginable point in the future …

Siân: … That might never come.

Therapist: Yup, that might never come. And that's a choice too Siân. That's a choice.

As with the logotherapeutic, existential-humanistic and 'Laingian' approach to practice, we can see here that the philosophical existential-phenomenological approach can be quite challenging to clients. However, while the logotherapeutic approach challenges clients to find meanings, and the existential-humanistic and 'Laingian' approaches challenge clients to be true to themselves and to their therapists, van Deurzen's challenge to clients is more one of being true to 'life'. That is, it is less about challenging clients to be honest about themselves and their experiences, and more about challenging clients to acknowledge the reality of the human condition.

Within the four dimensions of existence, there are also numerous paradoxes that clients can be encouraged to explore and come to terms with (van Deurzen-Smith, 1995a). In the social dimension, for instance, there is the paradox that the more someone chases after us, the less interested we often end up being in them. Similarly, in the personal plane, the more we strive for happiness, the more we can end up feeling dissatisfied; and the more we stop chasing happiness, the better we may end up feeling. Our client Siân, for instance, is trying to 'keep things OK' with Hanako by not telling her about Rachel but, paradoxically, she seems to be making things that much worse in the long term. Here, therapists from a philosophical phenomenological-existential position may bring these paradoxes into the therapeutic work as a way of helping clients to understand the unattainability of their unrealistic expectations. For instance, a therapist might point out to Siân that, as is often the case, the more she tries to smooth over things with Hanako, the more she is actually making problems.

A challenging stance

As this last vignette with Siân suggests, in helping clients face up to the reality of their lives, van Deurzen (2012a) advocates an approach that can be challenging – even 'ruthless' – at times. For her, therapists should act as 'surrogate consciences', gently but firmly calling their clients back to the actuality of their existences – in all their anxiety- and guilt-invoking realities – even if this means that clients may become perturbed for a period of time. For van Deurzen, it is of particular importance that therapists challenge their clients' unexamined assumptions: those beliefs that they hold true without questioning, but which may blind them to the realities of existence. In Siân's case, for instance, this might be her belief that things can work out with Hanako by her doing nothing. From a philosophical existential-phenomenological position, we might suggest that this is a convenient and reassuring belief for Siân, but it is also a form of self-deception, and one that the therapist – warmly and with care – challenges her on.

From a van Deurzen-ian standpoint, challenging *contradictions* in clients' narratives can also be an important way of helping them to develop a deeper understanding of their lived-world. Siân, for instance, talks about loving Hanako and deeply caring for her, but her affair with Rachel seems to contradict this basic narrative. From a philosophical existential-phenomenological position, we might feed this contradiction back to Siân, so that she is more able to reflect on, and clarify, the true nature of her feelings towards Hanako: for instance, that she feels that she *should* care for her, but actually cannot get past her anger.

Clarifying values

The aim of van Deurzen's (2012a: 124) existential therapy, however, is not simply to challenge clients' assumptions and highlight the irrationality of their thinking. Rather, the ultimate aim 'is to assist the client in grasping the principles that will turn out to withstand questioning': that is, to identify what it is that really matters to them. Van Deurzen's existential therapy, then, is particularly concerned with helping clients to identify their core values: the things that they think are worth living or dying for (see also Jacobsen, 2005). As with the logotherapeutic approach, it is also fundamentally concerned with helping clients uncover the meanings and goals to which they truly wish to strive.

This means that the philosophical existential-phenomenological approach of van Deurzen (2012a), in contrast to the existential-humanistic approach, is focused not only on immediate, emotional experiences but also on the 'spiritual world' of values, meanings and assumptions. While van Deurzen does see the exploration of emotions as an integral part of the therapeutic process, for her, this is a means towards identifying clients' underlying values and meanings, rather than a goal in itself. 'Emotions are our most sensitive barometers,' she writes, 'and they give us accurate information about what we value' (2010: 308). An example of this can be given in the work with Siân:

> Therapist: Siân, you're saying that you feel an incredible guilt towards Hanako. What is that guilt about?
> Siân: It's – I know I've really let her down. Just incredibly.
> Therapist: Is that – you were saying about being someone who doesn't slink around life. Is it – is that about you wanting to be honest?
> Siân: I – Yes, I think – I see myself as someone who's really honest and I've really – always valued that in myself. Been proud of it.
> Therapist: But you're feeling guilty. There's a sense of falling short. In a sense, there's something you really value and you're not doing it.
> Siân: Yes, I feel guilty.
> Therapist: It sounds like you feel guilty because you know you are capable of more. And you feel that, as you love Hanako, she deserves this honesty from you, rather than this slinking around.

Here, as van Deurzen (2010: 311) suggests, 'Guilt is the emotional colouring of having failed to achieve or obtain something that is important to us', and the therapist's role with Siân is to help uncover what that important thing is. Through such activity, the therapist aims to help the client re-establish their own moral principles for living (van Deurzen, 2009). Note, in contrast to the existential-humanistic approach, there is less emphasis on going into the feelings *per se* (through questions like 'Where do you experience the guilt in your body?' or through experiential exercises; see Chapter 5, this volume). Rather, the focus is more on making sense of the emotions in terms of meanings and values. This brings it closer to the meaning-centred approaches (Chapter 4, this volume). For van Deurzen, helping clients to explore their dreams and fantasies can also be a way of helping them to identify – and feel motivated towards – their underlying goals.

Having developed a deeper understanding of their values, meanings and goals, van Deurzen (2012a) suggests that therapy can then help clients to consider how to proceed into their future. In the work with Siân, for instance, this might go as follows:

> Therapist: So there's your guilt Siân, and it feels like this is really helping you understand who you are and what it is you want from – and for – yourself. But what are you – how are you going to live with that, what are you going – *need* to do? You're saying it's really important for you to be honest in your life.
> Siân: I do – that *is* really important to me. That honesty. I know I've let myself down. And Hanako. I – there's something about needing to be that me again. I need to be that me.

For van Deurzen (2012a), an important part of this future-moving process is helping clients to identify their talents, strengths and hidden potentials. Just as an art tutor helps their students develop their own particular style, so van Deurzen writes that clients should be encouraged to discover what they are best at, so that they can develop their way of being to the best of their abilities. Moreover, van Deurzen encourages clients not only to identify specific strengths, but also to see that they have the strength to face the challenges of life: that they have been, are, and will be able to ride the storm of existence, and forge constructive and positive ways forward.

The therapist as guide

For van Deurzen (2010, 2015) each client must come to find their own personal answers to life's challenges. At the same time, as we have seen, she argues that the problems, dilemmas and paradoxes that clients face are not unique ones, but shared challenges for all of humankind. It is not only Siân, for instance, who struggles between the desire to be honest with others and the desire not to anger them – many of us have a similar tension in our lives. For van Deurzen, then, existential therapy is not just a personal, psychological exploration but a philosophical dialogue: where universal human questions are brought to the fore and guiding principles for living are distilled.

In this philosophical dialogue, the therapist, as a fellow human being, is likely to 'resonate' with many of the challenges and difficulties that clients face. They too, for instance, may have found it difficult to be honest with people if they knew it was going to provoke their anger and cause a rift. Furthermore, through their training, they will have explored many of their clients' concerns from a range of different perspectives: philosophical, psychological and therapeutic. For van Deurzen (2012a) then, the therapist – and particularly the more seasoned one – is not only a fellow traveller, but a 'mentor', 'wise person', or 'expert guide' who can bring a special wisdom and experience to the client's journey. And, argues van Deurzen, they should not be afraid of sharing doing so. Here, van Deurzen is not suggesting that therapists should lead the therapeutic work, or that they should prescribe to their clients certain solutions to their problems in living. Rather, she is suggesting that it is legitimate for therapists to present to their clients different ways of seeing things – an 'extra pair of eyes' (van Deurzen & Adams, 2011: 12) – such that clients can consider a wider range of standpoints than just their own. In the work with Siân, this might look like the following:

Therapist: Siân, it is – it can be really difficult to be honest with people. No doubt about it. It's something that most of us struggle with, especially when it matters so much. You don't want to annoy people, hurt them. It feels easier and seems kinder to keep things hidden. But my own personal experience is that hiding things doesn't always help things in the long run and often makes things worse. Things don't just magically sort themselves out – maybe we have to

> take responsibility for sorting things out. And somehow when things are hidden it just drains the life out of the intimacy you can have with someone .... You know, there's something about a relationship that can't flourish if there's not the truth – if people aren't real in it. It becomes – two people in a mask.

'There is no single recipe for living the good life,' writes van Deurzen (2009: 53), 'But there are certain culinary secrets.' In this respect, like cookery teachers, existential therapists cannot instruct their clients on how to live, but they can teach them certain skills and insights that may help them on their way: 'Try using fresh herbs instead of dried ones', 'Taste the food as you go', 'Face up to life's difficulties rather than hide from them'. Here, for van Deurzen, we can always learn about making meals more tasty and satisfying; and, similarly, life 'can be served up with more zest and flavour when we know more about it'.

Critical perspectives

Undoubtedly, van Deurzen (2012a) is committed to a therapeutic approach that aims to help clients take the lead, and which respects and values their points of view: 'directional', rather than 'directive' (van Deurzen, 2014b: 165). 'I judge my daily therapy practice,' she states, 'by the highest standards of whether clients are actually finding a path of their own or not and whether they can manage contradictions better and in their own way. I never try to make them conform to my values or my philosophy' (personal communication, 31 December 2015). An excellent illustration of this, and of van Deurzen's sensitivity in her therapeutic work, is the client study of Rita, presented in the second edition of *Everyday Mysteries* (van Deurzen, 2010: Chapter 35). At the same time, however, there can be a more evangelical element to her writings (as she, herself, acknowledges), and a more prescriptive sentiment: in particular, that we should be facing life with courage, vigour and determination. 'We need to learn to say "yes" to life', she writes (2015: 104), but this would seem to provide little validation for clients who, at the most fundamental level, may want to say 'no', and hide themselves away with their daydreams, fantasies and 'untruths'. In this sense, then, van Deurzen has a tendency to smuggle normative judgements back into therapy (Wolf, 2000); and while her way of working may place less stress on the illness–health dimension than most other existential therapies, it still tends towards valuing certain ways of being over and above others. Put another way, there is something of a contradiction between van Deurzen's (2009: 53) statement that, 'There is not just one way to lead a good life', and such statements as 'Truth and the good life are to be found not by avoiding life or by living in hiding, but rather by facing the daily struggle of human existence with courage and determination' (van Deurzen, 2009: 29). To her credit, however, van Deurzen (personal communication, 2001) acknowledges that the latter 'is clearly a value judgement and a basic assumption on my part'; she does not attempt to portray herself as adopting a 'neutral' perspective in which all values are bracketed.

To some extent, van Deurzen's claims might be less problematic if she provided evidence to support their universality. However, in most instances this is absent. She writes, for instance, that, 'The consequences of embracing anxiety is a feeling of aliveness, excitement and is the source of creativity' (van Deurzen & Adams, 2011: 91), but gives no evidence to show that this is generally the case. And, indeed, while her approach tends to emphasise that we are better off bravely facing up to life, there is evidence to suggest that a certain degree of illusion, distortion and self-deception may be integral to the way 'well-adjusted' people perceive their world (Baumeister, 1991). That is, those who adopt an unrealistically optimistic outlook can often fare better than those who face up to the brute reality of their situation (Armor & Taylor, 1998). Van Deurzen does not consider such evidence and, in this respect, her writings can be seen as promoting a particular opinion – and, indeed, encouraging other therapists to promote a particular opinion – that may be counterproductive to some clients.

As a counter to this criticism, van Deurzen (2014b) has specifically argued that one of the unique features of the existential approach – as she defines it – is that it is not dependent on psychological evidence, but instead draws knowledge from the long-established traditions of philosophy. Indeed, she states that, 'Kierkegaard's observations about his anxiety are more convincing to me than any other form of research' (personal communication, 30 December 2015). This does beg the question, however, of whether philosophical ideas from hundreds, or even thousands, of years ago should be privileged over contemporary research findings. However, van Deurzen does acknowledge that empirical research can play a valuable part in helping to develop and refine philosophical insights. 'I am greatly in favour of using new data to inform our existential ways of thinking,' she states.

Finally, as with all the existential-phenomenological therapies, there is little empirical evidence to provide direct support for the helpfulness of this approach. As with the existential-humanistic approach (Chapter 5, this volume), there is some indirect evidence from the common factors literature, as well as positive outcomes from non-systematic case studies, but rigorous, independent evaluations have yet to be conducted. However, Vos et al.'s (2014) review of the outcomes of existential therapies – as well as psychotherapy research more broadly (e.g., Castonguay & Beutler, 2006; Emmelkemp, 2013) – suggests that therapies which challenge clients to face up to their anxieties and issues, and which have some pedagogic element, may be of particular value. If this is the case, then the philosophical existential-phenomenological approach may be expected to fare well in any outcome evaluation.

Conclusion

Van Deurzen is one of the most inspiring, creative and original thinkers in the existential field today. Not only has she been a key contributor to the regeneration of existential thought and practice across Europe, but also the philosophical existential-phenomenological approach that she has developed makes a unique contribution to the field. There are those within the existential-phenomenological approach who find her writings and style of therapy too didactic for their tastes. However, it is, perhaps, van Deurzen's belief in the truth – and her seeking of it – that has led her to be such a powerful agent of change in the existential therapies field.

Relational existential-phenomenological therapy – Ernesto Spinelli

The work of Ernesto Spinelli (2001, 2005, 2006a, 2006b, 2015) provides a valuable contrast to that of van Deurzen. Spinelli trained as a developmental psychologist, and was a faculty member at Regent's College School of Psychotherapy and Counselling from 1989 to 2009. Spinelli's work is particularly influenced by Husserl and the phenomenologists, as well as by contemporary relational and social constructionist thinkers such as Kenneth Gergen (see Gergen, 2011). Hence, rather than conceptualising therapists as 'experts in living', Spinelli puts particular emphasis on therapists bracketing their assumptions and beliefs and encountering clients from a place of *un-knowing*. This emphasis on bracketing also means that Spinelli's approach has a strong focus on working descriptively. In contrast to van Deurzen, Spinelli's approach is also strongly influenced by the more intersubjective and dialogic existential-phenomenologists, such as Buber, Binswanger and Farber. In this respect, he puts particular emphasis on the quality of the relationship between therapists and clients, suggesting that the way in which things are talked about in therapy is often of far more importance than what is discussed. 'My clients remind me over and over again,' he states, 'that what they take from me is, first and foremost, the me who they experience being there with them. What I say to them, what we discuss, what knowledge I have is way down the line in terms of its significance to their lives' (personal communication, 2002).

Worlding and worldview

The starting point for Spinelli's (2015) existential-phenomenological approach is that being, as discussed in Chapter 2 (this volume), is not a noun-like thing but a verb-like flow. Spinelli uses the term *worlding* to describe this immediate, unrepeatable, embodied, holistic flux of experiencing. This term highlights the way that, from an existential-phenomenological standpoint, being is not something 'within' us, but involves a continual engagement and construction of our lived-worlds. Along these lines, Spinelli (2015: 16) suggests that one of the three key features of our being is *relatedness*: 'Everything that exists is always in an inseparable relation to everything else.' This leads on to a second key feature: *uncertainty*. As relational beings, we will always be impacted upon by the world, and in ways that we cannot fully predict or control. And, argues Spinelli, through the lived-experience of relational uncertainty comes a third key feature of human existence: *anxiety*.

For Spinelli (2015: 58), our worlding is 'linguistically elusive'. As a pre-reflective experiencing, it can never be directly expressed through words. However, Spinelli argues that we each come to develop a *worldview* – of ourselves, of others, and of the wider world around us – which is a reflective conceptualisation of this worlding: structuring and thing-ifying it into a substance. Like a frozen waterfall, our worldview is a snapshot of our worlding, but it is also one that inevitably misrepresents the actuality of our lived-flow of being. This is because it will always be partial and incomplete. So, for instance, it is likely that our client, Siân, experiences a complex swirl of emotions when she is arguing with Hanako – including, for instance, hurt, anger, boredom, frustration, vulnerability, sadness and resentment. However, her worldview of herself at these times inevitably foregrounds certain aspects of her worlding (such as her vulnerability and hurt), and forecloses others (such as her boredom and feelings of resentment).

Box 7.2   Understanding existentialism in terms of worlding and worldview

In *Practising Existential Therapy*, Spinelli (2015: Chapter 2) reinterprets a number of classic existential themes using worlding and worldview. For instance, he describes the anxiety of choice in terms of the risk inherent to moving beyond a particular worldview, and embracing a novel, unknown and unpredictable existence. Authenticity, from this perspective, can be understood as a close alignment between worldview and worlding: an openness to '*that which is there in the way that it is there*' (2015: 48). And, from this perspective, death anxiety can be understood as the fear of a catastrophic breakdown in our self-construct. Here, everything that we have substantiated in our selves, crafted to be 'us', is threatened with annihilation. Interestingly, too, Spinelli uses his theoretical framework to explore the question of meaning, and comes to a somewhat different conclusion from that of the meaning-centred therapists (Chapter 4, this volume). Here, while he acknowledges the importance of meaning to people's lives, he also emphasises the value of allowing the meaningless to emerge (worlding), without too quickly imposing a meaning (worldview) on it.

Spinelli (2015) goes on to suggest that particular worldviews can become *sedimented*. By this, he means that they can become rigid and inflexible, to the point where they are impermeable to challenge from the individual's actual experiencing. Siân, for instance, develops an increasingly powerful sense of herself as a 'victim' of Hanako's anger, to the point where she can only construct experiences – even ones such as her shouting at Hanako – in terms of what *Hanako* has done to *her*. Note, this is not dissimilar from Laing's concept of *mystification* (see Chapter 6, this volume), in that the individual becomes alienated from their actual experiencing. Laing's focus, however, is on how such alienation is *done* to the individual, while Spinelli focuses more on how individuals bring about their own self-estrangement.

To maintain such sedimentations, Spinelli (2015) suggests that people may *dissociate* from their experiencing. One way they might do this is by attributing these experiences to other people or forces. He gives the example of a client, Clive, a fundamentalist lay-preacher, who believed that he had 'conquered the evils of the flesh' by no longer experiencing sexual arousal:

> But, lo and behold!, at times his response to women is obviously one which expresses sexual arousal. In order that the sedimented self-construct can remain in a way that it can deny or disown these challenging experiences, Clive 'explains' such occurrences in terms of 'being possessed by Satan'. Via this explanation, it is an 'alien construct' that responds in a sexually-arousing fashion. (Spinelli, 1996c: 65)

For Spinelli (2015), our attempts to create fixed and sedimented worldviews arise, in part, as a means of trying to manage the anxieties of an uncertain, relationally-embedded existence. However, as with all moves away from authentic being (see Chapter 2, this volume), such defensive processes are seen as having the potential to cause more harm than good. Despite his dissociation, for instance, Clive (above) is likely to continue experiencing sexual arousal in the presence of women, and therefore will be constantly challenged with a threat to his sense of self. In this respect, Spinelli argues that existential anxiety arises not just from the uncertainty of being, but also from the unease that accompanies the worldview's partial and limiting attempts to reflect relational uncertainty from a structural perspective.

Box 7.3   The present and future in the past

Spinelli's philosophical and therapeutic perspective is based around a critique of the ways in which worlding becomes sedimented into fixed and rigid worldviews. As with Boss (1963), then, much of his writings have critiqued sedimented assumptions within the therapeutic world, such as 'transference', 'the unconscious', 'intrapsychic dynamics', and the concept of the 'self' (see, in particular, Spinelli, 2006a).

One very prominent assumption that Spinelli (2006a) has challenged is the belief that clients' present lives are caused by their past experiences. Instead, Spinelli argues that the ways people remember their pasts are often a consequence of the ways they see themselves in the present, or would like to see themselves in the future. That is, individuals' reconstructions of their pasts can never be wholly accurate – they are always interpretations – and the way in which individuals selectively recall certain events, while selectively overlooking others, may say much about their current self-structures and future-directed motivations. An individual, for instance, who only tends to remember the happy events in her past may be trying to reinforce her self-structure as a happy-go-lucky person. Indeed, Spinelli suggests that the very search for past experiences may be part of an attempt to maintain a particular self-structure. Clients, for instance, who long to recall *the* event in their past that has caused them to experience such misery and sadness may be desperately trying to preserve a 'my-life-will-get-better' self-structure, rather than acknowledging the desperateness of their present circumstances.

The aims of therapy

With its rejection of sedimented worldviews, Spinelli's (2006b, 2015) approach almost entirely brackets off any assumptions as to what constitutes 'good' mental health. In contrast to daseinsanalytic, logotherapeutic or existential-humanistic approaches, there is no assumption that it is better to be open to the world, meaning-orientated, or courageously facing the givens of existence. Furthermore, in contrast to van Deurzen's approach, Spinelli does not assume that it is better to face up to the challenges and vicissitudes of life. Spinelli also makes very few assumptions about the aetiology of clients' difficulties, although there is a tendency to see them as arising from the disjunction between worlding and worldview, and particularly where the latter is highly sedimented. Here, therapy can be seen as a way of helping clients to de-sediment fixed stances and re-own dissociated experiences. However, Spinelli also argues that too *much* consonance between worlding and the worldview can be problematic, leaving the individual with a fragmented and empty sense of being. Hence, for Spinelli (2001) it would be quite legitimate and appropriate for clients to decide that they did not want to adopt – or even consider – alternative ways of seeing themselves and their world. Here, Spinelli (2006b) emphasises the importance of respecting and accepting the client's existence *as it is currently being lived*, rather than as it could be.

For Spinelli (2001, 2015), then, the aim of therapy is not to *do* something to clients: to encourage them to change or to adopt a more existential way of living. Rather, 'its primary concern lies with attempts to clarify descriptively that which the client experiences as disruptive to the continuity of the worldview so that its sedimentations and dissociations can be explored inter-relationally' (2015: 87). In other words, the aim of therapy, from Spinelli's perspective, is to help clients descriptively explore their worldviews and their lived experiences, so that they can come to understand more about the disparities and disjunctions that might be related to their dilemmas and difficulties.

A stance of un-knowing

These theoretical foundations have led Spinelli (2006b, 2015) to suggest that therapists should encounter their clients from a stance of *un-knowing*. Here, he is not referring to the feigning of ignorance, but of a willingness to bracket one's assumptions: striving to hold in abeyance fixed beliefs, values and interpretations. In this respect, un-knowing involves an openness and receptivity to that which emerges in the therapeutic encounter in all its novelty, mystery and otherness. It is an 'acceptance of, and curiosity about, the client's accounts of how it is for him or her to exist both in the wider-world and in the therapy-world *in the way that the client chooses to present them*' (Spinelli, 2014: 147).

Being-with and being-for

In addition to holding a stance of un-knowing, Spinelli (2006a, 2014) writes that therapists should both *be-with* and *be-for* their clients. By being-with, Spinelli means respecting and accepting the client's expressed truth – their worldview – as it is being related, rather than seeking to question or confirm its validity. With Siân, for instance, this might mean listening and staying with her view of herself as a victim of Hanako's behaviour. By being-for, Spinelli means being prepared to step into the client's lived-world as fully as possible: to try to experience their world as they experience it and to help them explore it descriptively. This being-for, writes Spinelli (2006a), is not unlike the task of the method actor whose essential aim revolves around immersing themselves in a specific character. Being-for Siân, then, might involve entering into her experiences of arguing with Hanako, and helping her to uncover a richer and more nuanced descriptive understanding of her experiencing. For Spinelli, being-with and being-for can be a powerful therapeutic combination: helping clients to feel that their perceptions are legitimate and accepted, but also providing them with the opportunity to delve more deeply into their experiences.

Phase one of therapy: Co-creating the therapy world

Spinelli (2015) proposes a three-phase structure for understanding and practising existential therapy. The first phase focuses on setting up the 'therapy-world', which includes establishing the boundaries and contract for the therapeutic work. In this phase, there is a particular focus on helping clients to descriptively articulate, express and explore their worldviews and lived-experiences, as related to their presenting concerns. Here, the therapist aims to attune to their clients through the process of being-with and being-for them, and by adopting a stance of un-knowing (see above). In this phase, the therapist also aims to facilitate a descriptively-focused inquiry: inviting the client to describe, in increasing levels of detail, their worldview and the tensions within it. *Other-focused listening* is central here, in which the therapist strives to remain with the client's narrative as it is being expressed and recounted. In this phase, the therapist may also ask *strategic questions*: to make increasingly explicit that which has remained implicit within the client's narrative. This may include asking *idiot questions*: 'questions that would normally be deemed to be too obvious or too basic to ask' (Spinelli, 2015: 155). With our client Siân, for instance, a therapist might ask, 'When you say you are depressed, what do you actually mean by "depressed"?' or 'What is "guilt" for you, Siân?' Another descriptive method suggested by Spinelli is *narrational scene-setting*, in which the client is asked to focus on a single specific example of what they are concerned with.

Phase two of therapy: Co-habiting the therapy-world

As trust begins to grow in the therapy relationship and the client becomes more open to challenges – both from the therapist and from themselves – the therapy may be ready to move into the next stage. In this second phase, there is an intensification of challenges to the client's worldview, and an exploration of sedimentations and dissociations. Here, the therapist becomes a more fully-fledged 'other': willing to introduce their own understandings, experiences and presence, more explicitly, into the therapeutic work. As part of this, as with Yalom (2001) and Laing, this may involve a focus on the immediacy of the here-and-now therapeutic encounter, with the client being invited to describe how they experience the therapist, and the therapist being willing to self-disclose their experiences in response. Through such work, the client can come to deepen their understanding of their relational being outside the therapy-world. As Spinelli (2015: 110) writes: 'The therapist acts as both the representative of all others in the client's wider world relations and, just as importantly, is also the other who challenges the client's self-, other- and world-constructs simply through the inter-relational impact of his or her presence.'

Much of this work may focus on a relational, here-and-now exploration of the sedimentations and dissociations in the client's self-construct. In the work with Siân, this might look something like the following:

Therapist:	Siân, I want to ask you something. What are – who are you when you're arguing with Hanako? What do – what do you become?
Siân:	I see – I feel … a child. Sitting there. Grey school skirt. Some godawful stripy school tie and jacket; perched on a chair. I'm – I'm just a child.
Therapist:	Like you feel – like you've felt with me when you're late for sessions?
Siân:	Like I feel in my life: a 'woman-child'.
Therapist:	And now … do you feel – is it a woman-child sitting opposite me now?
Siân:	I don't – in some ways maybe. It's – you're the expert, you know what's – But, no, there's also – part of me also thinks, 'I'm OK'. I feel OK sitting here. I

	know – I don't know therapy. You're the – it's you who's the expert on that but … I'm not, you know, I'm not totally wasted. I've got, like if I asked you to play guitar or something stupid …
Therapist:	Say more Siân. What were you – were you going to say?
Siân:	Just that, you know, if we were both sitting – here with guitars and playing. You'd – I'd be OK and you – God knows [Siân laughs]. No – no offence or anything. Just …
Therapist:	What's it like to say that? To say, you know, that there's something you can do and I – that I probably can't. You're right: I can't.
Siân:	It's – I don't want to offend – upset you.
Therapist:	But, you know, fine, because it's – that's right. You would be better. And – it's – it's totally fine with me. I'm really fine with that.
Siân:	[Siân smiles uncomfortably and looks at the therapist. After a while, her smile gradually disappears and she looks more serious. She holds the therapist's gaze for a few seconds.]

Through this here-and-now immediacy work, Siân's concept of herself as a 'woman-child' begins to be challenged. Instead, she has the opportunity to experience herself as a knowledgeable and able adult woman, in relation to another human being. This here-and-now focus is similar to an existential-humanistic or 'Laingian' approach, but its emphasis is less on disclosure and honesty *per se*; rather, it is on how clients *construct* themselves in relationship, and how they might construct themselves otherwise.

The inter-relational realms of encounter

For Spinelli (2006a), however, this self-concept is not an independent entity, but something that is constructed and maintained in relationship to others. With Siân, for instance, it is not just that she sees herself as a child, but that she sees herself as a child *in relation to* more mature and sophisticated others. Furthermore, Spinelli argues that this relational self-structure is merely one of four inter-relational realms of encounter that can be explored in therapy. For not only has an individual developed some sense of themselves, but they have developed some sense of the other that they are encountering, some sense of what goes on between the two of them, and some sense of how that other relates to further others in their world (see Table 7.2).

Table 7.2   Spinelli's inter-relational realms of encounter

I-focused realm	My experience of my self in any given relationship. What I tell myself about my current experience of me in this relationship.
You-focused realm	My experience of the other being in relationship with me. What I tell myself about my current experience of you being in the encounter.
We-focused realm	My experience of us being in relation with one another. What I tell myself about us in the immediacy of our encounter.
They-focused realm	My experience of the other's experience of others in his or her world. What I tell myself about the other's experience with further others.

Spinelli (2001) suggests that the structured exploration of these four realms of encounter is what provides existential therapy with its uniqueness. In other words, in the therapeutic relationship, therapists should keep an awareness of these four different realms in the back of their minds, and encourage their clients to explore them. This can be both as they manifest in the therapeutic encounter, and as they exist in relation to others in the clients' lives. As well as thinking about her self-construct, for instance, Siân could be invited to reflect on her construct of Hanako in relation to her, her construct of them together, and her construct of Hanako in relation to other people. Are there ways in which there are also sedimentations and dissociations here? For instance, has she developed a fixed worldview of Hanako as a critic and aggressor towards her, and closed off an awareness of Hanako's more caring, vulnerable or sexual sides?

For Spinelli (2006a), the therapeutic relationship provides a particular opportunity for therapist and client to explore the third, interactional realm – an exploration that can throw light on the client's experiencing of the other three realms. An interesting example of this comes from Spinelli's (2006b) work with Jennifer, a 'studiously guarded' young woman who was racked with a multitude of concerns, among them bulimia. At one point in the therapeutic dialogue, Jennifer and Spinelli speak simultaneously, to which Jennifer quickly apologises (we-focused realm). Spinelli encourages Jennifer to stay focused on this interaction, and he asks her what kind of messages she picked up from him as a consequence of it (you-focused realm). She says that she heard a critical one. Spinelli (2006b: 144) then asks her to explore the kinds of things she was saying to herself when she spoke at the same time as him (I-focused realm). 'I'm awful! Despicable! How could I be so stupid and arrogant' she states. To explore the generalisability of these experiences, Spinelli then asks her whether these are common messages she hears from others and says to herself when she feels she's done something wrong. She replies in the affirmative.

Through this process, Jennifer is helped to develop a greater awareness of how she experiences interpersonal interactions – and, with it, self and others. For Spinelli (2006a: 332), however, the particular specialness of therapy lies in the fact that it allows client and therapist an opportunity to explore 'the various *conjunctions or points of contact* between the participants' relational realms'. For it is not only the client, but the therapist, too, who experiences self, other, we and they in the therapeutic encounter; and, by sharing these experiences with the client, the client may be helped to revise and reconsider her own relational understandings. Jennifer, for instance, assumes that Spinelli (2006b) is angry with her for interrupting him. In fact, as he lets her know, he is angry with himself for blurting out what he did. By letting her know this, he gives her an opportunity to revise her view of the relational encounter, and thereby her views of self and other. We also saw this in the work with Siân, where the therapist's disclosure that they are OK with Siân being better than him allows Siân to reframe her self-, other- and we-construct.

Self-disclosure

Spinelli (2006b), then, can be quite disclosing in his therapeutic work – particularly where the focus is on the third, inter-relational realm. Drawing on the American psychotherapist Leslie Farber (2000), however, Spinelli (2001) goes beyond Yalom and Laing in arguing that one of the most helpful things a therapist can do is to reveal to clients their own uncertainties and vulnerabilities. For instance, a therapist might share with their client that they genuinely do not know how the client can overcome their anxieties, or they might disclose that they struggle with similar challenges themselves. Initially, a client might find this very disconcerting, but by realising that the therapist does not have the answers, they may come to revise their view of others as informed and themselves as ignorant. Instead, they may come to see that others, like themselves, are uncertain and powerless in the face of the 'impossible dilemmas of being human' (Spinelli, 2001: 168). Furthermore, by disclosing their vulnerabilities, the client may start to develop a true caring for the therapist (Farber uses the more challenging term 'pity'). This is a caring that may help them rediscover their ability to connect with others, and feel more empowered.

Phase three of therapy: Closing down the therapy-world

As the client begins to adopt a more challenging and fluid stance towards their sedimentations and dissociations, and as the ambiguities in their worldviews are no longer so disturbing, the therapeutic work may begin to shift into a third and final phase. This involves a particular focus on translating the insights gained in the therapy-world to the wider-world, and also closing down the therapeutic relationship.

As part of this process of translation, Spinelli (2001, 2015) suggests that therapists may want to help clients explore how their worldview – and any changes in it – may impact upon others in their lives. This is the fourth, they-focused realm. Spinelli (2001) argues that this exploration is important for two reasons. First, from an existential, intersubjective perspective, clients' experiences and choices cannot be isolated from the choices and experiences of those around them. 'In the inescapable interrelationship that exists between "a being" and "the world",' Spinelli (2001: 16) writes, 'each impacts upon and implicates the other, each is defined through the other and, indeed, each "is" through the existence of the other.' Second, Spinelli argues that a therapeutic approach which ignores the relational realms of those outside the therapeutic relationship abandons any sense of social responsibility or potential for social change, and instead becomes little more than vehicles for self-serving individualism.

An exploration of this they-focused realm is illustrated as the work with Siân comes towards a close:

Therapist: For me, Siân – for me, that position you're dev– you're adopting, that adult you've found. It's different but – I can feel – I like the seriousness there. You've – it feels a different way of being.

Siân: It's – Yes, it feels a different kind of – I feel a bit different inside. Feel like – more serious – take myself more serious. I can feel, kind of – it's an older self.

Therapist: And how it is – any thoughts on how it is for people around you. Like Hanako?

Siân: We spoke – Hana and I *did* talk about stuff during the week. I was going to say. For the – I said – I tried saying to her, 'Let's talk. Let's look at what's going on between us.'

Therapist: And how did that – What's your sense of how that was for her? You taking – being more the initiator?

Siân: Yeah. She was, like, I think she thought it was quite cool. She was kind of surprised. We – I said, 'Let's find some quiet time to talk. Away from Kai, when he's in bed.'

Therapist: So maybe she – maybe she quite liked you initiating that and taking the lead … setting it up.

Siân: It felt a different – different in how *we* are together. And – but it was a hard conversation. Really hard. I was going to say.

Therapist: What was – what was the difficult stuff Siân? What made it difficult?

Siân: Just … talking about stuff. So much for the first time. And I told her about, you know, Rachel. She said she'd – she'd already kind of worked it out. She knew Rachel from a while back and she knew I still had …. And she – turned out she'd also been – there was someone from Japan who'd been really close with her and she'd – wanted her to go back together. She'd been thinking about that a lot. Hadn't said. Just finding me so angry and pushing away all the time. But – I think she appreciated – she said she sensed I'd changed – was wanting to change. And trying to make things work …

Critical perspectives

One of the key strengths of Spinelli's (2001, 2015) relational existential-phenomenological approach is its focus on the 'social' dimensions of existence (see Table 7.1). However, the stress on this world means that, at least in his writings, there is less exploration of the physical, personal or spiritual realms of being.

From a philosophical existential-phenomenological standpoint, Spinelli's emphasis on working descriptively can also be criticised for being too limited. For Adams (2001: 78), the descriptive elicitation of experiencing is just the first stage of the phenomenological process, and without the more active stage of 'verification' – which seeks out structural invariants of the clients' experiences (Chapter 2, this volume) – there can be a 'morbid going round in circles when, almost literally, nothing happens'. Here, suggests Adams, 'You are both busy finding out things you already know.' Along similar lines, Adams also criticises the concept of un-knowing, arguing that a reluctance to rely on the authority of your own experience is a hiding-behind-ignorance. From this standpoint, if the therapist has their own insights or understandings to bring to the therapeutic dialogue, then they are doing the client a disservice to deny them. Indeed, van Deurzen and Adams (2016: 62) argue that such denial 'can lead to nihilism and insecurity in the client and can be as damaging as hiding behind theory'.

A closely related criticism of Spinelli's relational existential-phenomenological approach could be its lack of directionality. For some clients, an open-ended, exploratory therapy may be ideal. However, as the research indicates, there are many clients who are looking for a more goal-focused, structured and therapist-led approach to therapy (Cooper & Norcross, 2015). Such clients may find Spinelli's approach particularly unsuitable, and may do better in a more directive, or outcome-focused, therapeutic therapy – existential or otherwise.

Finally, as with many other forms of existential therapy, there is limited evidence to demonstrate the helpfulness of Spinelli's relational existential-phenomenological approach. To date, probably the best direct evidence comes from tests of Rayner's *existential experimentation* (Rayner & Vitali, 2015) (see below), as well as the general evidence for experiential humanistic approaches (Elliott et al., 2013). In addition, the common-factors evidence regarding the strong association between the quality of the therapeutic relationship and outcomes (Norcross, 2011) may be particularly relevant to this relational approach.

Brief existential therapies

With the emphasis – particularly in health settings – on developing briefer interventions, the last two decades have seen various attempts within the existential-phenomenological school to develop short-term existential therapies.

Time-limited existential therapy

The first of these was Freddie and Alison Strasser's (1997) *time-limited existential therapy*, which Alison Strasser (2015) is currently working to update. Strasser and Strasser suggest that, for existential therapists, there are some very distinct benefits to working in a time-limited way. Much of this revolves around the fact that a time-limited therapeutic encounter mirrors, in many respects, the time-limited nature of human existence. Hence, in contrast to longer-term therapies, clients are brought face-to-face with issues of finitude and temporality in very direct and immediate ways. This gives them an opportunity to become more aware of how they relate to finitude in the extra-therapeutic world, and to develop strategies for relating to it in more constructive and effective ways.

A client, for instance, who tends to treat the time-limited therapeutic relationship as if it will go on for ever may also tend to ignore the fact that their time on the earth is limited. If this is pointed out to the client and the possible connections explored, it may encourage the client to face up to the finitude of their being and make the most of the time that they do have.

Strasser and Strasser (1997) also suggest that a time-limited therapeutic approach may be particularly effective at helping clients overcome overly-high expectations of life. Just as clients may hope for a 'smooth and perfect life' (van Deurzen, 1998), so they may expect that therapy will provide them with either an 'instant cure and complete elimination of their presenting problem or some particular method or tool that can specifically help in overcoming their dilemma' (Strasser & Strasser, 1997: 54). With only 12 or so weeks to work in, however, clients are confronted with the fact that any change will inevitably be limited. The time-limited nature of the therapeutic process, then, may encourage clients to reduce their expectations to feasible and workable levels; and if this relaxation of standards can be generalised beyond the therapeutic environment, then clients may develop more realistic and achievable expectations in life as a whole.

The short-term, finite nature of time-limited existential therapy also means that the ending is likely to be a prominent feature of the therapeutic relationship. Strasser and Strasser (1997) write that the ending will inevitably evoke some kind of emotional response in clients – such as fear, anger or sadness – as well as recollections of previous losses and rejections. Here again, then, the time-limited nature of the therapeutic relationship may help clients to develop a greater awareness of a particular area of their extra-therapeutic life, as well as of their values and coping strategies.

Structurally, Strasser and Strasser (1997) have suggested that therapists and clients should meet for approximately 12 sessions, with one follow-up session approximately six weeks later, and a second follow-up session approximately six weeks after that. They also suggest that, at the final follow-up session, therapists and clients may choose to negotiate a further 'module' of 12-plus-2 sessions. However, more recently, Alison Strasser (2015) has proposed a more flexible 'modular' approach, in which the length of contract offered to clients may vary depending on their individual needs and preferences.

In terms of content and process, Strasser and Strasser's (1997) time-limited existential therapy has been structured around two *wheels of existence* (see Figures 7.1 and 7.2). The first of these is a diagrammatic representation of the existential givens that every human being faces, and which therapists might encourage their clients to explore. The second wheel is a representation of the methods and skills that therapists can use to address each of the corresponding possibilities and limitations. Hence, for instance, 'identifying value systems and polarities' (Segment 4) can be used to address the 'creation of patterns of value and behaviour systems'.

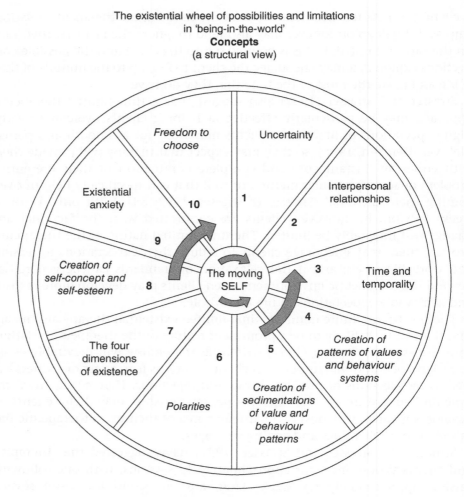

Figure 7.1 The existential wheel: concepts

Source: F. Strasser and A. Strasser (1997) *Existential time-limited therapy*. Reproduced by permission of John Wiley & Sons Limited.

Note. Those segments in roman script represent existential givens, whilst those in italics represent the human reactions and responses to these givens.

The case of Simona provides a good illustration of many of the key concepts, methods and skills of Strasser and Strasser's (1997) time-limited existential approach. Simona, a 25-year-old woman, was coming to the end of her university studies, but felt 'compulsively' unable to get up in the morning to attend lectures and study, and experienced uncontrollable feelings of rage, usually directed towards her boyfriend. In the first five to six sessions of the time-limited existential therapy, Simona was encouraged to explore her

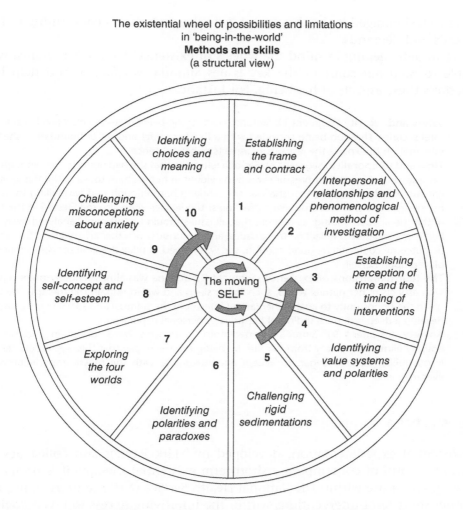

The existential wheel of possibilities and limitations
in 'being-in-the-world'
Methods and skills
(a structural view)

The diagram represents a non-chronological and non-linear
interconnection of the methods

Figure 7.2   The existential wheel: methods and skills

Source: F. Strasser and A. Strasser (1997) *Existential time-limited therapy*. Reproduced by permission of John Wiley & Sons Limited.

history, her worldview, and the motivations behind her value systems. It emerged that she had developed strong perfectionist tendencies as a means of coping with an uncertain and uncontrollable childhood; and her 'inability' to get up was motivated by a sense that if she could not do things perfectly – like achieving a first-class degree – then there was no point in doing them at all. Simona also came to see that her desire for perfection was accompanied by a strong desire to control the world around her, and this was leading her to feel enraged by her boyfriend, who was not always conforming to her needs and demands.

Through keeping in mind the wheels of existence, Simona's therapist was able to map out some of the key issues Simona was facing, and help her address these aspects of her being. For instance:

- **Safety and security** (Segment 1): Simona had a strong belief that she could reach a state of total security. Through being provided with a fixed contract and set of boundaries, she felt safe enough to explore the less secure aspects of her existence.
- **Time and temporality** (Segment 3): Simona felt guilty that she had not achieved enough for her age, and this sense of pressure was also evident in her attitude towards the therapeutic encounter, where she felt that she was not working hard enough and was failing to reach her desired goals. Her compulsive perfectionist tendencies were also manifested in the face of the therapeutic ending: as a desire that all issues should be 'properly' analysed away. By being encouraged to reflect on these issues, and to consider whether an imperfect therapeutic outcome could still be good enough, she was helped to relax the time pressures that she placed upon herself.
- **The four dimensions of existence** (Segment 7): Simona was almost entirely preoccupied with aspects of her natural world, such as her sleep and waking-up. In the therapy, she was given the opportunity to analyse her lack of interest in the spiritual and social worlds, and to develop a deeper understanding of her private, personal experiences.
- **Anxiety** (Segment 9): Simona's perfectionist tendencies were rooted in a desire to entirely eliminate anxiety from her life. By being helped to see that this was an existential impossibility, Simona began to accept and re-engage with the messy imperfections of everyday life.

Existential experimentation

Existential experimentation, developed by Mark Rayner and colleagues, is another form of contemporary short-term existential therapy. It is primarily designed for use within UK National Health Service (NHS) settings, alongside other short-term interventions within the Improving Access to Psychological Therapies (IAPT) programme, and is delivered directly at doctors' surgeries. The intervention is primarily inspired by the work of Spinelli, and is focused on helping clients to overcome sedimented assumptions and constructions of self (Rayner & Vitali, 2015).

Existential experimentation is delivered in six weekly sessions (Rayner & Vitali, 2015). In the initial sessions, there is a focus on helping clients to describe their difficulties, and to establish their goals for the therapeutic process. Clients are encouraged to 'own' the ways in which they understand their experiences. For instance, Siân might be encouraged to see that her sense of herself as weak is not a 'fact', but a particular construction of herself that she has chosen to adopt. In the middle part of the intervention, clients are then supported to reconsider the usefulness, or otherwise, of particular ways of interpreting their experiences, and to challenge sedimented or unhelpful constructs. Is it useful, for instance, for Siân to see herself in this way? Here, therapists may also support clients' attempts to experiment with alternative understandings of self, world and others. For instance, a therapist might encourage Siân to experiment with seeing herself as confident and attractive, or to 'stay with' an ambiguous and fluid sense of self. Finally, clients are helped to remain mindful of their achievements and how this might be applied in other situations in their lives.

Existential experimentation is one of the few forms of existential-phenomenological therapy that has been subjected to relatively rigorous evaluation, and its outcomes are promising. In a study of 52 adults meeting criteria for depression or anxiety, drop-out was only around 10 per cent, and participants who completed all six sessions showed large reductions in symptoms of depression, anxiety and psychological distress (Rayner & Vitali, 2015). A large majority of clients in existential experimentation also meet their personal goals for therapy, at least to a moderate extent (Rayner & Vitali, 2014).

Pluralism: An existential approach to existential therapy

As with Schneider's (2008) existential-integrative framework (Chapter 5, this volume), some authors within the third phase of the British existential-phenomenological tradition have tried to extend this way of working by proposing that existential thinking and practice can serve as the basis for a more integrative paradigm. Milton et al. (2003: 115) write that 'existential psychotherapy has the potential to augment and deepen narrow epistemological frameworks by providing a rich contextual base and soulfulness for understanding the overarching principles of what it means to be human.' Similarly, over the past decade, John McLeod, myself and colleagues have articulated a *pluralistic* approach to therapy, which is fundamentally based on existential-phenomenological principles (Cooper, 2015; Cooper & Dryden, 2016; Cooper & Stumm, 2016; Manafi, 2010; McLeod & Cooper, 2015). This pluralistic approach starts from the existential assumption that each person is fundamentally unique (Chapter 2, this volume). Hence, it assumes that different clients may want very different things from therapy at different points in time, and that there is no one 'right' way of working with clients. Drawing on phenomenology (Chapter 2, this volume), the pluralistic approach also holds that therapists should bracket their assumptions about what might be best for clients, and instead dialogue with clients about what *they* might find most helpful. On this basis (and in contrast to a purist existential standpoint) the pluralistic perspective holds that clients may find a range of different methods and understandings helpful in therapy – *existential or otherwise* – and that therapists should work collaboratively with their clients to identify the most suitable way of working. This does not mean that existential therapists should be proficient in every therapeutic approach going – clearly that would not be possible. It does suggest, however, that existential therapists should be respectful and valuing of other therapeutic approaches; able to talk to clients about what they can offer them and whether it might be helpful for them; and willing to refer on as and where appropriate (see Box 7.4).

Box 7.4   For whom might existential therapy be most helpful?

From a pluralistic standpoint, some clients (at some points in time) are likely to find existential therapy more helpful than others. So who is existential therapy most suited for? Based on a review of existential understandings and methods (Cooper, 2015: 207–208), and building on van Deurzen's (2012a) work, I have suggested that it might be most appropriate for clients who:

- Want to be engaged with on an 'equal' level, as a fellow, intelligible human being.
- Want to gain insight and understanding of their experiences rather than 'cure'.
- Want to develop a greater sense of their freedom and possibilities, and make more active choices in life.
- Accept that there are limitations to their lives, and want to work out the best way of thriving despite them.
- Want to develop a greater sense of meaning and purpose in life.
- Want to improve their interpersonal relationships and interpersonal understandings.
- Have a somewhat melancholic or pessimistic worldview, and feel comfortable with seeing the world in that way.
- Want to experience the full spectrum of human emotions: the downs as well as the ups.

Along these lines, we could also ask about the kinds of *practitioners* for whom working in an existential way may be most suited. Research, for example, indicates that existential therapists come to the approach because it fits their outlook in life: for instance, an attraction to philosophy and not seeing things in a deterministic way (Smith, Burr, & Leeming, 2015).

Moreover, a pluralistic approach suggests that it can be legitimate for existential therapists to draw on ideas and methods from non-existential orientations (just as non-existential therapists may want to draw on existential ones). From this pluralistic-existential standpoint, the key question is whether these choices emerge dialogically – with the client's active involvement in these 'metatherapeutic' decisions (see Cooper, Dryden, Martin, & Papayianni, 2016) – or whether they are solely the therapist's choice. From a pluralistic standpoint, then, the use of cognitive or behavioural methods, with a client who actively wants to engage with these techniques, may be more 'existential' than imposing phenomenological or existential methods on an unwilling or compliant client. This pluralistic approach can be criticised on the grounds that what clients say they want may not be what they need. However, if client intelligibility is assumed (see Chapter 6, this volume), as well as their rights to make choices for themselves, then attending to clients' explicitly-stated wants may be an important component of an existentially-informed therapy.

So what would a pluralistically-based existential therapy look like in the work with Siân? To a great extent, its distinctive features are likely to be most evident early on in the therapeutic process. For a start, in an initial session, the therapist would be likely to spend some time working out with Siân if an existential approach was suitable for her (see Box 7.4). In that session, Siân might also be asked about her goals for therapy, and also the ways in which she thought she might be most likely to get there. Would Siân, for instance, prefer a more directive approach from the therapist, or would she like therapy to progress at her own pace? And would Siân want her therapist to be supportive and gentle, or would she prefer a more challenging and confrontational approach? Based on Siân's answers, the therapist would then try to tailor their way of working with Siân – always practising within their own competences and understandings of what might be helpful. As part of this pluralistic process, the therapist might also invite Siân to regularly review her sense of progress and whether she felt she was getting from the existential work what she wanted. This might involve the use of 'outcome measures' such as the CORE-OM (Connell et al., 2007), to help clients reflect on their levels of wellbeing, or 'process measures' such as the Session Rating Scale (Duncan, Miller, Sparks, & Claud, 2003), to provide a means of reflecting on the therapeutic alliance.

Conclusion

Today, developments within the existential-phenomenological approach are forming the basis for a 'radical existential therapy' (van Deurzen-Smith, 1995b). This is one that moves away from diagnosis and pathologisation towards an exploration of the client's lived-world and their problems in living. In the UK alone, different versions of this radical approach have emerged. Some, like van Deurzen, take a more philosophically-informed stance, while others, like Spinelli, adopt a more relational and experiential style. But all these approaches have a similar goal: of helping clients be more conscious of how they are in the world, and how they might find different – and potentially more fulfilling – ways of doing things.

Questions for reflection

- If, as a philosophical existential-phenomenological therapist, you were going to give your clients three top tips on the art of living, what would they be?
- Think of a client you are currently working with. What sedimented assumptions might they have about self, others and their world? In what ways might you be able to work with them on this?
- What do you think would be important to consider in offering existential therapy to clients in a short-term context?
- At what points in therapy do you talk to clients about what they want from, and prefer in, the therapeutic work? Do you think it would be helpful to do this more?

Recommended resources

Introductory and general texts

Cohn, H. W. (1997). *Existential thought and therapeutic practice: An introduction to existential psychotherapy*. London: Sage.
Popular, brief text that lays out the foundations of an existential-phenomenological approach and compares it with psychodynamic therapy.

Cooper, M. (2012). *Existential counselling primer*. Ross-on-Wye: PCCS Books.
Succinct and accessible introduction to existential practice from an existential-phenomenological perspective. See also Adams' (2013) *A concise introduction to existential counselling* (London: Sage), and Iacovou and Weixel-Dixon's (2015) *Existential therapy: 100 key points and techniques* (London: Routledge).

du Plock (Ed.). (2016). *Case studies in existential therapy: Translating theory into practice*. Ross-on-Wye: PCCS Books.
Case studies of contemporary existential-phenomenological practice, covering such diverse areas as dream analysis, work with transgendered clients, and existential equine therapy.

Langdridge, D. (2012). *Existential counselling and psychotherapy*. London: Sage.
Rich and well-informed introduction to an existential-phenomenological approach, including an exploration of power, politics and language.

van Deurzen, E. (2014). Existential therapy. In W. Dryden & A. Reeves (Eds.), *The handbook of individual therapy* (4th ed., pp. 155–178). London: Sage.
Brief and clearly structured introduction to existential therapy, as viewed from a philosophical existential-phenomenological standpoint.

van Deurzen, E. (Ed.). (in press). Existential phenomenological therapy. Section 2 in *World handbook of existential therapy*. London: Wiley.
In-depth series of chapters on the key ideas and practices of the existential-phenomenological approach.

Existential Analysis (formerly known as *The Journal of the Society for Existential Analysis*). Twice-yearly journal that publishes a range of scholarly, practical and engaging papers on all aspects of existential therapy and philosophy. Available through the Society of Existential Analysis (see contacts).

Philosophical existential-phenomenological therapy

van Deurzen, E. (2010). *Everyday mysteries: A handbook of existential psychotherapy* (2nd ed.). London: Routledge.
In-depth presentation of van Deurzen's therapeutic approach, with a particular focus on the philosophical and therapeutic foundations of her work. The second most influential text, after Yalom (1980), on existential-phenomenological practice (Correia et al., 2014a).

van Deurzen, E. (2012). *Existential counselling and psychotherapy in practice* (3rd ed.). London: Sage.
Classic introduction to van Deurzen's existential approach: practical, accessible and illustrated throughout with illuminating and evocative case studies and examples of therapist–client dialogue. Ranked fourth in most influential existential-phenomenological texts (Correia et al., 2014a).

van Deurzen, E. (2015). *Paradox and passion in psychotherapy: An existential approach* (2nd ed.). Chichester: John Wiley.
Personal, passionate and well-illustrated presentation of existential ideas and practices, emphasising the importance of facing the challenges and paradoxes of life to forge an existence that is vibrant and full.

van Deurzen, E., & Adams, M. (2016). *Skills in existential counselling and psychotherapy* (2nd ed.). London: Sage.
Practical guide to philosophical existential counselling, with a range of reflective exercises.

Relational existential-phenomenological therapy

Spinelli, E. (1994/2006). *Demystifying therapy*. Ross-on-Wye: PCCS Books.
Highly accessible and popular critique of commonly-held assumptions within the therapeutic world – such as the existence of an 'unconscious' – outlining a range of existential-phenomenological alternatives.

Spinelli, E. (1997/2006). *Tales of un-knowing: Therapeutic encounters from an existential perspective*. Ross-on-Wye: PCCS Books.
A compelling, moving and insightful collection of case studies that reveals something of the warmth, humour and humility of Spinelli's therapeutic approach. An excellent introduction to his work and the existential therapies in general.

(Continued)

(Continued)

Spinelli, E. (2014). *Practising existential psychotherapy: The relational world* (2nd ed.). London: Sage.

First published in 2007, this is already ranked as the third most influential text on practice across the existential field (Correia et al., 2014a). Original, complex, yet highly practical, this is the definitive guide to Spinelli's relational existential-phenomenological approach.

Brief existential therapies

Rayner, M., & Vitali, D. (2015). Short-term existential psychotherapy in primary care: A quantitative report. *Journal of Humanistic Psychology*. Advance online publication.

Brief review of, and evidence for, existential experimentation.

Strasser, F., & Strasser, A. (1997) *Existential time-limited therapy*. Chichester: John Wiley and Sons.

Presents Strasser and Strasser's time-limited existential model. Due to be updated by Alison Strasser.

Existential therapy and pluralism

Cooper, M. (2015). *Existential psychotherapy and counselling: Contributions to a pluralistic practice*. London: Sage.

Detailed, practical guide to existential understandings and methods, framed from within a pluralistic stance. Includes video and online resources.

8

DIMENSIONS OF EXISTENTIAL THERAPEUTIC PRACTICE

This chapter discusses:

- Key commonalities across the existential therapies.
- Key dimensions across which the existential therapies vary:

  - Knowing–Un-knowing
  - Directive–Non-directive
  - Explanatory–Descriptive
  - Pathologising–De-pathologising
  - Technique-based–Non-technique-based
  - Immediacy orientated–Extra-therapeutically orientated
  - Philosophically orientated–Psychologically orientated
  - Individualising–Universalising
  - Subjective–Inter-worldly.

Ending with Siân

Drawing the work with Siân to a close gives an opportunity to reflect on what it tells us about the existential therapies, and how they compare and contrast.

In the final few sessions of therapy, Siân begins to talk more about the future. She decides that she *does* want to work on things in her relationship with Hanako, and to try to be more proactive with her. 'I can see,' she says, 'that some of what I was doing was driving Hanako up the wall. I was just acting like a stroppy teen.' Siân is uncertain about whether things will work out, and open to the idea that the relationship may come to a close, but she wants to try as hard as she can. She says, 'I know that Hanako really loves me and cares for me; and also with Kai. I don't want to just chuck that away.' As for Rachel, Siân says that she wants to 'put things on hold' for now. 'It's – she's a lovely woman but it's not going to go anywhere, and Hanako and Kai are what I need to think about.'

In terms of career, Siân still feels a bit despondent, but at least is now more aware of what *isn't* right for her. 'I know,' she says, 'that I have to get away from the web work. It's driving me crazy.' In the penultimate session, Siân says that she is planning to enrol on an introductory course to music therapy: a way, she feels, of combining her love of music with her love of working with kids. 'And,' says Siân with a grin, 'I still get to be a child!'

In the last session of therapy, Siân is asked what she feels that she got out of it. She says:

> I think the main thing was just learning to grow up a lot. I was – I feel like I came into therapy still a child, still mucking about and it – it made me look at what *I* need to do to make things different. It's not that I *don't* want to be a child; just that I need to be an adult sometimes as well and do difficult adult things.
>
> It was like – in the therapy it was someone holding your hand while you work out what to do, but also, kind of, encouraging you to do it. It did make me feel a lot stronger. More able to be 'me' whatever anyone else thought or wanted. It wasn't some kind of magic solution, but I – I do feel I know myself better: know what triggers me and saddens me and also what I can do to feel better. I'm not there yet but at least I have some sense of where I want to go.
>
> I still feel that elephant sitting and shitting on my head sometimes – no doubt – and I do get to feeling overwhelmed; but it does feel a bit lighter now and I think I get less panicked – I can still breathe. It's a godawful horrible stench sometimes but – and maybe sometimes now I just say, *'and that's the way the world is'*. A godawful horrible stench of elephant dung but, you know, I'm OK, I kind of feel more able to face it.

Siân's description of what she got out of existential therapy encapsulates many of the shared aims of the existential approaches (see Box 8.1). Each of them encouraged Siân to acknowledge, and 'own', her capacity for choice – to encounter the world from the position of an agentic adult. They also encouraged Siân to 'stay with' and learn from her more distressing feelings: for instance, her anger, her fears of being judged by the therapist, and her deep sense of isolation. Each of the existential approaches also encouraged Siân to understand more about her present experiences, and to work out what she wanted to do for the future. Through all this different work, each of the existential therapies aimed to help Siân understand more about her being in the world, and to live more in tune with her genuine experiences, values and wants.

Box 8.1   Shared existential practices

In summary, the following practices tend to be shared across the existential approaches:

- The aim of the therapeutic work is to help clients become more authentic: to become more aware of their actual existence, and to live more in accordance with their true values, beliefs and experiences.
- Therapists tend to work with the concrete actuality of clients' experiences, rather than viewing these experiences in terms of abstract or hypothetical constructs.
- Clients are encouraged to acknowledge, and act on, their freedom and responsibility.

- Clients are encouraged to acknowledge, accept and learn from the more 'negative' feelings, such as anxiety, guilt, despair and a sense of tragedy.
- Clients are encouraged to explore their present and future experiences, as well as their past ones.
- Clients are encouraged to explore all aspects of their being – emotions, beliefs, behaviours, physiological responses, etc. – and to see these aspects as fundamentally interconnected.
- Therapists tend to be relatively genuine and direct with their clients, rather than adopting the role of a blank screen.
- Flexibility and adaptability of practice tend to be emphasised over fixed and immovable boundaries.

However, there were also differences in how each of the existential therapies approached the work with Siân. In daseinsanalysis, she was provided with a supportive, reflective space to explore her experiences, and to develop a deeper trust and openness towards others and her world. In meaning-centred therapy, by contrast, she was encouraged towards identifying meanings and purposes in her life. Existential-humanistic therapy aimed to help her be more present and real, and to acknowledge the existential given of choice, while a 'Laingian' approach challenged her to be more honest in her interactions with others. In philosophical existential-phenomenological therapy, Siân was encouraged to accept the limitations and paradoxes of being, while the relational existential-phenomenological approach aimed to help her understand more of how she constructed self, other and relating. Elements of all these change processes can be seen in how Siân described the outcomes of the work, suggesting that they are compatible – rather than mutually exclusive – aims, which can be integrated together in an existential practice.

Dimensions of existential practice

Another way of looking at these differences across the existential therapies is to think of them as *dilemmas of practice*. That is, rather than thinking of each of these different existential therapies as discrete practices, we can think of them as varying from each other along a range of dimensions (see Table 8.1). This may be more helpful for the individual existential practitioner, who can then consider where they would position themselves across each of these dimensions, rather than having to subscribe to one particular model of existential therapy.

Knowing–Un-knowing

Perhaps the most fundamental dimension across the existential therapies is the extent to which they encounter clients holding a range of assumptions

Table 8.1 Dimensions of existential therapies (informed by Correia et al., 2016c)

Knowing	meaning-cen.	van Deurzen ex.-humanistic daseinsanalysis Laing	Spinelli	Un-knowing
Directive	meaning-cen.	Laing daseinsanalysis ex.-humanistic van Deurzen	Spinelli	Non-directive
Explanatory		daseinsanalysis ex.-humanistic meaning-cen.	ex.-phenomen. Laing	Descriptive
Pathologising	meaning-cen. daseinsanalysis	ex.-humanistic	Laing ex.-phenomen.	De-pathologising
Technique-based	meaning-cen.	ex.-humanistic	daseinsanalysis ex.-phenomen. Laing	Non-technique-based
Immediacy orientated	ex.-humanistic Laing Spinelli	daseinsanalysis	meaning-cen. van Deurzen	Extra-therapeutically orientated
Philosophically orientated	van Deurzen	meaning-cen.	daseinsanalysis ex.-humanistic Laing	Psychologically orientated
Individualising	ex.-humanistic daseinsanalysis Laing	meaning-cen.	van Deurzen	Universalising
Subjective	ex.-humanistic Laing	van Deurzen meaning-cen.	daseinsanalysis Spinelli	Inter-worldly

Note: meaning-cen. = meaning-centred; ex.-humanistic = existential-humanistic, ex.-phenomen. = existential-phenomenological

and beliefs, as opposed to encountering clients from a position of openness and 'un-knowing'. In meaning-centred therapy, for instance, the therapist worked with Siân, assuming that she needed to find meanings in her life and that there were meanings to be found. Similarly, the existential-humanistic therapist assumed that she, like all of us, had a fundamental fear of acknowledging her freedom, and that this might be underlying her problems. By contrast, the relational existential-phenomenological therapist tended to offer Siân a more open-ended exploration of her experiences, striving to hold any fixed assumptions in abeyance. To some extent, this knowing–un-knowing dimension maps onto an 'existential–phenomenological' dimension, with the knowing-based therapists applying a set of existential assumptions to their clients, and the un-knowing-based therapists aiming to bracket all assumptions, including existential ones. However, as phenomenological inquiry can also include an eidetic and transcendental search for universal essences (see Chapter 2, this volume), these dimensions are not entirely synonymous.

For those approaches that do tend to orientate the therapeutic work around certain existential assumptions, there are also a number of dimensions along which these assumptions sit. First, there is a contrast between those therapies that encourage clients to discover the meaning and purpose of their lives (for instance, Frankl, 1986), as opposed to those approaches which encourage clients to accept that life is devoid of intrinsic meanings (e.g., Yalom, 2001). Second, there are those approaches that encourage clients to face their fundamental aloneness (e.g., Yalom, 1980), in contrast to those approaches that encourage clients to acknowledge their fundamental being-ness-with-others (e.g., Cohn, 1997). Third, there are those approaches that encourage clients to face up to their existence with resolution and fortitute (e.g., May, 1958), in contrast to those approaches that put greater emphasis on helping clients adopt an attitude of openness, contemplation and *gelassenheit* (e.g., Boss, 1963).

Directive–Non-directive

A second, closely related dimension (and one that underlies many variations across the wider therapy field; Cooper & Norcross, 2015) is the extent to which the therapeutic approach is directive. This is the degree to which it 'influences the therapy process and content, by raising issues, asking questions, and suggesting content as opposed to encouraging the client to choose his or her own topics and modes of processing' (Sachse & Elliott, 2002: 89). Hence, for instance, in meaning-centred therapy, Siân was specifically directed to think about what was meaningful to her, and in a philosophical existential-phenomenological approach, she was encouraged to face her fears of telling Hanako about Rachel. By contrast, in the relational existential-phenomeno-logical approach, there was no specific guidance about how she might move forward in her life or, indeed, use the therapeutic time.

As this suggests, this directive–non-directive dimension is closely related to the knowing–un-knowing dimension, in that those approaches that assume certain existential 'truths' incorporate, by their very nature, an element of directivity. At the same time, however, they are not synonymous: in a 'not-knowing' way of working, for instance, clients might still be directed to explore certain aspects of their experiencing.

To some extent, the location of the different existential therapies on this directive–non-directive dimension is related to their views about the unconscious and self-deception. The more that an existential therapist believes that clients *repress* their true concerns into their unconscious (for instance, Yalom, 1980) – as opposed to simply being *reluctant* to face what they know to be true (for instance, van Deurzen, 2012a) – the more they are likely to feel that direction and challenge are necessary to 'unearth' clients' real experiences. Where therapists sit on this dimension is also likely to be related to their views on therapeutic growth. If, for instance, therapists believe that clients *can* move towards a 'better' way of being, and have some sense of what that way of being is (for instance, Schneider & May, 1995c), then they are more likely to feel that it is legitimate to point their clients in that particular direction. If, on the other hand, they hold that life will always be a struggle between polarities (e.g., van Deurzen, 2012a), and make few assumptions about the best way to live (e.g., Spinelli, 2001), then they are less likely to want to point their clients in any particular direction.

Explanatory–Descriptive

A third dimension across the existential therapies is the extent to which they encourage clients to look for reasons and explanations for how they have come to think, feel and behave in the way that they do (for instance, Yalom, 2001), as opposed to facilitating a descriptive exploration of their lived-experiences (e.g., Spinelli, 2006b). With respect to the former, for example, an existential-humanistic therapist might suggest to Siân that her playfulness and self-depreciation are a means of avoiding making adult choices in her life, while the relational existential-phenomenological therapist may just accompany Siân on a descriptive exploration of these experiences. This, again, is quite similar to the knowing–un-knowing dimension – in the sense that therapists who adopt an un-knowing stance are more likely to work descriptively – but a therapist who works from certain assumptions will not necessarily use those assumptions to try to explain the client's experiences (for instance, Cohn, 1997).

For those existential therapies that are more explanatory, there are also dimensions across which they vary. Along psychodynamic lines, some of the existential therapists discussed in this book tend to account for present experiences in terms of childhood experiences (Laing, 1976b; May, 1969a). In the case of the meaning-centred therapies, however, explanations may primarily be in terms of future fears or hopes. Explanations may also be offered in terms of underlying fears or concerns in the present. As we have seen, for instance, Yalom (1980, 2001) may account for a client's preoccupation with sex in terms of their fear of death, or their desire for attention in terms of a fear of isolation.

In contrast with other forms of therapy, such as psychoanalysis, however, it should be noted that all of the existential therapies tend to sit fairly close to the descriptive end of the descriptive–explanatory spectrum. Indeed, even Yalom (2001), drawing on the empirical evidence, acknowledges that clients generally value his intellectual interpretations far less than he does.

Pathologising–De-pathologising

Following on from this is the extent to which the existential approaches tend to construe clients' difficulties in terms of individual 'pathologies' and 'disorders' (e.g., Holzhey-Kunz & Fazekas, 2012), as opposed to more universal 'problems in living' (e.g., van Deurzen, 2012a). With Siân, for instance, the existential-humanistic therapist introduces into the therapy the idea that her jokiness may be a defence against the reality of her freedom, while a relational existential-phenomenological therapist would be more likely to withhold any assumptions about the functionality or dysfunctionality of her current behaviour. Those at the pathologising end of this spectrum are more likely to draw on diagnostic terms in their therapeutic work and thinking, and may also be more ready to make judgements about their clients' ways of being. For instance, the contemporary Austrian logotherapist Lilo Tutsch (2003) writes about clients with 'narcissistic personality disturbance', describing such individuals as pushy, impenetrable, superficial, childish and naïve.

Technique-based–Non-technique-based

A fifth dimension along which the existential therapies vary is the extent to which they draw on specific therapy methods and techniques, as opposed to encountering the client in a more natural, dialogical way. Techniques can be defined as 'well-defined therapeutic procedures implemented to accomplish a particular task or goal' (Cooper, 2008a: 127). With respect to the former, for instance, the existential-humanistic therapist introduced an embodied meditation exercise into the work with Siân, and a meaning-centred therapist might have invited her to describe her life as a film. By contrast, with the Laingian-style therapist, there were no specific procedures that were implemented. Rather, the therapeutic work took the form of a free-flowing dialogue. Again, however, in contrast to other therapeutic approaches, all of the existential therapies – apart from the meaning-centred approaches – tend to be at the relatively non-technique-based end of this dimension.

Immediacy orientated–Extra-therapeutically orientated

A sixth dimension across the existential therapies is the extent to which the work focuses on the immediate here-and-now therapeutic relationship. In the existential-humanistic, 'Laingian' and relational existential-phenomenological work with Siân, we saw how the therapist brought the focus of the dialogue specifically on the client–therapist interaction. These approaches also tend to put greater emphasis on therapist self-disclosure. In contrast, in the meaning-centred and philosophical existential-phenomenological approaches there was less of a direct focus on this interaction – though it is unlikely that either would avoid it if it specifically emerged.

Philosophically orientated–Psychologically orientated

A further dimension along which the existential therapies vary is the extent to which the therapeutic process is seen as an exploration of psychological experiences and processes, as opposed to a more philosophical exploration of how to live life in a constructive and meaningful way. Despite being based on philosophical principles, most of the existential therapies tend towards the former, psychological focus. Indeed, the daseinsanalyst Holzhey-Kunz (2014) is very critical of the explicit use of philosophical ideas in a therapeutic conversation. However, as we saw in the work with Siân, the philosophical existential-phenomenological approach – as the name suggests – tends to bring in a consideration of wider philosophical issues, such as whether or not it is possible for people to get what they want without making choices.

This psychological–philosophical dimension can also be conceptualised in terms of those approaches that tend towards encouraging clients to explore their emotions (e.g., Schneider & May, 1995c), as opposed to those approaches that place an equal, or greater, emphasis on encouraging clients to explore the world of values and meanings (e.g., van Deurzen, 2012a). Does the therapist, for instance, principally encourage Siân to look at what she *felt* when she was at the doctors with Hanako and Kai, or does the therapist encourage her to look more at her *beliefs* or values in this situation?

Individualising–Universalising

This leads on to a closely related, but not identical, dimension: the extent to which the therapeutic approach encourages clients to focus in on the individual, personal dimensions of their experiences, as opposed to the more universal, transpersonal dimensions. Again, most of the existential therapies tend to emphasise the former but, as we saw with Siân, van Deurzen's approach brings in broader questions about the nature of living and being *per se*.

Subjective–Inter-worldly

A final dimension, related to the individualising–universalising one, is the extent to which the therapeutic approach encourages clients to focus *in* on their personal, subjective experiences, as opposed to focusing *out* on their in-the-world contextual and intersubjective experiences. The relational existential-phenomenological work with Siân is an example of the latter, where she was encouraged to reflect on her assumptions about Hanako's relationships with others. Another example of this inter-worldly focus is the logo-therapeutic technique of dereflection, where clients are specifically encouraged to take their attention off themselves.

While those existential therapists who adopt a more subjectivist standpoint tend to want to help clients get in touch with their own needs, those therapists who adopt a more inter-worldly and intersubjective standpoint may also be interested in helping clients get in touch with the experiences and needs of others. In addition, such therapists may be keen to help clients explore their ethical responsibilities towards others in their lives.

Discussion

Although nine dimensions of existential practice have been presented here, the first five of these can be seen as manifestations of a more generic *hard–soft* dimension (Cooper, 2008b), or what Meg-John Barker (personal communication, 2014) has termed a *firm–gentle* dimension. Here, at the former end, are those existential therapists who work in relatively directive and challenging ways, bringing in more assumptions, interpretations and existential techniques into their work. At the latter end, by contrast, are those existential therapists who work in a relatively non-directive and gentle way, staying closer to the client's own narrative, pace and phenomenological experiencing. Similarly, the latter three of these nine dimensions can be clustered together into a more generic *intrapersonal–interpersonal* factor, with some existential therapists tending to focus *in* on the clients' experiences, and others focus *out* on their relationship to the world.

Of course, in mapping out the existential therapies along the dimensions discussed in these chapters, there are some important caveats to bear in mind. First, there is inevitably a great deal of variation within the different approaches, such that practitioners within the same school can only be very loosely located at one particular point on these dimensions. Second, even within a single practitioner's practice, there is likely to be a great deal of variation, such that they might be quite hard and challenging with one client, but soft and gentle with the next, and even varying with the same client at different points in time. Hence, rather than identifying particular existential approaches or therapists at specific points on these spectra, it is probably more helpful to suggest that each of them is likely to cover particular 'scopes' across each of these dimensions. That is, there are a range of ways in which they would be willing to work, but some things that they would not be willing to stretch to. For instance, an existential-phenomenological therapist may be able to work from being very descriptive to fairly explanatory, but would not be willing to practise at the wholly explanatory end of the dimension.

As suggested earlier, it may also be useful to think about these different dimensions as practice *dilemmas*. That is, just as human beings are consistently pulled between the poles of different tensions (see Chapter 7, this volume), so existential therapists – indeed, all therapists – are consistently pulled between various dilemmas of practice. For example, 'Should I offer the client an explanation here or stay working descriptively?' or 'Should I bring in the here-and-now relationship or keep the focus on extra-therapeutic issues?' Here, as with life tensions, there may be no 'right' answers, and no easy resolutions – just an ongoing pull between different opportunities and possibilities. However, it is important to note that, from a pluralistic existential-phenomenological standpoint (see Chapter 7, this volume), such practice dilemmas are tensions that therapists and clients can face *together*. That is, therapists can lay out the options to clients and find out what their clients would prefer. A therapist might ask, for instance, 'Would it be helpful to try to understand this by focusing on what goes on between us, or would it make more sense to explore things outside therapy?' In this way, the dimensions identified above become opportunities for both therapists and clients to think through how they would like to work, and to find a style of existential practice that is of greatest benefit to the client at that particular moment in time.

Question for reflection

On each of the dimensions below, circle the scope within which you would feel comfortable practising. For instance, if you would be willing to work entirely from a place of knowing, and also entirely from a place of un-knowing (and anywhere in between), then circle the whole line. However, if you would only work from an un-knowing stance, circle that end of the dimension.

Take some time to reflect, and perhaps discuss with a partner, what you have circled and why. Why are you comfortable with some areas of existential practice and not others?

Knowing	Not knowing
Directive	Non-directive
Explanatory	Descriptive
Pathologising	De-pathologising
Techniques	Not techniques
Immediacy	Non-immediacy
Psychological	Philosophical
Individualising	Universalising
Subjective	Inter-worldly

9

DISCUSSION: CHALLENGES AND POSSIBILITIES FOR THE EXISTENTIAL THERAPIES

This chapter discusses:

- The extent to which the existential therapy field has met the challenges set out in the 2003 edition of this book.
- Moves towards greater convergence, internationally, of the existential therapies.
- The opportunity for local variants of existential thought and practice to emerge.
- The challenge of clarifying what existential therapists actually do.
- The challenge of developing the evidence base for the existential therapies.
- The challenge of exploring and articulating the kinds of clients that might be most helped by existential therapies.
- The challenge of developing existential work across difference and diversity.

In the 2003 edition of this book, I identified five challenges facing existential therapy in the years ahead. So how has the existential field fared?

1. *Demonstrating therapeutic efficacy.* Recent years have seen a growth in the evaluations of existential practice (e.g., Rayner & Vitali, 2015), as well as attempts to draw the research evidence together (e.g., Vos et al., 2014). However, this remains an ongoing challenge for the existential field (see below).
2. *Establishing a dialogue with other approaches.* Recent years have seen attempts to combine existential therapy with a range of approaches, including solution-focused therapy (Langdridge, 2006), CBT (Hickes & Mirea, 2012; Wolfe, 2008) and mindfulness (Nanda, 2012). However, extended dialogues with other orientations, exploring commonalities and differences, remain relatively limited.
3. *Postmodernism.* In 2003, I wrote that postmodern thought was increasingly penetrating the world of therapy. I think I was wrong. With the emergence of the evidence-based therapies movement, the present challenges to the existential field would seem to come more from the modernist direction than the postmodernist one.
4. *Unpacking existential thought.* A wealth of ideas from existential philosophy remains untapped. Perhaps the more pressing concern today, however, is to understand what it is that existential therapists actually do, and the particular aspects of this that are helpful (see below).
5. *A new openness.* In recent years, there has been a growing recognition among existential writers that 'there is no one way of being an existential thinker, and it is this very diversity and difference that is the life-blood of the existential therapeutic field' (Cooper, 2003: 151). I would like to think that the first edition of this book has made some contribution to this increased openness in the field, along with other developments, such as the World Congress of Existential Therapy.

So what are the challenges and opportunities for the existential field, today, in 2016? Below are some of the key issues that I, personally, believe the existential field will face as it moves forward into its future.

An evolving international consensus?

This book is founded on the principle that the existential field consists of several distinctive therapeutic practices. However, in recent years, there seems to be something of a coming-together of the different existential schools, and an increasing blurring of the boundaries between them. Längle's existential analysis (Chapter 4, this volume), for instance, has taken logotherapy in a direction that is closer to the existential-phenomenological school (Chapter 7). Similarly, Kirk Schneider's recent work – with its relatively descriptive, de-pathologising stance – also brings the existential-humanistic approach towards a more existential-phenomenological understanding (Chapter 5). Indeed, interestingly, in recent debates within the World Confederation of Existential Therapy about a definition of existential therapy, differences have been as much *within* schools as it has been *between* them.

A number of drivers may be behind this coming-together. First is the growing ease of international communication – through, for instance, email and social media – which may have helped to foster links and exchanges between existential authors and schools across national boundaries. Second is the publication of texts such as *Existential Therapy: Legacy, Vibrancy and Dialogue* (Barnett & Madison, 2012), and the *World Handbook of Existential Therapy* (Ed. van Deurzen, in press), which bring together authors from a range of schools. Third, and very importantly, was the founding of a World Confederation of Existential Therapy in 2015 – along with its international congress – which aims to 'foster communication between existential therapists throughout the world' (www.existentialpsychotherapy.net/). Closely linked to this is the establishment of existential societies and training institutes around the globe, which allows more opportunities for the interfacing and intermingling of different existential traditions.

What might a more universal existential practice look like? Given the current predominance of the existential-phenomenological and existential analysis traditions, it would likely have a strong emphasis on the quality of the therapeutic relationship, and on helping clients to phenomenologically explore their lived-worlds. Therapists would draw from existential understandings and insights – and be ready to introduce them into the therapeutic dialogue – but they would probably not use them in a strongly interpretative or directive way.

Should such a convergence of the existential therapies take place, the one approach that might remain outside this integrative perspective would be the more structured meaning-centred interventions (Chapter 4, this volume). Indeed, for the future, it is possible to envision a bifurcated existential field with, on the one hand, a set of exploratory, relational, existential-phenomenological therapies and, on the other, a set of structured, empirically-based, meaning-centred programmes for specific client groups. Research, as discussed in Chapter 4 (this volume), already indicates that meaning-centred practices stand somewhat apart from other existential therapies (Correia et al., 2016c), and it is quite possible that this separation will widen for the foreseeable future.

At the same time, it must be acknowledged that evidence in support of the meaning-centred therapies – particularly those targeted to particular groups of clients – is striking (see Chapter 4, this volume). Maybe it will turn out that these findings are spurious, or that they are the product of *allegiance effects* (Luborsky et al., 1999), whereby researchers 'prove' the effectiveness of therapies that they, themselves, are aligned with. However, as things stand, there is compelling evidence to suggest that helping clients to find meaning and direction in their lives – through relatively structured and directive methods – can be of considerable value, and this finding is consistent with the well-established link between the presence of meaning in life and wellbeing. This suggests that, for the wider existential field, it may be a mistake to maintain too great a separation from the meaning-centred practices. Rather, for the non-meaning-centred existential therapies, there may be much to learn from the structured meaning-centred programmes, just as meaning-centred therapies (through, for instance, the work of Längle) have been enriched by the incorporation of more relational and phenomenological methods.

The development of local variations of existential thought and practice

While the existential field may see greater convergence in the future, the development of local variants of existential thought and practice is, perhaps, one of the most exciting advances at the present time (see, for instance, Box 5.1 on *zhi mian* and Box 7.1 on *oistros*). Developments of this type open up a whole range of possibilities. What, for instance, might a Portuguese-specific existential therapy look like, or an existential-phenomenological approach informed by Siberian culture and history? Not only can such developments help to ensure that existential therapy is tailored to specific cultures, but also they can generate new ideas and practices that could contribute to the work of existential therapists globally.

In the coming years, then, it is possible that the existential field might see the emergence of a highly constructive dialectical process. This would consist of increasing communication and interchange at the school and international level (as above), but fed by increasing differentiation and generation of new ideas at the local one. For this to happen, however, it will be imperative that any convergence of the existential schools does not become a *standardisation* of what existential therapy is, or a *mandate* to practise in any one particular way. As van Deurzen and Adams (2011: 3) write, 'It is crucial to the future freedom of existential therapy that no one single form of existential therapy should be seen as the standard or definitive way of practising.' Rather, the existential field might benefit from encouraging local variation and innovation, while at the same time providing fora – such as the World Congress for Existential Therapy – where these new ideas and methods can be discussed and integrated.

What do existential therapists actually do?

Alongside developing definitions and models of existential practice, an essential challenge for the future will be to develop a better understanding of what existential therapy actually looks like – or could look like – in practice. It is one thing, for instance, to talk about the Heideggerian roots of existential therapy, or to develop new concepts like *oistros*, but what will be essential to show is how these ideas translate into actual clinical practices. To some extent, movement in this direction has started to take place. Over the last decade, for instance, a number of books have provided a clear and concrete description of actual existential work (e.g., Adams, 2013; Cooper, 2015; Spinelli, 2015; van Deurzen & Adams, 2016). More importantly, perhaps, existential researchers have started to look at what actually takes place in existential therapy: interviewing and surveying therapists about their practice (Correia, 2015; Wilkes & Milton, 2006), interviewing clients about their experiences in existential therapy (Olivereira, Sousa, & Pires, 2012), and analysing actual therapy transcripts (Alegria et al., 2016; Correia, 2015). However, there is a need for such work to continue, and analysing transcripts or video recordings of actual existential therapy sessions – through, for instance, content or conversational analysis – would be a valuable means of pursuing this.

Conducting such research will be essential in being able to answer questions like: 'How do the schools of existential therapy differ from each other (if at all)?' and 'How does existential therapy differ from other therapeutic orientations (if at all)?' It could also serve as the basis for process-outcome research – both qualitative and quantitative – into the aspects of existential therapy that are more, or less, helpful for different clients. Clarifying the nature of existential practices in this way would be very helpful too for developing competences for existential therapies (e.g., Farber, 2010), which could then serve as the basis for training curricula. Of course, there is always the danger that such competence frameworks and curricula could end up becoming fixed and standardised 'manuals' of practice. But, developed with openness and flexibility, they could also become a means of communicating more clearly the nature of existential therapeutic work, and of incorporating innovative and helpful methods into an evolving existential framework.

Researching existential therapies

The evidence-based therapies movement has not gone away. Indeed, with developments such as the Improving Access to Psychological Therapies (IAPT) programme in the UK, there is probably more pressure now – more than ever before – for therapies to demonstrate the empirical validity of their work. There is also every reason to assume that these pressures will continue, or even intensify, for the foreseeable future (Cooper & Reeves, 2012).

This puts existential therapists in a difficult position. On the one hand, the mechanistic, nomothetic, medical-model assumptions behind most outcome research are antithetical to the very essence of existential thinking (Cooper, 2015; see Chapter 1, this volume). On the other hand, if existential therapists do not generate evidence to support their therapeutic practices, there is a very real danger that the existential therapies will be wiped from the face of publicly supported mental health care.

There are a range of responses that existential therapists can have to this tension, all of which have some degree of legitimisation from an existential standpoint. At one of the spectrum is a Heideggerian resolve to withstand the forces of reductionism and 'empiricalisation', and a refusal to engage with the evidence-based agenda whatever the cost. At the other end of the spectrum is an existential pragmatism, which holds that the benefits of making existential therapies publicly available are worth the cost of compromising some epistemological ground. Between these two positions are a range of other stances (see Finlay, 2012). Some existential therapists, for instance, have looked towards research methods that are more compatible with an existential-phenomenological outlook – such as practice-based research (Finlay, 2012) or in-depth case studies (e.g., Schneider, 2001) – as a means of generating evidence for the approach. Another stance, consistent with a pluralistic existential perspective (see Chapter 7, this volume), is to consider positivist outcome research as just one of many methods – both empirical and non-empirical – that can be used to understand more about the process and value of therapy. Whatever way existential therapists choose to respond to the evidence-based therapy agenda, however, one thing is clear: not choosing is not an option.

For existential therapists, one of the limitations of the evidence-based agenda is that 'outcomes' are often defined in medical-model terms, such as reductions in symptoms. Research into the existential therapies, therefore, might benefit from the development and validation of measures that could evaluate the outcomes and processes of existential therapies in ways that are consistent with existential theory. For instance, Wood et al. (2008) have developed the Authenticity Scale, which assesses levels of self-alienation, authentic living, and resistance to external influence. Another 'existential-friendly' measure, as discussed in Chapter 4 (this volume), is the Existence Scale (Kundi, Wurst, & Längle, 2003), which assesses self-reported levels of freedom, responsibility, self-distancing and self-transcendence. New, creative methods for assessing outcomes may also be important developments, such as online tools or cognitive tasks, which can access deeper levels of existential meaning and lived-experiencing (Craig et al., 2016).

Another important area for research in the existential field will be to look at what clients find helpful, and unhelpful, in existential therapy (see, for instance, Olivereira et al., 2012). Qualitative methods such as Client Helpfulness Interview studies (Cooper & McLeod, 2015) may be very useful here, although quantitative methods, such as meta-analyses and process-outcome research, could also contribute to the development of this knowledge. Through such research, existential therapists would be supported to develop and refine their practices: evolving forms of existential therapy that helped more clients, more of the time.

For the future, the existential therapies might also benefit from drawing more fully from the psychological research (see, for instance, Cooper & Joseph, 2016). As we have seen in this book, for instance, there is a wealth of research on the relationship between meaning and wellbeing (Chapter 4), as well as on the effects of increased mortality salience (Chapter 5). Drawing on such evidence, again, could help existential therapists to evolve their practices, and to increase their fit for specific clients or client groups. Research, for instance, indicates that people who behave in antisocial ways tend to have lower meaning in life (Steger, 2013). Knowing this evidence, existential therapists may be particularly sensitised to issues around meaning and meaninglessness when working with clients from this group.

For whom might existential therapy be most helpful?

Linked to the above point, the existential therapies would almost certainly benefit from developing a clearer sense of whom, or for what kinds of issues, their approaches may be suited (see Box 7.4). Today, in public mental health-care, interventions are increasingly determined by the kind of problem being experienced (for instance, computerised cognitive behavioural therapy for 'persistent subthreshold depressive symptoms'; National Collaborating Centre for Mental Health, 2010). The existential therapies would not need to go down such a diagnosis-based route, but developing some kinds of indicators of whom the approach might be most helpful for would benefit clients, referrers, commissioners and existential therapists themselves.

Such indicators may be on a range of dimensions. For instance, *client issues* may be an important factor, with existential therapies, say, being most suited to clients who are experiencing existential crises, or facing such existential problems as death, choices or a lack of meaning. Another important factor might be *client characteristics*: for instance, existential therapies may be more suited to clients with a melancholic worldview, and less so for clients who are cheerily optimistic (see Box 7.4 and Chapter 7, this volume). Certainly, *client preferences* would also be important, with existential therapies, for instance, more suited to those clients who are looking for insight rather than cure (see Box 7.4 and Chapter 7, this volume).

Working across difference and diversity

We exist in a world in which issues of difference and diversity are becoming increasingly salient. Gender fluidity, migrant crises, transgenderism, disability rights, Islamophobia: these are all issues that psychotherapists and counsellors across the globe are increasingly likely to face. And, in many respects, the existential approach is ideally well-placed to help clients face them:

> Here, as with a 'social model' of disability (Crow, 1996), the emphasis is not on what is 'wrong' with the client. Rather, it is on the client's experiences as they confront a world that may oppress, objectify and discriminate against them. And, as the research suggests (e.g., Liddle, 1996), engaging with clients in such a de-pathologising way may be experienced as profoundly helpful, validating and empowering. (Cooper, 2015: 201)

To date, the involvement of existential therapists with issues of difference, diversity and social justice has been relatively limited. However, there are some encouraging shoots of growth. In particular, as discussed in Chapter 5 (this volume), there is the work of Louis Hoffman and other existential-humanistic colleagues on developing the multicultural dimensions of existential theory and practice (Hoffman, 2016; Hoffman et al., 2014; Schneider, 2008). In the UK existential community, too, there has been an increasing focus on such issues as sexuality and gender identity (e.g., Milton, 2014, see Chapter 7, this volume). Perhaps, in years to come, the existential approaches will not only be considering these issues, but leading the way in addressing them – that is, encouraging the counselling and psychotherapy field as a whole to value the uniqueness and difference of every client who we encounter, and to engage with them in deeply respectful and validating ways.

Conclusion

As stated in the introduction (Chapter 1), the aims of this book have been fourfold: first, to introduce readers to the rich tapestry of existential therapies; second, to provide readers with ideas and practices that they can incorporate into their own work; third, to help readers identify – and follow up – areas of existential therapy that are of particular interest to them; and fourth, to contribute to a range of debates within the existential therapy field. It is my hope that this book has achieved these aims and, in particular, has served to interest and stimulate readers in the existential field.

Today, the existential therapies face a range of challenges. There are calls to provide evidence that our work is effective, to specify what it is that we do, to understand more about why our work might be helpful, and to identify for whom our approaches may be most beneficial. And, to some extent, such challenges *are* challenges because they fly in the face of existential thinking, with its emphasis on understanding people in holistic, non-mechanistic, idiographic ways. Yet, at the heart of the existential approach is also an acknowledgement that being challenged is part of life and that, rather than shirk away, we should 'stand naked in the storm of life' and meet such challenges head on. Perhaps the greatest challenge for the existential therapies, then, is to remain open to the manifold pushes and pulls that currently confront us: to 'greet it festively' and say 'Now I am ready'. This involves an attitude of resolve – the courage to stay true to our radical agenda – but also a willingness to engage and dialogue with others, and to be creative and constructive in our responses. The existential field knows much but, as existential therapists, there is also much that we are committed to holding un-known. Sitting in this tension between resolution and openness, between confidence and humility, may be the most valuable place from which we can take the existential field forward.

Questions for reflection

- What do you see as the main challenges for the existential field in the coming years?
- To what extent do you think that existential therapists should strive to generate outcome evidence to support their work?
- For whom do you think existential therapy would be best suited?

REFERENCES

Adams, M. (2001). Practicing phenomenology: some reflections and considerations. *Journal of the Society for Existential Analysis, 12*(1), 65–84.

Adams, M. (2013). *A concise introduction to existential counselling.* London: Sage.

Alegria, S., Carvalho, I., Sousa, D., et al. (2016). Process and outcome research in existential psychotherapy. *Existential Analysis, 27*(1), 78–92.

Armor, D. E., & Taylor, S. E. (1998). Situated optimism: Specific outcome expectancies and self-regulation. In M. P. Zanna (Ed.), *Advances in experimental social psychology.* San Diego, CA: Academic Press.

Arndt, J., Cook, A., & Routledge, C. (2004). The blueprint of terror management. In J. Greenberg, S. L. Koole & T. Pyszczynski (Eds.), *Handbook of experimental existential psychology.* New York: Guilford Press.

Aronson, E., Wilson, T. D., & Akert, R. M. (1999). *Social psychology.* New York: Longman.

Ascher, L. M., & Pollard, C. A. (1983). Paradoxical intention. In J. Hariman (Ed.), *The therapeutic efficacy of the major psychotherapeutic techniques.* Springfield, IL: Charles C. Thomas.

Bargh, J. A. (2004). Being here now: Is consciousness necessary for human freedom? In J. Greenberg, S. L. Koole & T. Pyszczynski (Eds.), *Handbook of experimental existential psychology.* New York: Guilford Press.

Barker, M. (2014). Open non-monogamies: Drawing on de Beauvoir and Sartre to inform existential work with romantic relationships. In M. Milton (Ed.), *Sexuality: Existential perspectives.* Ross-on-Wye: PCCS Books.

Barnes, M., & Berke, J. (1971). *Mary Barnes: Two accounts of a journey through madness.* Harmondsworth: Pelican Books.

Barnett, L. (2008). *When death enters the therapeutic space: Existential perspectives in psychotherapy and counselling.* London: Routledge.

Barnett, L., & Madison, G. (Eds.). (2012). *Existential psychotherapy: Vibrancy, legacy and dialogue.* London: Routledge.

Bateson, G., Jackson, D. D., Haley, J., & Weakland, J. (1956). Towards a theory of schizophrenia. *Behavioral Science, 1,* 251–264.

Batthyány, A. (2016). The state of empirical research on logotherapy and existential analysis. In A. Batthyány (Ed.), *Logotherapy and existential analysis: Proceedings of the Viktor Frankl Institute, Vienna.* Cham, Switzerland: Springer International.

Baumeister, R. F. (1991). *Meanings of life.* New York: Guilford Press.

Beck, A. T., John, R. A., Shaw, B. F., & Emery, G. (1979). *Cognitive therapy of depression.* New York: Guilford Press.

Becker, E. (1973). *The denial of death.* New York: Free Press Paperbacks.

Berne, E. (1961). *Transactional analysis in psychotherapy.* New York: Grove Press.

Binswanger, L. (1958). The case of Ellen West: An anthropological-clinical study. In R. May, E. Angel & H. F. Ellenberger (Eds.), *Existence: A new dimension in psychiatry and psychology*. New York: Basic Books.

Binswanger, L. (1963). *Being-in-the-World: Selected papers of Ludwig Binswanger* (J. Needleman, Trans.). London: Condor Books.

Blackham, H. J. (1961). *Six existentialist thinkers: Kierkegaard, Nietzsche, Jaspers, Marcel, Heidegger, Sartre*. London: Routledge.

Boss, M. (1957). *The analysis of dreams* (A. J. Pomerans, Trans.). London: Rider.

Boss, M. (1963). *Psychoanalysis and daseinsanalysis*. New York: Basic Books.

Boss, M. (1977). *'I dreamt last night ... '* (S. Conway, Trans.). New York: John Wiley and Sons.

Boss, M. (1979). *Existential foundations of medicine and psychology* (S. Conway & A. Cleaves, Trans.). Northvale, NJ: Jason Aronson.

Boss, M. (1988). Recent considerations in daseinsanalysis. *The Humanistic Psychologist, 16*(1), 58–73.

Boss, M., & Kenny, B. (1987). Phenomenological or daseinsanalytical approach. In J. L. Fusshage & C. A. Loew (Eds.), *Dream interpretation*. New York: PMA.

Breitbart, W., Rosenfeld, B., Gibson, C., et al. (2010). Meaning-centered group psychotherapy for patients with advanced cancer: A pilot randomized controlled trial. *Psycho-Oncology, 19*(1), 21–28.

Brouwers, A., & Tomic, W. (2016). Factor structure of Längle's Existence Scale. In A. Batthyány (Ed.), *Logotherapy and existential analysis: Proceedings of the Viktor Frankl Institute, Vienna*. Cham, Switzerland: Springer International.

Brownell, P. (2016). Contemporary gestalt therapy. In D. Cain, K. Keenan & S. Rubin (Eds.), *Humanistic psychotherapies* (2nd ed.). Washington, DC: American Psychological Association.

Buber, M. (1947). *Between man and man* (R. G. Smith, Trans.). London: Fontana.

Buber, M. (1958). *I and thou* (2nd ed.) (R. G. Smith, Trans.). Edinburgh: T. & T. Clark.

Buber, M. (1988). *The knowledge of man: Selected essays* (M. Friedman & R. G. Smith, Trans.). Atlantic Highlands, NJ: Humanities Press International.

Bugental, J. F. T. (1978). *Psychotherapy and process: The fundamentals of an existential-humanistic approach*. Boston, MA: McGraw-Hill.

Bugental, J. F. T. (1981). *The search for authenticity: An existential-analytic approach to psychotherapy* (Exp. ed.). New York: Irvington.

Bugental, J. F. T. (1987). *The art of the psychotherapist: How to develop the skills that take psychotherapy beyond science*. New York: W. W. Norton and Co.

Bugental, J. F. T. (1999). *Psychotherapy isn't what you think: Bringing the psychotherapeutic engagement in the living moment*. Phoenix, AZ: Zeig, Tucker and Co.

Bugental, J. F. T., & Sterling, M. M. (1995). Existential-humanistic psychotherapy: New perspectives. In A. S. Gurman & S. B. Messer (Eds.), *Essential psychotherapies: Theory and practice*. New York: Guilford Press.

Bulka, R. P. (1982). Logotherapy and Judaism – some philosophical comparisons. In R. P. Bulka & M. H. Spero (Eds.), *A psychology-Judaism reader*. Springfield, IL: Charles C. Thomas.

Burston, D. (1996). *The wing of madness: The life and work of R. D. Laing*. Cambridge, MA: Harvard University Press.

Burston, D. (2000). *The crucible of experience: R. D. Laing and the crisis of psychotherapy*. Cambridge, MA: Harvard University Press.

Cain, D. J. (2002). Defining characteristics, history, and evolution of humanistic psychotherapies. In D. J. Cain & J. Seeman (Eds.), *Humanistic psychotherapies: Handbook of research and practice*. Washington, DC: American Psychological Association.

Calton, T., Ferriter, M., Huband, N., & Spandler, H. (2008). A systematic review of the Soteria paradigm for the treatment of people diagnosed with schizophrenia. *Schizophrenia Bulletin, 34*(1), 181–192.

Camus, A. (1955). *The myth of Sisyphus* (J. O'Brien, Trans.). London: Penguin.

Cannon, B. (1991). *Sartre and psychoanalysis: An existentialist challenge to clinical metatheory*. Lawrence, KN: University Press of Kansas.

Cannon, B. (2012). Applied existential psychotherapy: An experiential-psychodynamic approach. In L. Barnett & G. Madison (Eds.), *Existential psychotherapy: Vibrancy, legacy and dialogue*. London: Routledge.

Castonguay, L. G., & Beutler, L. E. (Eds.). (2006). *Principles of therapeutic change that work*. New York: Oxford University Press.

Chan, A. (2014). Chinese existential givens: The building blocks of Chinese indigenous existential psychotherapy. Paper presented at the Third International Conference on Existential Psychology. Retrieved from http://iiehp.org/downloads/

Cohn, H. W. (1993). Authenticity and the aims of psychotherapy. *Journal of the Society for Existential Analysis, 4*, 48–55.

Cohn, H. W. (1997). *Existential thought and therapeutic practice: An introduction to existential psychotherapy*. London: Sage.

Cohn, H. W. (2002). *Heidegger and the roots of existential therapy*. London: Continuum.

Collier, A. (1977). *R. D. Laing: The philosophy and politics of psychotherapy*. London: Harvester Press.

Comas-Diaz, L. (2008). Latino spirituality. In K. J. Schneider (Ed.), *Existential-integrative psychotherapy: Guideposts to the core of practice*. New York: Routledge.

Condrau, G. (1998). *Martin Heidegger's impact on psychotherapy*. Dublin: Edition Mosaic.

Connell, J., Barkham, M., Stiles, W. B., et al. (2007). Distribution of CORE-OM scores in a general population, clinical cut-off points and comparison with the CIS-R. *British Journal of Psychiatry, 190*, 69–74.

Cooper, M. (1999). The discourse of existence: Existential-phenomenological psychotherapy in a postmodern world. *Journal of the Society for Existential Analysis, 10*(2), 93–101.

Cooper, M. (2003). *Existential therapies*. London: Sage.

Cooper, M. (2004). Viagra for the brain: Psychotherapy research and the challenge of existential therapeutic practice. *Existential Analysis, 15*(1), 2–14.

Cooper, M. (2006). Socialist humanism: A progressive politics for the twenty-first century. In G. Proctor, M. Cooper, P. Sanders & B. Malcolm (Eds.), *Politicising the person-centred approach: An agenda for social change*. Ross-on-Wye: PCCS Books.

Cooper, M. (2008a). *Essential research findings in counselling and psychotherapy: The facts are friendly*. London: Sage.

Cooper, M. (2008b). Existential psychotherapy. In J. LeBow (Ed.), *Twenty-first century psychotherapies: Contemporary approaches to theory and practice*. London: Wiley.

Cooper, M. (2012). *Existential counselling primer*. Ross-on-Wye: PCCS Books.

Cooper, M. (2015). *Existential psychotherapy and counselling: Contributions to a pluralistic practice*. London: Sage.

Cooper, M., & Dryden, W. (Eds.). (2016). *Handbook of pluralistic counselling and psychotherapy*. London: Sage.

Cooper, M., Dryden, W., Martin, K., & Papayianni, F. (2016). Metatherapeutic communication and shared decision-making. In M. Cooper & W. Dryden (Eds.), *Handbook of pluralistic counselling and psychotherapy*. London: Sage.

Cooper, M., & Joseph, S. (2016). Psychological foundations for humanistic psychotherapeutic practice. In D. Cain, K. Keenan & S. Rubin (Eds.), *Humanistic psychotherapies* (2nd ed.). Washington, DC: American Psychological Association.

Cooper, M., & McLeod, J. (2011). *Pluralistic counselling and psychotherapy*. London: Sage.

Cooper, M., & McLeod, J. (2015). *Client helpfulness interview studies: A guide to exploring client perceptions of change in counselling and psychotherapy* (working paper). Download from https://www.researchgate.net/profile/Mick_Cooper

Cooper, M., & Norcross, J. C. (2015). A brief, multidimensional measure of clients' therapy preferences: The Cooper-Norcross Inventory of Preferences (C-NIP). *International Journal of Clinical and Health Psychology*, *16*(1), 87–98.

Cooper, M., & Reeves, A. (2012). The role of randomised controlled trials in developing an evidence-base for counselling and psychotherapy. *Counselling and Psychotherapy Research*, *12*(4), 303–307.

Cooper, M., Schmid, P. F., O'Hara, M., & Bohart, A. C. (Eds.). (2013). *The handbook of person-centred psychotherapy and counselling* (2nd ed.). Basingstoke: Palgrave.

Cooper, M., & Stumm, G. (2016). Existential approaches and pluralism. In M. Cooper & W. Dryden (Eds.), *Handbook of pluralistic counselling and psychotherapy*. London: Sage.

Cooper, M., Vos, J., & Craig, M. (2011). *Protocol for EXIST review*. Glasgow: University of Strathclyde Press.

Cooper, R., Friedman, J., Gans, S., et al. (Eds.). (1989). *Thresholds between philosophy and psychoanalysis*. London: Free Association.

Correia, E. (2015). *Practices and characteristics of existential counsellors and psychotherapists: A worldwide survey and observational study*. Glasgow: University of Strathclyde Press.

Correia, E., Cooper, M., & Berdondini, L. (2014a). Existential psychotherapy: An international survey of the key authors and texts influencing practice. *Journal of Contemporary Psychotherapy*, *45*(1), 3–10.

Correia, E., Cooper, M., & Berdondini, L. (2014b). The worldwide distribution and characteristics of existential psychotherapists and counsellors. *Existential Analysis*, *25*(2), 321–337.

Correia, E., Cooper, M., & Berdondini, L. (2016a). Existential therapy institutions worldwide: An update of data and the extensive list. *Existential Analysis*, *27*(1), 155–200.

Correia, E., Cooper, M., & Berdondini, L. (2016b). Worldwide list of existential psychotherapy institutions. *Dasein*, *5*(Special issue), 83–131.

Correia, E., Cooper, M., Berdondini, L., & Correia, K. (2016c). Existential psychotherapies: Similarities and differences among the main branches. [doi: 10.1177/0022167816 653223] *Journal of Humanistic Psychology*.

Correia, E., Correia, K., Cooper, M., & Berdondini, L. (2014). Práticas da psicoterapia existencial em Portugal e no Brasil: Alguns dados comparativos. In A. M. L. C. de Feijoo & M. B. M. F. Lessa (Eds.), *Fenomenologia e práticas clínicas: Textos apresentados no 10 Congresso Luso-Brasileiro de Práticas Clínicas Fenomenológico-Existenciais: Diálogos entre a clínica e a filosofia*. Rio de Janeiro: IFEN.

Cox, G. (2009). *How to be an existentialist: Or how to get real, get a grip and stop making excuses*. London: Bloomsbury.

Cox, G. (2012). *The existentialist's guide to death, the universe and nothingnesss*. London: Continuum.

Craig, E. (1988a). Daseinsanalysis today: A brief critical reflection. *The Humanistic Psychologist, 16*(1), 224–232.

Craig, E. (1988b). An encounter with Medard Boss. *The Humanistic Psychologist, 16*(1), 24–55.

Craig, E. (1993). Remembering Medard Boss. *The Humanistic Psychologist, 21*, 258–276.

Craig, E. (2015). The lost language of being: Ontology's perilous destiny in existential psychotherapy. *Philosophy, Psychiatry, & Psychology, 22*(2), 79–92.

Craig, M., Vos, J., Cooper, M., & Correia, E. (2016). Existential psychotherapies. In D. Cain, K. Keenan & S. Rubin (Eds.), *Humanistic psychotherapies* (2nd ed.). Washington, DC: American Psychological Association.

Crossley, N. (1996). *Intersubjectivity: The fabric of social becoming*. London: Sage.

Crow, L. (1996). Including all of our lives: Renewing the social model of disability. In C. Barnes & G. Mercer (Eds.), *Exploring the divide*. Leeds: Disability Press.

Crumbaugh, J. C. (1977). The seeking of noetic goals test (SONG): A complementary scale to the purpose in life test (PIL). *Journal of Clinical Psychology, 33*(3), 900–907.

Crumbaugh, J. C. (1979). Exercises of logoanalysis. In J. B. Fabry, R. P. Bulka & W. S. Sahakian (Eds.), *Logotherapy in action*. New York: Jason Aronson.

Crumbaugh, J. C., & Maholick, L. T. (1964). An experimental study in existentialism: The psychometric approach to Frankl's concept of noogenic neurosis. *Journal of Clinical Psychology, 20*(2), 200–207.

Dallas, E., Georganda, E. T., Harisiadis, A., & Zymnis-Georgalos, K. (2013). Zhi mian and 'oistros' of life. *Journal of Humanistic Psychology, 53*(2), 252–260.

DeCarvalho, R. J. (1996). James F. T. Bugental: Portrait of a humanistic psychologist. *Journal of Humanistic Psychology, 36*(4), 42–57.

Derrida, J. (1974). *Of grammatology* (G. C. Spivak, Trans.). Baltimore, MD: Johns Hopkins University Press.

Diamond, N. (1996). Embodiment. *Journal of the Society for Existential Analysis, 7*(1), 129–133.

Diamond, S. A. (1996). *Anger, madness and the daimonic: The psychological genesis of violence, evil and creativity*. Albany, NY: State University of New York Press.

Dreyfus, H. L. (1997). *Being-in-the-world: A commentary on Heidegger's Being and Time, Division 1*. Cambridge, MA: MIT Press.

Dryden, W. (1999). *Rational emotive behavioural counselling in action* (2nd ed.). London: Sage.

Duncan, B. L., Miller, S. D., Sparks, J. A., & Claud, D. A. (2003). The Session Rating Scale: Preliminary psychometric properties of a 'working' alliance measure. *Journal of Brief Therapy, 3*(1), 3–12.

Dunlop, F. (1991). *Thinkers of our time: Scheler*. London: Claridge Press.

Du Plock, S. (Ed.). (1997). *Case studies in existential psychotherapy and counselling*. Chichester: John Wiley.

Eleftheriadou, Z. (1997). The cross-cultural experience – integration or isolation. In S. Du Plock (Ed.), *Case studies in existential psychotherapy and counselling*. Chichester: John Wiley.

Ellenberger, H. F. (1958). A clinical introduction to psychiatric phenomenology and existential analysis. In R. May, E. Angel & H. F. Ellenberger (Eds.), *Existence: A new dimension in psychiatry and psychology*. New York: Basic Books.

Elliott, R., Greenberg, L. S., Watson, J. C., Timulak, L., & Freire, E. (2013). Research on humanistic-experiential psychotherapies. In M. J. Lambert (Ed.), *Bergin and Garfield's handbook of psychotherapy and behavior change* (6th ed.). Hoboken, NJ: John Wiley.

Emmelkemp, P. M. G. (2013). Behavior therapy with adults. In M. J. Lambert (Ed.), *Bergin and Garfield's handbook of psychotherapy and behavior change* (6th ed.). Hoboken, NJ: John Wiley.

Fabry, J. (1980). *The pursuit of meaning: Viktor Frankl, logotherapy and life* (rev. ed.). San Francisco, CA: Harper & Row.

Fabry, J. B., Bulka, R. P., & Sahakian, W. S. (Eds.). (1979). *Logotherapy in action.* New York: Jason Aronson.

Fanon, F. (1991). *Black skin, white masks* (C. L. Markmann, Trans.). London: Pluto.

Farber, E. W. (2010). Humanistic-existential psychotherapy competencies and the supervisory process. [doi:10.1037/a0018847]. *Psychotherapy: Theory, Research, Practice, Training, 47*(1), 28–34.

Farber, L. H. (2000). *The ways of the will* (exp. ed.). New York: Basic Books.

Feijoo, A. M. L. (2010). *A escuta e a fala em psicoterapia: Uma proposta fenomenológico-existencial.* Rio de Janeiro: IFEN.

Fillion, L., Duval, S., Dumont, S., et al. (2009). Impact of a meaning-centered intervention on job satisfaction and on quality of life among palliative care nurses. *Psycho-Oncology, 18*(12), 1300–1310.

Finlay, L. (2012). Research: An existential predicament for our profession? In L. Barnett & G. Madison (Eds.), *Existential psychotherapy: Vibrancy, legacy and dialogue.* London: Routledge.

Frankl, V. E. (1965). Fragments from the logotherapeutic treatment of four cases. In A. Burton (Ed.), *Modern psychotherapeutic practice.* Palo Alto, CA: Science and Behaviour Books.

Frankl, V. E. (1984). *Man's search for meaning* (revised and updated ed.). New York: Washington Square Press.

Frankl, V. E. (1986). *The doctor and the soul: From psychotherapy to logotherapy* (R. Winston & C. Winston, Trans., 3rd ed.). New York: Vintage Books.

Frankl, V. E. (1988). *The will to meaning: Foundations and applications of logotherapy* (exp. ed.). London: Meridian.

Frankl, V. E. (1998). The unconditional human: Metaclinical lectures (W. J. Maas, Trans.): Unpublished translation.

Frankl, V. E. (2000). *Recollections: An autobiography* (J. Fabry & J. Fabry, Trans.). Cambridge, MA: Perseus Publishing.

Freud, S. (1916). *Introductory lectures on psycho-analysis* (Vol. 15). London: Hogarth Press.

Freud, S. (1923). The ego and the id (J. Strachey, Trans.). *The standard edition of the complete psychological works of Sigmund Freud.* London: Hogarth Press.

Frie, R. (1997). *Subjectivity and intersubjectivity in modern philosophy and psychoanalysis: A study of Sartre, Binswanger, Lacan and Habermas.* Lanham, MD: Rowman & Littlefield.

Friedman, M. (1985). *The healing dialogue in psychotherapy.* New York: Jason Aronson.

Fromm, E. (1963). *Art of loving.* New York: Bantam Books.

Gans, S. (1989). The play of difference: Lacan versus Derrida on Poe. In R. Cooper, J. Friedman, S. Gans, J. M. Heaton, C. Oakley, H. Oakley & P. Zeal (Eds.), *Thresholds between philosophy and psychoanalysis.* London: Free Association.

Gans, S. (2015). Awakening to love: R. D. Laing's phenomenological therapy. In M. G. Thompson (Ed.), *The legacy of R. D. Laing: An appraisal of his contemporary relevance*. Hove: Routledge.

Gavin, V. J. (2013). Creative existential therapy for children, adolescents and adults (with special reference to training). *Existential Analysis*, *24*(2), 318–341.

Gendlin, E. T. (1977). Phenomenological concepts vs. phenomenological method: A critique of Medard Boss on dreams. In C. E. Scott (Ed.), *On dreaming: An encounter with Medard Boss*. Chico, CA: Scholars Press.

Gendlin, E. T. (1996). *Focusing-oriented psychotherapy: A manual of the experiential method*. New York: Guilford Press.

Gergen, K. (2011). *Relational being: Beyond self and community*. New York: Oxford University.

Giorgi, A. (Ed.). (1985). *Phenomenological and pychological research*. Pittsburgh, PA: Duquesne University Press.

Gire, J. T. (2002). How death imitates life: Cultural influences on conceptions of death and dying. In W. J. Lonner, D. L. Dinnel, S. A. Hayes & D. N. Sattler (Eds.), *Online readings in psychology and culture*. Bellingham, WA: Center for Cross-Cultural Research, Western Washington University.

Goldberg, L. R. (1990). An alternative description of personality: The big-five factor structure. *Journal of Personality and Social Psychology*, *59*, 1216–1229.

Gould, W. B. (1993). *Viktor E. Frankl – Life with meaning*. Pacific Grove, CA: Brooks/Cole.

Greenberg, J., & Mitchell, S. A. (1983). *Object relations in psychoanalytic theory*. Cambridge, MA: Harvard University Press.

Guignon, C. B. (2002). Existentialism. Available at www.rep.routledge.com (accessed 18 April 2016).

Halling, S., & Nill, J. D. (1995). A brief history of existential-phenomenological psychiatry and psychology. *Journal of Phenomenological Psychology*, *26*(1), 1–45.

Heaton, J. M. (1991). The divided self: Kierkegaard or Winnicott? *Journal of the Society for Existential Analysis*, *2*, 30–37.

Heaton, J. M. (1995). The self, the divided self, and the other. *Journal of the Society for Existential Analysis*, *6*(1), 31–60.

Heaton, J. M. (2006). The early history and ideas of the Philadelphia Association. *Existential Analysis*, *17*(1), 181–191.

Heidegger, M. (1949). What is metaphysics? In *Existence and being*. Chicago, IL: Henry Regnery Co.

Heidegger, M. (1962). *Being and time* (J. Macquarrie & E. Robinson, Trans.). Oxford: Blackwell.

Heidegger, M. (1966). *Discourse on thinking* (J. M. Anderson & E. H. Freund, Trans.). London: Harper Colophon Books.

Heidegger, M. (1996a). *Being and time* (J. Stambaugh, Trans.). Albany, NY: State University of New York Press.

Heidegger, M. (1996b). Letter on humanism. In L. Cahoone (Ed.), *From modernism to postmodernism: An anthology*. Cambridge, MA: Blackwell.

Heidegger, M. (2001). *Zollikon seminars: Protocols–conversations–letters* (F. Mayr & R. Askay, Trans.). Evanston, IL: Northwestern University Press.

Henry, M., Cohen, S. R., Lee, V., et al. (2010). The Meaning-Making intervention (MMi) appears to increase meaning in life in advanced ovarian cancer: A randomized controlled pilot study. *Psycho-Oncology*, *19*(12), 1340–1347.

Hickes, M., & Mirea, D. (2012). Cognitive behavioural therapy and existential-phenomenological psychotherapy: Rival paradigms or fertile ground for therapeutic synthesis? *Existential Analysis, 23*(1), 15–31.

Hicklin, A. (1988). The significance of life-history in daseinsanalytic psychotherapy. *The Humanistic Psychologist, 16*(1), 130–139.

Hill, C. E., & Knox, S. (2002). Self-disclosure. In J. C. Norcross (Ed.), *Psychotherapy relationships that work: Therapist contributions and responsiveness to patients*. New York: Oxford University Press.

Hoeller, K. (1999). Introduction. *Review of Existential Psychology and Psychiatry, 24*, v–viii.

Hoffman, L. (2009). Introduction to existential psychology in a cross-cultural context: An east-west dialogue. In L. Hoffman, M. Yang & F. J. Kaklauskas (Eds.), *Existential psychology east-west*. Colorado Springs, CO: University of the Rockies.

Hoffman, L. (2016). Multiculturalism and humanistic psychology: From neglect to epistemological and ontological diversity. *The Humanistic Psychologist, 44*(1), 56–71.

Hoffman, L., Cleare-Hoffman, H. P., & Jackson, T. (2014). Humanistic psychology and multiculturalism: History, current status, and advancements. In K. J. Schneider, J. F. Pierson & J. F. T. Bugental (Eds.), *The handbook of humanistic psychology: Leading edges of theory, research, and practice* (2nd ed.). Thousand Oaks, CA: Sage.

Hoffman, L., Yang, M., & Kaklauskas, F. J. (2009). *Existential psychology east-west*. Colorado Springs, CO: University of the Rockies.

Hoffman, P. (1993). Death, time, history: Division II of *Being and Time*. In C. B. Guignon (Ed.), *The Cambridge companion to Heidegger*. Cambridge: Cambridge University Press.

Holzhey-Kunz, A. (2014). *Daseinsanalysis* (S. Leighton, Trans.). London: Free Association.

Holzhey-Kunz, A. (2015). What connects psychic suffering to existential ontology? *International Journal of Psychotherapy, 19*(1), 39–46.

Holzhey-Kunz, A. (2016). Why the distinction between ontic and ontological trauma matters for existential therapists. *Existential Analysis, 27*(1), 16–27.

Holzhey-Kunz, A., & Fazekas, T. (2012). Daseinsanalysis: A dialogue. In L. Barnett & G. Madison (Eds.), *Existential psychotherapy: Vibrancy, legacy and dialogue*. London: Routledge.

Iacovou, S., & Weixel-Dixon, K. (2015). *Existential therapy: 100 key points and techniques*. London: Routledge.

Ihde, D. (1986). *Experimental phenomenology: An introduction*. Albany, NY: State University of New York Press.

Jacobsen, B. (2005). Values and beliefs. In E. van Deurzen & C. Baker (Eds.), *Existential perspectives on human issues: A handbook for therapeutic practice*. London: Palgrave.

Janoff-Bulman, R. (1997). *Shattered assumptions*. New York: Simon & Schuster.

Jaspers, K. (1932). *Philosophy* (E. B. Ashton, Trans., Vol. 2). Chicago, IL: University of Chicago Press.

Jaspers, K. (1963). *General psychopathology* (J. Hoenig & M. W. Hamilton, Trans., Vol. 1). Baltimore, MD: Johns Hopkins University Press.

Jaspers, K. (1986). *Karl Jaspers: Basic philosophical writings* (E. Ehrlich, L. H. Ehrlich & G. B. Pepper, Trans.). Trenton, NJ: Humanities Press.

Jones, M. A., Botsko, M., & Gorman, B. S. (2003). Predictors of psychotherapeutic benefit of lesbian, gay, and bisexual clients: The effects of sexual orientation matching and other factors. *Psychotherapy: Theory, Research, Practice, Training, 40*(4), 289–301.

Kaufmann, W. (Ed.). (1975). *Existentialism from Dostoevsky to Sartre*. New York: New American Library.

Kazantzakis, N. (2008). *Zorba the Greek*. London: Faber & Faber.

Keshen, A. (2006). A new look at existential psychotherapy. *American Journal of Psychotherapy*, *60*(3), 285–298.

Kierkegaard, S. (1980a). *The concept of anxiety: A simple psychologically orienting delibera-tion on the dogmatic issue of hereditary sin* (R. Thomte, Trans., Vol. 8). Princeton, NJ: Princeton University Press.

Kierkegaard, S. (1980b). *The sickness unto death: A Christian psychological exposition for upbuilding and awakening* (H. V. Hong & E. H. Hong, Trans., Vol. 19). Princeton, NJ: Princeton University Press.

Kierkegaard, S. (1992). *Concluding unscientific postscript to philosophical fragments* (H. V. Hong & E. H. Hong, Trans., Vol. 12: 1). Princeton, NJ: Princeton University Press.

King, L. A., & Hicks, J. A. (2013). Positive affect and meaning in life. In P. T. P. Wong (Ed.), *The human quest for meaning: Theories, research, and applications* (2nd ed.). New York: Routledge.

Kirsner, D. (2015). 'Human, all too human': The life and work of R. D. Laing – interview. In M. G. Thompson (Ed.), *The legacy of R. D. Laing: An appraisal of his contemporary relevance*. Hove: Routledge.

Kissane, D. W., Bloch, S., Smith, G. C., Clarke, D. M., Miach, P., & Love, A. (2000). A randomised controlled trial of cognitive-existential group therapy for women (n303) with early stage breast cancer. *Psycho-Oncology*, *9*(5), 212.

Kissane, D. W., Love, A., Hatton, A., et al. (2004). Effect of cognitive-existential group therapy on survival in early-stage breast cancer. *Journal of Clinical Oncology*, *22*(21), 4255–4260.

Klingberg, H., Jr (1995). Tracing logotherapy to its roots. *Journal des Viktor-Frankl-Instituts*, *1*, 9–20.

Klinger, E. (2013). The search for meaning in evolutionary goal-theory perspective and its clinical implications. In P. T. P. Wong (Ed.), *The human quest for meaning: Theories, research, and applications* (2nd ed.). New York: Routledge.

Kohn, A. (1984). Existentialism here and now. *Georgia Review*, *38*(2), 381–397.

Kolden, G. G., Klein, M. H., Wang, C.-C., & Austin, S. B. (2011). Congruence. In J. C. Norcross (Ed.), *Psychotherapy relationships that work: Evidence-based responsiveness* (2nd ed.). New York: Oxford University Press.

Krycka, K. C., & Ikemi, A. (2016). Focusing-oriented-experiential psychotherapy. In D. Cain, K. Keenan & S. Rubin (Eds.), *Humanistic psychotherapies* (2nd ed.). Washington, DC: American Psychological Association.

Kundi, M., Wurst, E., & Längle, A. (2003). Existential analytical aspects of mental health. *European Psychotherapy*, *4*(1), 109–118.

Kwee, J. L., & Längle, A. (2013). Phenomenology in psychotherapeutic praxis: An intro-duction to personal existential analysis. *Presencing EPIS*. Retrieved from http://epis journal.com/journal-2013/phenomenology-in-psychotherapeutic-praxis (accessed 4 May 2016).

Laing, R. D. (1965a). *The divided self: An existential study in sanity and madness*. Harmondsworth: Penguin.

Laing, R. D. (1965b). Mystification, confusion and conflict. In I. Boszormenyi-Nagy & J. Framo (Eds.), *Intensive family therapy*. New York: Harper & Row.

Laing, R. D. (1967). *The politics of experience and the bird of paradise*. Harmondsworth: Penguin.

Laing, R. D. (1969). *Self and others* (2nd ed.). London: Penguin Books.

Laing, R. D. (1970). *Knots*. London: Penguin.

Laing, R. D. (1976a). *Do you love me?* New York: Pantheon Books.

Laing, R. D. (1976b). *The facts of life*. London: Penguin.

Laing, R. D. (1985). *Wisdom, madness and folly: The making of a psychiatrist 1927–1957*. London: Macmillan.

Laing, R. D., & Esterson, A. (1964). *Sanity, madness and the family*. London: Penguin Books.

Laing, R. D., Phillipson, H., & Lee, A. R. (1966). *Interpersonal perception: A theory and a method of research*. London: Tavistock.

Langdridge, D. (2006). Solution-focused therapy: A way forward for brief existential therapy? *Existential Analysis, 17*(2), 359–370.

Langdridge, D. (2012). *Existential counselling and psychotherapy*. London: Sage.

Längle, A. (2003a). The art of involving the person: Fundamental existential motivations as the structure of the motivation process. *European Psychotherapy, 4*(1), 47–58.

Längle, A. (2003b). The method of 'personal existential analysis'. *European Psychotherapy, 4*(1), 59–75.

Längle, A. (2012). The Viennese School of Existential Analysis: The search for meaning and affirmation in life. In L. Barnett & G. Madison (Eds.), *Existential psychotherapy: Vibrancy, legacy and dialogue*. London: Routledge.

Längle, A. (2015). The power of logotherapy and the need to develop existential analytic psychotherapy. *International Journal of Psychotherapy, 19*(1), 73–80.

Längle, A., Orgler, C., & Kundi, M. (2003). The Existence Scale: A new approach to assess the ability to find personal meaning in life and to reach existential fulfilment. *European Psychotherapy, 4*(1), 157–174.

Längle, S. (2003). Levels of operation for the application of existential-analytical methods. *European Psychotherapy, 4*(1), 77–92.

Längle, S., & Wurm, C. (Eds.). (2016). *Living your own life: Existential analysis in action*. London: Karnac.

Lantz, J. (1993). *Existential family therapy*. New York and London: Jason Aronson.

Lantz, J., & Gregoire, T. (1996). Basic concepts in existential psychotherapy with couples and families. *Contemporary Family Therapy: An International Journal, 18*(4), 535–548.

Lantz, J., & Gregoire, T. (2000). Existential psychotherapy with Vietnam veteran couples: A twenty-five year report. [doi:10.1023/A:1007766431715]. *Contemporary Family Therapy: An International Journal, 22*(1), 19–37.

Lantz, J., & Gregoire, T. (2003a). Couples, existential psychotherapy, and myocardial infarction: A ten year evaluation study. [doi:10.1023/A:1027304618120]. *Contemporary Family Therapy: An International Journal, 25*(4), 367–379.

Lantz, J., & Gregoire, T. (2003b). Existential trauma therapy with men after a heart attack. [doi:10.1023/A:1021451610123]. *Journal of Contemporary Psychotherapy, 33*(1), 19–33.

Lantz, J., & Walsh, J. (2007). *Short-term existential intervention in clinical practice*. Chicago, IL: Lyceum Books.

Lee, V. (2008). The existential plight of cancer: Meaning making as a concrete approach to the intangible search for meaning. *Supportive Care in Cancer, 16*(7), 779–785.

Lee, V., Cohen, S. R., Edgar, L., Laizner, A. M., & Gagnon, A. J. (2006). Meaning-making intervention during breast or colorectal cancer treatment improves self-esteem, optimism, and self-efficacy. *Social Science & Medicine, 62*(12), 3133–3145.

LeMay, K., & Wilson, K. G. (2008). Treatment of existential distress in life-threatening ill-ness: A review of manualized interventions. *Clinical Psychology Review, 28*(3), 472–493.

Levinas, E. (1969). *Totality and infinity: An essay on exteriority* (A. Lingis, Trans.). Pittsburgh, PA: Duquesne University Press.

Liddle, B. J. (1996). Therapist sexual orientation, gender, and counseling practices as they relate to ratings on helpfulness by gay and lesbian clients. *Journal of Counseling Psychology, 43*, 394–401.

Linsenmayer, M. (2011). Three types of 'reduction' in phenomenology. Retrieved from www.partiallyexaminedlife.com/2011/12/22/three-types-of-reduction-in-phenome-nology/ (accessed 18 April 2016).

Loewenthal, D. (2010). Post-existentialism instead of CBT. *Existential Analysis, 21*(2), 320–330.

Loewenthal, D. (2011). *Post-existentialism and the psychological therapies: Towards a therapy without foundations.* London: Karnac.

Loewenthal, D. (2016). *Existential psychotherapy and counselling after post-modernism: The collected works of Del Loewenthal.* London: World Library of Mental Health, Routledge.

Luborsky, L., Diguer, L., Seligman, D. A., et al. (1999). The researcher's own therapy allegiances: A 'wild card' in comparisons of treatment efficacy. *Clinical Psychology: Science and Practice, 6*(1), 95–106.

Lyotard, J.-F. (1984). *The postmodern condition: A report on knowledge* (G. Bennington & B. Massumi, Trans., Vol. 10). Manchester: Manchester University Press.

MacKinnon, C. J., Smith, N. G., Henry, M., et al. (2014). Meaning-based group coun-seling for bereavement: Bridging theory with emerging trends in intervention research. *Death Studies, 38*(3), 137–144.

Macquarrie, J. (1972). *Existentialism.* Harmondsworth: Penguin Books.

Madison, G. (2010). Focusing on existence: Five facets of an experiential–existential model. *Person-Centered & Experiential Psychotherapies, 9*(3), 189–204.

Madison, G. (Ed.). (2014). *Theory and practice of focusing-oriented psychotherapy: Beyond the talking cure.* London: Jessica Kingsley.

Madison, G. (2015). What is the living body in existential therapy? *International Journal of Psychotherapy, 19*(1), 81–88.

Madison, G., & Gendlin, E. (2012). Palpable existentialism: An interview with Eugene Gendlin. In L. Barnett & G. Madison (Eds.), *Existential psychotherapy: Vibrancy, legacy and dialogue.* London: Routledge.

Manafi, E. (2010). 'Amor Fati': Existential contributions to pluralistic practice. In M. Milton (Ed.), *Therapy and beyond: Counselling psychology contributions to therapeu-tic and social issues.* London: Wiley-Blackwell.

Marcel, G. (1949). *The philosophy of existence* (M. Harai, Trans.). Freeport, NY: Books for Libraries Press.

Martin, L., Campbell, W. K., & Henry, C. D. (2004). The roar of awakening: Mortality acknowledgement as a call to authentic living. In J. Greenberg, S. L. Koole & T. Pyszczynski (Eds.), *Handbook of experimental existential psychology.* New York: Guilford Press.

Maslow, A. H. (1968). *Towards a Psychology of Being* (2nd ed.). New York: D. van Nostrand.

Maslow, A. H. (1971). *The farther reaches of human nature.* London: Penguin.

Mautner, T. (Ed.). (1996). *Dictionary of philosophy.* London: Penguin.

May, R. (1953). *Man's search for himself*. New York: W. W. Norton and Co.

May, R. (1958). Contributions of existential psychotherapy. In R. May, E. Angel & H. F. Ellenberger (Eds.), *Existence: A new dimension in psychiatry and psychology*. New York: Basic Books.

May, R. (1969a). *Love and will*. New York: W. W. Norton and Co.

May, R. (Ed.). (1969b). *Existential psychology* (2nd ed.). New York: Random House.

May, R. (1972). *Power and innocence: A search for the sources of violence*. New York: W. W. Norton and Co.

May, R. (1978). Response to Bulka's article. *Humanistic Psychology, 18*(4), 55.

May, R. (1981). *Freedom and destiny*. New York and London: W. W. Norton and Co.

May, R. (1999). Creativity and the unconscious. *Review of Existential Psychology and Psychiatry, 24*, 33–39.

May, R., Angel, E., & Ellenberger, H. F. (Eds.). (1958). *Existence: A new dimension in psychiatry and psychology*. New York: Basic Books.

May, R., & Yalom, I. (1989). Existential psychotherapy. In R. J. Corsini & D. Wedding (Eds.), *Current psychotherapies*. Itasca, IL: F. E. Peacock Publishers.

McLeod, J., & Cooper, M. (2015). Pluralistic counselling and psychotherapy. In S. Palmer (Ed.), *The beginner's guide to counselling and psychotherapy* (2nd ed.). London: Sage.

Mearns, D., & Cooper, M. (2005). *Working at relational depth in counselling and psychotherapy*. London: Sage.

Merleau-Ponty, M. (1962). *The phenomenology of perception* (C. Smith, Trans.). London: Routledge.

Mezan, P. (2015). Who was R. D. Laing? In M. G. Thompson (Ed.), *The legacy of R. D. Laing: An appraisal of his contemporary relevance*. Hove: Routledge.

Milton, M. (2010). Coming home to roost: Counselling psychology and the natural world. In M. Milton (Ed.), *Therapy and beyond: Counselling psychology contributions to therapeutic and social issues*. London: Wiley-Blackwell.

Milton, M. (Ed.). (2014). *Sexuality: Existential perspectives*. Ross-on-Wye: PCCS Books.

Milton, M., Charles, L., Judd, D., O'Brien, M., Tipney, A., & Turner, A. (2003). The existential-phenomenological paradigm: The importance for psychotherapy integration. *Existential Analysis, 14*(1), 112–136.

Monheit, J. (2008). A lesbian and gay perspective: The case of Marcia. In K. J. Schneider (Ed.), *Existential-integrative psychotherapy: Guideposts to the core of practice*. New York: Routledge.

Moran, D. (2000). *Introduction to phenomenology*. London: Routledge.

Morgan-Williams, S. (1996). All real living is meeting. *Journal of the Society for Existential Analysis, 6*(2), 76–96.

Mosher, L. R., & Hendrix, V. (2004). *Soteria: Through madness to deliverance*. Bloomington, IN: Xlibris.

Mullan, B. (1995). *Mad to be normal: Conversations with R. D. Laing*. London: Free Association Books.

Mullan, B. (1999). *R. D. Laing: A personal view*. London: Duckworth.

Murphy, D., & Joseph, S. (2016). Person-centered therapy: Past, present, and future orientations. In D. Cain, K. Keenan & S. Rubin (Eds.), *Humanistic psychotherapies* (2nd ed.). Washington, DC: American Psychological Association.

Nanda, J. (2010). Embodied integration: Reflections on mindfulness-based cognitive therapy (MBCT) and a case for mindfulness-based existential therapy (MBET). A single-case illustration. *Existential Analysis, 21*(2), 331–350.

Nanda, J. (2012). Why mindfulness-based existential coaching? In E. van Deurzen & M. Hanaway (Eds.), *Existential perspectives on coaching*. London: Palgrave.

National Collaborating Centre for Mental Health. (2010). *Depression: The NICE guidelines on the treatment and management of depression in adults*. London: National Institute for Health and Clinical Excellence.

Nietzsche, F. (1967). *Thus spake Zarathustra* (T. Common, Trans.). London: George Allen and Unwin.

Norcross, J. C. (1987). A rational and empirical analysis of existential psychotherapy. [doi:10.1177/0022167887271005]. *Journal of Humanistic Psychology, 27*(1), 41–68.

Norcross, J. C. (Ed.). (2011). *Psychotherapy relationships that work: Evidence-based responsiveness* (2nd ed.). New York: Oxford University Press.

Norcross, J. C., & Wampold, B. E. (2011). Evidence-based therapy relationships: Research conclusions and clinical practices. In J. C. Norcross (Ed.), *Psychotherapy relationships that work: Evidence-based responsiveness* (2nd ed.). New York: Oxford University.

Oakley, C. (1989). Introducing an incomplete project. In R. Cooper, J. Friedman, S. Gans, J. M. Heaton, C. Oakley, H. Oakley & P. Zeal (Eds.), *Thresholds between philosophy and psychoanalysis*. London: Free Association Books.

Olivereira, A., Sousa, D., & Pires, A. P. (2012). Significant events in existential psychotherapy: The client's perspective. *Existential Analysis, 23*(2), 288–304.

Park, N., Park, M., & Peterson, C. (2010). When is the search for meaning related to life satisfaction? *Applied Psychology: Health and Well-Being, 2*(1), 1–13.

Perls, F., Hefferline, R. F., & Goodman, P. (1951). *Gestalt therapy: Excitement and growth in the human personality*. New York: Julian Press.

Polt, R. (1999). *Heidegger: An introduction*. London: UCL Press.

Pyszczynski, T., Greenberg, J., & Koole, S. L. (2004). Experimental existential psychology: Exploring the human confrontation with reality. In J. Greenberg, S. L. Koole & T. Pyszczynski (Eds.), *Handbook of experimental existential psychology*. New York: Guilford Press.

Quinn, F. (2010). The right to choose: Existential-phenomenological psychotherapy with primary school-aged children. *Counselling Psychology Review, 25*(1), 41–48.

Randall, E. (2001). Existential therapy of panic disorder: A single system study. *Clinical Social Work Journal, 29*(3), 259–267.

Rayner, M., & Vitali, D. (2014). CORE blimey! Existential therapy scores GOALS! *Existential Analysis, 25*(2), 296–312.

Rayner, M., & Vitali, D. (2015). Short-term existential psychotherapy in primary care: A quantitative report. *Journal of Humanistic Psychology*. Advance online publication.

Resnick, J. (1997). Jan Resnick. In B. Mullan (Ed.), *R. D. Laing: Creative destroyer*. London: Cassell.

Rice, D. L. (2008). An African-American perspective: The case of Darrin. In K. J. Schneider (Ed.), *Existential-integrative psychotherapy: Guideposts to the core of practice*. New York: Routledge.

Robles, Y. A. M., & Signorelli, S. (2015). Brief review of the history of existential psychotherapy in Latin America. *International Journal of Psychotherapy, 19*(1), 89–94.

Rogers, C. R. (1957). The necessary and sufficient conditions of therapeutic personality change. *Journal of Consulting Psychology, 21*(2), 95–103.

Rogers, C. R. (1959). A theory of therapy, personality and interpersonal relationships as developed in the client-centered framework. In S. Koch (Ed.), *Psychology: A study of science*. New York: McGraw-Hill.

Romero, E. (2004). *As dimensões da vida humana: Existência e experiência* (4th ed.). São Paulo: Della Bídia Editora.

Ryan, R. M., & Deci, E. L. (2004). Autonomy is no illusion: Self-determination theory and the empirical study of authenticity, awareness and will. In J. Greenberg, S. L. Koole & T. Pyszczynski (Eds.), *Handbook of experimental existential psychology*. New York: Guilford Press.

Sachse, R., & Elliott, R. (2002). Process-outcome research on humanistic therapy variables. In D. J. Cain & J. Seeman (Eds.), *Humanistic psychotherapies: Handbook of research and practice*. Washington, DC: American Psychological Association.

Sartre, J.-P. (1958). *Being and nothingness: An essay on phenomenological ontology* (H. Barnes, Trans.). London: Routledge.

Sartre, J.-P. (1996). Existentialism. In L. Cahoone (Ed.), *From modernism to postmodernism: An anthology*. Cambridge, MA: Blackwells.

Scalzo, C. (2010). *Therapy with children: An existentialist perspective*. London: Karnac.

Schneider, K. J. (1990). *The paradoxical self: Towards an understanding of our contradictory nature*. New York: Plenum Press.

Schneider, K. J. (2000). R. D. Laing's existential-humanistic practice: What was he actually doing? *Psychoanalytic Review, 87*(4), 591–600.

Schneider, K. J. (2001). Multiple-case depth research: Bringing experience-near closer. In K. J. Schneider, J. F. T. Bugental & J. F. Pierson (Eds.), *The handbook of humanistic psychology: Leading edges in theory, research and practice*. London: Sage.

Schneider, K. J. (2003). Existential-humanistic psychotherapies. In A. S. Gurman & S. B. Messer (Eds.), *Essential psychotherapies*. New York: Guilford Press.

Schneider, K. J. (Ed.). (2008). *Existential-integrative psychotherapy: Guideposts to the core of practice*. New York: Routledge.

Schneider, K. J. (2016). Existential-integrative therapy: Foundational implications for integrative practice. *Journal of Psychotherapy Integration, 26*(1), 49–55.

Schneider, K. J., & Krug, O. T. (2010). *Existential-humanistic therapy*. Washington, DC: American Psychological Association.

Schneider, K. J., & May, R. (1995a). Existential-integrative psychology: A beginning. In K. J. Schneider & R. May (Eds.), *The psychology of existence: An integrative, clinical perspective*. New York: McGraw-Hill.

Schneider, K. J., & May, R. (1995b). Guidelines for an existential-integrative (EI) approach. In K. J. Schneider & R. May (Eds.), *The psychology of existence: An integrative, clinical perspective*. New York: McGraw-Hill.

Schneider, K. J., & May, R. (Eds.). (1995c). *The psychology of existence: An integrative, clinical perspective*. New York: McGraw-Hill.

Schrader, G. A., Jr (1967). Resurgent humanism. In G. A. Schrader Jr (Ed.), *Existential philosophers: Kierkegaard to Merleau-Ponty*. New York: McGraw-Hill.

Schulenberg, S. E., Hutzell, R. R., Nassif, C., & Rogina, J. M. (2008). Logotherapy for clinical practice. *Psychotherapy: Theory, Research, Practice, Training, 45*(4), 447–463.

Schwartz, B. (2005). *The paradox of choice*. London: Harper.

Scully, M. (1995). Viktor Frankl at ninety: An interview. *First Things, 52*(April), 39–43.

Semyon, M. (1997). Mina Semyon. In B. Mullan (Ed.), *R. D. Laing: Creative destroyer*. London: Cassell.

Shapiro, L. S. (2016). *Pragmatic existential counseling and psychotherapy*. Thousand Oaks, CA: Sage.

Smith, V., Burr, V., & Leeming, D. (2015). Philosophy in practice: An exploration of the relationship between existential philosophy and therapeutic practice from the therapists' perspective. Paper presented at the Annual Conference, Society of Existential Analysis, 21 November, London.

Soon, C. S., Brass, M., Heinze, H. J., & Haynes, J. D. (2008). Unconscious determinants of free decisions in the human brain. *Nature Neuroscience, 11*(5), 543–545.

Spiegel, D., Bloom, J. R., & Yalom, I. (1981). Group support for patients with metastatic cancer. *Archive of General Psychiatry, 38*, 527–533.

Spiegelberg, H. (1972). *Phenomenology in psychology and psychiatry: A historical introduction.* Evanston, IL: Northwestern University Press.

Spinelli, E. (1996a). The existential-phenomenological paradigm. In R. Woolfe and W. Dryden (Eds.), *Handbook of counselling psychology.* London: Sage.

Spinelli, E. (1996b). Martin Heidegger's influence upon British psychology and psychotherapy. *Journal of the Society for Existential Analysis, 8*(1), 28–38.

Spinelli, E. (1996c). The vagaries of the self: An essay in response to Emmy van Deurzen-Smith's 'The survival of the self' and Mick Cooper's 'Modes of existence': Towards a phenomenological polypsychism. *Journal for the Society of Existential Analysis, 7*(2), 57–68.

Spinelli, E. (1997). Foreword. In F. Strasser & A. Strasser, *Existential time-limited therapy: The wheel of existence.* Chichester: John Wiley.

Spinelli, E. (2001). *The mirror and the hammer: Challenges to therapeutic orthodoxy.* London: Continuum.

Spinelli, E. (2005). *The interpreted world: An introduction to phenomenological psychology* (2nd ed.). London: Sage. (First published 1989.)

Spinelli, E. (2006a). *Demystifying therapy.* London: Constable.

Spinelli, E. (2006b). *Tales of un-knowing: Therapeutic encounters from an existential perspective.* London: Duckworth.

Spinelli, E. (2014). An existential challenge to some dominant perspectives in the practice of contemporary counselling psychology. *Counselling Psychology Review, 29*(2), 7–24.

Spinelli, E. (2015). *Practising existential psychotherapy: The relational world* (2nd ed.). London: Sage.

Spinelli, E., & Horner, C. (2007). The existential-phenomenological paradigm. In S. Palmer & A. Whybrow (Eds.), *The handbook of coaching psychology: A guide for practitioners* (2nd ed.). London: Routledge.

Starck, P. L. (1993). Logotherapy: Applications to nursing. *Journal des Viktor-Frankl-Instituts, 1*, 94–98.

Steger, M. F. (2013). Experiencing meaning in life. In P. T. P. Wong (Ed.), *The human quest for meaning: Theories, research, and applications* (2nd ed.). New York: Routledge.

Steger, M. F., Frazier, P., Oishi, S., & Kaler, M. (2006). The Meaning in Life questionnaire: Assessing the presence of and search for meaning in life. *Journal of Counseling Psychology, 53*(1), 80–93.

Stern, P. J. (1977). Foreword. In M. Boss (Ed.), *'I dreamt last night ...'* (S. Conway, Trans.). New York: John Wiley and Sons.

Strasser, A. (2015). The relational world of existential therapy and counselling. In C. Noble & E. Day (Eds.), *Psychotherapy and counselling: Reflections on practice.* Melbourne: Oxford University Press.

Strasser, F., & Strasser, A. (1997). *Existential time-limited therapy: The wheel of existence.* Chichester: John Wiley.

Sullivan, H. S. (1953). *The interpersonal theory of psychiatry.* New York: W. W. Norton and Co.

Tengan, A. (1999). *Search for meaning as the basic human motivation: A critical examination of Viktor Emil Frankl's logotherapeutic concept of man* (Vol. 556). Frankfurt am Main: Peter Lang.

Thompson, M. G. (1996). Deception, mystification, trauma: Laing and Freud. *Psychoanalytic Review, 83*, 827–847.

Thompson, M. G. (1997). Michael Guy Thompson. In B. Mullan (Ed.), *R. D. Laing: Creative destroyer.* London: Cassell.

Thompson, M. G. (2012). 'A road less travelled': The dark side of R. D. Laing's conception of authenticity. *Psychotherapy in Australia, 18*(2), 20–29.

Thompson, M. G. (2015). A note on living in one of R. D. Laing's post-Kingsley Hall households: Portland Road. In M. G. Thompson (Ed.), *The legacy of R. D. Laing: An appraisal of his contemporary relevance.* Hove: Routledge.

Thompson, M. G., & Heaton, J. M. (2012). R. D. Laing revisited: A dialogue on his contribution to authenticity and the sceptic tradition. In L. Barnett & G. Madison (Eds.), *Existential psychotherapy: Vibrancy, legacy and dialogue.* London: Routledge.

Tillich, P. (2000). *The courage to be* (2nd ed.). New Haven, CT: Yale University Press.

Tutsch, L. (2003). Of the phenomenology and therapy of narcissistic personality disturbance. *European Psychotherapy, 4*(1), 93–107.

van Deurzen, E. (1998). *Paradox and passion in psychotherapy: An existential approach to therapy and counselling.* Chichester: John Wiley and Sons.

van Deurzen, E. (2002). Existential therapy. In W. Dryden (Ed.), *Handbook of individual therapy* (4th ed.). London: Sage.

van Deurzen, E. (2009). *Psychotherapy and the quest for happiness.* London: Sage.

van Deurzen, E. (2010). *Everyday mysteries* (2nd ed.). London: Routledge.

van Deurzen, E. (2012a). *Existential counselling and psychotherapy in practice* (3rd ed.). London: Sage.

van Deurzen, E. (2012b). The existential ideology and framework for coaching. In E. van Deurzen & M. Hanaway (Eds.), *Existential perspectives on coaching.* London: Palgrave.

van Deurzen, E. (2014a). Becoming an existential therapist. *Existential Analysis, 25*(1), 6–16.

van Deurzen, E. (2014b). Existential therapy. In W. Dryden & A. Reeves (Eds.), *The handbook of individual therapy* (4th ed.). London: Sage.

van Deurzen, E. (2015). *Paradox and passion in psychotherapy: An existential approach* (2nd ed.). Chichester: John Wiley and Sons.

van Deurzen, E. (Ed.). (in press). *World handbook of existential therapy.* London: Wiley.

van Deurzen, E., & Adams, M. (2011). *Skills in existential counselling and psychotherapy.* London: Sage.

van Deurzen, E., & Adams, M. (2016). *Skills in existential counselling and psychotherapy* (2nd ed.). London: Sage.

van Deurzen, E., & Arnold-Baker, C. (Eds.). (2005). *Existential perspectives on human issues: A handbook for therapeutic practice.* Basingstoke: Palgrave.

van Deurzen, E., & Hanaway, M. (Eds.). (2012). *Existential perspectives on coaching.* London: Palgrave.

van Deurzen, E., & Iacovou, S. (Eds.). (2013). *Existential perspectives on relationship therapy*. London: Palgrave.

van Deurzen, E., & Kenward, R. (2005). *Dictionary of existential psychotherapy and counselling*. London: Sage.

van Deurzen, E., & Young, S. (2009). *Existential perspectives on supervision: Widening the horizon of psychotherapy and counselling*. London: Palgrave.

van Deurzen-Smith, E. (1988). *Existential counselling in practice* (1st ed.). London: Sage.

van Deurzen-Smith, E. (1991). The paradoxical self: Towards an understanding of our contradictory nature, by Kirk J. Schneider – book review'. *Journal of the Society for Existential Analysis*, (2), 71–73.

van Deurzen-Smith, E. (1994). Questioning the power of psychotherapy: Is Jeffrey Masson onto something? *Journal of the Society for Existential Analysis, 5*, 36–44.

van Deurzen-Smith, E. (1995a). *Existential therapy*. London: Society for Existential Analysis.

van Deurzen-Smith, E. (1995b). Heidegger and psychotherapy. *Journal of the Society for Existential Analysis, 6*(2), 13–25.

van Deurzen-Smith, E. (1997). *Everyday mysteries*. London: Routledge.

Vohs, K. D., & Baumeister, R. F. (2004). Ego depletion, self-control, and choice. In J. Greenberg, S. L. Koole & T. Pyszczynski (Eds.), *Handbook of experimental existential psychology*. New York: Guilford Press.

von Kirchbach, G. (2003). Existential analysis. *European Psychotherapy, 4*(1), 33–46.

Vos, J. (2015). Meaning-centered group training for physically ill individuals: Basic treatment manual. University of Roehampton.

Vos, J. (2016a, in press). Working with meaning in life in chronic or life-threatening disease: A review of its relevance and effectiveness of meaning-centred therapies. In P. Russo-Netzer, S. E. Schulenberg & A. Batthyány (Eds.), *To thrive, to cope, to understand: Meaning in positive and existential psychotherapy*. New York: Springer.

Vos, J. (2016b). Working with meaning in life in mental health care: A systematic literature review and meta-analysis of the practices and effectiveness of meaning-centered therapies. In P. Russo-Netzer, S. E. Schulenberg & A. Batthyány (Eds.), *To thrive, to cope, to understand: Meaning in positive and existential psychotherapy*. New York: Springer.

Vos, J., Craig, M., & Cooper, M. (2014). Existential therapies: A meta-analysis of their effects on psychological outcomes. *Journal of Consulting and Clinical Psychology, 83*(1), 115–128.

Vos, J., & Vitali, D. (2016). Psychological treatments supporting clients to live a meaningful life: A meta-analysis of the effects of meaning-centered therapies on quality-of-life and psychological-stress. Submitted for publication.

Walsh, R. A., & McElwain, B. (2002). Existential psychotherapies. In D. J. Cain & J. Seeman (Eds.), *Humanistic psychotherapies: Handbook of research and practice*. Washington, DC: American Psychological Association.

Wampold, B. E., & Imel, Z. E. (2015). *The great psychotherapy debate: The evidence for what makes psychotherapy work* (2nd ed.). New York: Routledge.

Wang, X. (2009). Spiritual warrior in search of meaning: An existential view of Lu Xun through his life incidents and analogies. In L. Hoffman, M. Yang & F. J. Kaklauskas (Eds.), *Existential psychology east-west*. Colorado Springs, CO: University of the Rockies.

Wang, X. (2011). Zhi Mian and existential psychology. *The Humanistic Psychologist, 39*(3), 240–246.

Wang, X. (2016). Zhi Mian: Approaching healing/therapy through facing reality: A Chinese approach to existential thinking and pratice. *Existential Analysis, 27*(1), 4–15.

Warnock, M. (1970). *Existentialism* (rev. ed.). Oxford: Oxford University Press.

Wartenberg, T. E. (2008). *Existentialism: A beginner's guide.* London: Oneworld.

Watson, J. B. (1925). *Behaviourism.* New York: W. W. Norton and Co.

Wilkes, R. S., & Milton, M. (2006). Being an existential therapist: An I.P.A. study of existential therapists' experiences. *Existential Analysis, 17*(1), 71–83.

Wolf, D. (2000). Everything you wanted to know about Heidegger (but were afraid to ask your therapist). *Journal of the Society for Existential Analysis, 11*(1), 54–62.

Wolfe, B. E. (2008). Existential issues in anxiety disorders and their treatment. In K. J. Schneider (Ed.), *Existential-integrative psychotherapy: Guideposts to the core of practice.* New York: Routledge.

Wong, P. T. P. (1998). Meaning-centred counseling. In P. T. Wong & P. Fry (Eds.), *The quest for human meaning: A handbook of theory, research and application.* Mahwah, NJ: Lawrence Erlbaum.

Wong, P. T. (2010). Meaning therapy: An integrative and positive existential psycho-therapy. *Journal of contemporary psychotherapy, 40*(2), 85–93.

Wong, P. T. (2013). From logotherapy to meaning-centred counselling and therapy. In P. T. P. Wong (Ed.), *The human quest for meaning: Theories, research, and applications* (2nd ed.). New York: Routledge.

Wong, P. T. P., & Wong, L. C. J. (2013). The challenge of communication: A meaning-centred perspective. In E. van Deurzen & S. Iacovou (Eds.), *Existential perspectives on relationship therapy.* London: Palgrave.

Wood, A. M., Linley, P. A., Maltby, J., Baliousis, M., & Joseph, S. (2008). The authentic personality: A theoretical and empirical conceptualization and the development of the Authenticity Scale. *Journal of Counseling Psychology, 55*(3), 385–399.

Woolf, D. (2000). Everything you wanted to know about Heidegger (but were afraid to ask your therapist). *Journal of the Society for Existential Analysis, 11*(1), 54–62.

World Confederation for Existential Therapy. (2016). *Existential therapy.* Retrieved from www.nspc.org.uk/about-nspc/the-existential-approach.html (accessed 18 April 2016).

Yalom, I. D. (1980). *Existential psychotherapy.* New York: Basic Books.

Yalom, I. D. (1989). *Love's executioner and other tales of psychotherapy.* London: Penguin Books.

Yalom, I. (1992). *When Nietzsche wept: A novel of obsession.* New York: Harper Collins.

Yalom, I. D. (2001). *The gift of therapy: Reflections on being a therapist.* London: Piatkus.

Yalom, I. D. (2008). *Staring at the sun.* London: Piatkus.

Yalom, I. D. (2015). *Creatures of a day.* London: Piatkus.

Yalom, I. D., & Elkin, G. (1974). *Every day gets a little closer: A twice-told therapy.* New York: Basic Books.

INDEX